Elizabeth Bishop
THE GEOGRAPHY OF GENDER

Feminist Issues: Practice, Politics, Theory
Alison Booth and Ann Lane, Editors

Carol Siegel
Lawrence among the Women: Wavering Boundaries
in Women's Literary Traditions

Harriet Blodgett, Editor
Capacious Hold-All: An Anthology of
Englishwomen's Diary Writings

Joy Wiltenburg
Disorderly Women and Female Power in the Street
Literature of Early Modern England and Germany

Diane P. Freedman
An Alchemy of Genres: Cross-Genre Writing
by American Feminist Poet-Critics

Jean O'Barr and Mary Wyer, Editors
Engaging Feminism: Students Speak Up and Speak Out

Kari Weil
Androgyny and the Denial of Difference

Anne Firor Scott, Editor
Unheard Voices: The First Historians of Southern Women

Anne Wyatt-Brown and Janice Rossen, Editors
Aging and Gender in Literature: Studies in Creativity

Alison Booth, Editor
Famous Last Words: Changes in Gender and Narrative Closure

Marilyn May Lombardi, Editor
Elizabeth Bishop: The Geography of Gender

Heidi Hutner, Editor
Rereading Aphra Behn: History, Theory and Criticism

Elizabeth Bishop

THE GEOGRAPHY
OF GENDER

Edited by

Marilyn May Lombardi

University Press of Virginia

Charlottesville and

London

The University Press of Virginia
Copyright © 1993
by the Rector and Visitors
of the University of Virginia

First published 1993

Library of Congress Cataloging-in-Publication Data

Elizabeth Bishop : the geography of gender / edited by Marilyn May Lombardi.
p.   cm. — (Feminist issues)
Includes bibliographical references (p.   ) and index.
ISBN 0-8139-1444-2 (cloth). — ISBN 0-8139-1445-0 (pbk.)
1. Bishop, Elizabeth, 1911-1979—Political and social views.
2. Feminism and literature—United States—History—20th century.
3. Women and literature—United States—History—20th century.
4. Sex role in literature.
I. Lombardi, Marilyn May.   II. Series: Feminist issues (Charlottesville, Va.)
PS3503.1785Z68   1993
811'.54–dc20   93-908
CIP

Printed in the United States of America

Contents

Contents

Contents

Epilogue

VICTORIA HARRISON

BRETT CANDLISH MILLIER

Acknowledgments

Excerpts from the unpublished writings of Elizabeth Bishop are used here with the permission of her estate, copyright © 1993 by Alice Helen Methfessel. All rights reserved.

Quotations from the unpublished writings of Robert Lowell are used with the permission of his estate, copyright © 1993 by Frank Bidart.

Quotations from the unpublished writings of Marianne Moore are used with the permission of her estate, copyright © 1993 by Marianne Craig Moore.

Quotations from the unpublished writings of Elizabeth Bishop, Robert Lowell, and Marianne Moore are also used with the permission of the Vassar College Library, Houghton Library (Harvard University), the Princeton University Library, the Rosenbach Museum & Library, and the Washington University Library.

Excerpts from *The Collected Prose* by Elizabeth Bishop. Copyright © 1984 by Alice Methfessel. Reprinted by permission of Farrar, Straus & Giroux, Inc.

Excerpts from *The Complete Poems, 1927–1979* by Elizabeth Bishop. Copyright © 1979, 1983 by Alice Helen Methfessel. Reprinted by permission of Farrar, Straus & Giroux, Inc.

"Bishop's Sexual Poetics" from *Women Poets and the American Sublime* by Joanne Feit Diehl, copyright © 1990 by Indiana University Press. Reprinted by permission.

"The Closet of Breath: Elizabeth Bishop, Her Body and Her Art" by Marilyn May Lombardi from *Twentieth Century Literature* (Summer 1992), copyright © 1992 by *Twentieth Century Literature*. Reprinted by permission of William McBrien and *Twentieth Century Literature*.

"The Body's Roses" from *Elizabeth Bishop: The Biography of a Poetry* by Lorrie Goldensohn, copyright © 1992 by Columbia University Press, New York. Used by permission of the publisher.

"The Geography of Gender: Elizabeth Bishop's 'In the Waiting Room'" by Lee Edelman from *Contemporary Literature* (Summer 1985), copyright © 1985 by *Contemporary Literature*. Reprinted by permission of *Contemporary Literature* and the University of Wisconsin Press.

Acknowledgments

"Attractive Mortality." Reprinted by permission of the publishers from *Elizabeth Bishop: Questions of Mastery* by Bonnie Costello, Cambridge, Mass.: Harvard University Press, Copyright © 1991 by the President and Fellows of Harvard College.

"Elizabeth Bishop: *Perversity* as Voice" by Jacqueline Vaught Brogan from *American Poetry* (1990), copyright © 1990 by *American Poetry*. Reprinted by permission of Lee Bartlett, Peter White, and *American Poetry*.

"Recording a Life: Elizabeth Bishop's Letters to Ilse and Kit Barker" by Victoria Harrison from *Contemporary Literature* (1988), copyright © 1988 by *Contemporary Literature*. Reprinted by permission of *Contemporary Literature* and the University of Wisconsin Press.

"Elusive Mastery: The Drafts of Elizabeth Bishop's 'One Art' " by Brett Candlish Millier from *New England Review* (Winter 1990), copyright © 1990 by Brett Candlish Millier. Reprinted by permission.

Abbreviations

CP	*Elizabeth Bishop: The Complete Poems*
CProse	*Elizabeth Bishop: The Collected Prose*
HL	Houghton Library, Harvard University, Cambridge, Mass.
KWN	Key West/Nemer notebooks
NYP	New York Public Library
PU	Elizabeth Bishop Collection, Princeton University Library, Princeton, New Jersey
RM	Rosenbach Museum and Library, Philadelphia, Pa.
VC	Elizabeth Bishop Collection, Vassar College Library, Poughkeepsie, New York
WU	Washington University Library, St. Louis, Mo.

Elizabeth Bishop
THE GEOGRAPHY OF GENDER

MARILYN MAY LOMBARDI

Prologue
"Another Way of Seeing"

ELIZABETH Bishop received her share of accolades during her life-time. The Pulitzer Prize, the National Book Award, the National Book Critics Circle Award—she won all the major literary awards. But when Robert Lowell called her poetry "the best written by a woman in the twentieth century" (Lowell 1987, p. 78), Bishop accepted her friend's gallantry with some misgivings: "Most of my writing life I've been lucky about reviews," she admitted in a late interview with George Starbuck (1983). "But at the very end they often say 'The best poetry by a woman in this decade, or year, or month.' Well, what's that worth?" (p. 324). The whole thrust of Bishop's early public experience, as Lorrie Goldensohn observes, "seems to have been to avoid being ghettoized as a woman."[1] In her interview with Starbuck, Bishop traced her reluctance to have her work included in all-women anthologies back to "feminist principles, stronger than I was aware of"—principles that led her to question the role that gender played in her literary reputation (p. 322). Though rarely articulated, these principles made themselves felt in the poet's instinc-tive refusal to be defined. As David Kalstone (1983a, p. 3) reminds us, Bishop's poetic voice is "to her credit, hard to 'place.'"

An inveterate traveler, Bishop came to be regarded by the New York literary world as a remote figure. While many of her contemporaries were quarrying art directly out of personal tragedy, Bishop maintained a style that was equivocal and ambiguous about the contours of her pri-vate life; while others of her generation were fully engaged in literary politics she kept her distance in Key West, Mexico, and Brazil, refus-ing enlistment in the ranks of any particular aesthetic movement. Her

Marilyn May Lombardi

psychological and geographical remoteness, combined with her dignified refusal to promote herself, encouraged early readers to stress the self-effacing properties of her poetry. Reviewing her first volume of poetry, Oscar Williams (1983) praised her "charming little stained-glass bits," and her delicate observation of domestic detail, relegating Bishop to the niche conceded women of her generation by established literary opinion—and delaying the full recognition of her achievement (p. 185).[2] Late in life, she spoke with quiet bitterness of the way conventional views of the feminine unfairly colored her status as a poet. Faced with condescension on the basis of her gender, age, or unmarried status, Bishop tried to meet the slighting references with good humor, but as she once told her friends U. T. and Joseph Summers, patronizing reviewers "brought [her] feminist facet uppermost."[3]

For most of her career, Bishop was cast in the role of a "much-prized, plain-spoken, pleasantly idiosyncratic maiden aunt, one who has observed, considered, and savored the world, for the most part alone" (Elliott 1969, p. 13). As Thomas Travisano argues, those earlier reviewers who transformed the poet into a prudish eccentric "either did not know, or chose to ignore" the fact that Bishop was "by no means alone in the personal sense." She observed, considered, and savored the world in the company of other women—women with whom she had long-term intimate relationships. Indeed, as Travisano suggests in his essay in this volume, the life of voluntary exile that Bishop led was unabashedly bohemian, certainly cosmopolitan, and "far more physically adventurous, and far more diverse in what it offered to the eye, than the lives of her mostly professorial (and male) poetic colleagues."[4]

A modest person leading an adventurous, unconventional life, Bishop developed both a public persona and a poetic style that vibrated "between two frequencies—the domestic and the strange" (Vendler 1983, p. 32). In a television interview, her close friend James Merrill remembered "the wonderful way in which she impersonated an ordinary woman," concealing from view the "incredible fresh genius who wrote the poems" (Merrill 1988). As Merrill (1979) explained in his memorial piece for the *New York Review of Books,* this mask of ordinariness was the one artificiality the poet permitted herself—a bit of theater that offered her some degree of relief, "from what must have been an at times painful singularity" (p. 6). Although discerning friends like Merrill appreciated the rich ambiguities of her public and poetic performances,

2

critics like Oscar Williams and Charles Elliott continued to take an un-complicated view of Bishop's poetry. As Lee Edelman argues, Bishop's reviewers often "colluded unself-consciously with Bishop's own efforts to efface or minimize the strangeness of her work" (letter to the author, 10 March 1991)—and the role that her personal sense of difference played in its creation.[5]

When Bishop became the first American, and the first woman, to win the distinguished Neustadt International Prize for Literature in 1976, John Ashbery (1977) reminded those friends, critics, and artists gathered together to honor her that Bishop's great subject had always been "the strangeness, the unreality of our reality"—a strangeness that her "rooted, piercing vision" continually rediscovers (p. 10). Astute readers like Howard Moss, Helen Vendler, John Ashbery, Lynn Keller, and Chris-tanne Miller were among the first to recognize that Bishop's poems speak to her own sense of estrangement. The poet shows a protective interest in "off creatures" who escape conventional definition, hyphenated pro-tagonists poised on a threshold between the organic and the inorganic, the mechanical and the sensual. Until the final years of her life, how-ever, few readers could have sensed the enormity of Bishop's alienation; only Bishop's circle of intimates would have been aware of all the ways in which her life and art violated accepted decorums and social norms. Not until the publication of her last and warmest book, *Geography III,* did Bishop begin to speak publicly of herself as a feminist and more candidly about the limiting factors that shaped her art: her "era, sex, situation, education." As Goldensohn notes in her essay for this collec-tion, Bishop's lesbianism "seems an inseparable if mostly puzzling part of the other factors she herself named as limiting." The relative candor of Bishop's later years makes it impossible for contemporary readers to continue to take an uncomplicated view of her poetic "reticence."[6]

When Bishop published *Geography III* she revealed for the first time how autobiographical her poems had always been, despite their practiced indirection and reserve. The new work also confirmed the impression already held by her most sympathetic readers that Bishop's great sub-ject had always been "strangeness" and that her empathy for the exiled, liminal creature, and the peripheral perspective, was drawn from her own profound sense of difference. With late poems like "In the Wait-ing Room" and stories like "In the Village" and "Memories of Uncle Neddy," Bishop unveiled the origins of her attraction to geographical peripheries and her adoption of the fugitive stance: the early death of her father, the insanity that claimed her mother when Bishop was four years old, the illnesses that isolated Bishop in her early years, and the terrible sense of being a guest in the homes of her relations. In the years after the poet's death, more information has come to light about her sexuality, alcoholism, and courageous resolve in the face of physical and emotional trauma, and a new generation of readers have found fresh and suggestive sources for Bishop's implicative style.

Making extensive use of the poet's newly discovered diaries, her private correspondence, and a series of candid unpublished poems, Bishop scholars are in the process of opening up new perspectives on the geographies of sex, race, and gender as they appear in the poet's art. Emerging from this radical reconsideration of Bishop's achievement is a portrait of an enduring artist whose poetry proves compelling and challenging in previously unimagined ways. With the publication of David Kalstone's *Becoming a Poet: Elizabeth Bishop with Marianne Moore and Robert Lowell* in 1989, the appearance just two years later of major studies by Lorrie Goldensohn and Bonnie Costello, and the promise of several revelatory biographies and critical studies in the near future, Bishop scholarship is at last coming of age.

Elizabeth Bishop: The Geography of Gender takes its place in this new critical terrain. This collection aims to make the most important current criticism easily accessible for both the scholar and the general reader of Bishop's work. Eight of the essays were published previously in various books and journals; three have never appeared before in print. This anthology gathers together the work of pioneering scholars in the field, critics who are exploring the psychosexual tensions within Bishop's vision and the uncanny way her poetics of dislocation challenge our assumptions about placement and orientation. Readers already familiar with Lee Edelman's essay, "The Geography of Gender: Elizabeth Bishop's 'In the Waiting Room' " will recognize the origin of the collection's subtitle. Edelman's work has become a classic and central essay for reading gender in Bishop's poetry and supplies the collection as a whole with its touchstone. Each essay contributes to the mapping of Bishop's sense of difference as an orphan, a woman artist, and a lesbian. Despite their own differences in approach and emphasis, the contributors agree on one point: Bishop's gender plays a significant role in the questioning of aesthetic, ethical, and sexual boundaries that constitutes so much a part of her poetic practice. Drawing on the crucial issues of Bishop's personal life—her early sense of maternal deprivation, her lesbianism, her struggles with alcoholism and debilitating asthma—the essays consider the ways in which the poet's art confronts the imprisonings and problematic releases of the female body, the sexual politics of a male-dominated literary tradition, and the pleasures and the perils of language itself.

Viewing Bishop's poetry through the lens of gender, the authors address questions vital to contemporary feminist criticism. How does a woman poet tap the resources of her female experience when she writes? What is a woman writer's relation to literary tradition? Can an autonomous woman's tradition in American literature be defined without arguing for some problematic notion of feminine essence? The reasons for Bishop's belated and somewhat uneasy assimilation into the feminist critical canon are multiple and germane to any discussion of feminism's role in mapping such a tradition. Bishop's poetry emerges from this reconsideration as more amenable to feminist interpretation than previously imagined. At the same time, her art expands our narrow definitions of the "woman poet" or "woman's poetry" and so poses a greater challenge to feminist orthodoxies than earlier readers may have been willing to admit.[7]

Adrienne Rich was among the first to offer a feminist rereading of Elizabeth Bishop's art, and her 1983 review of the poet's posthumously published *Complete Poems* marks the shift in thinking about Bishop's poetics and person that has led to this present collection of essays. Intent on placing Bishop's poetry within an empowering female tradition, Rich's review highlights how Bishop commented on the unempowered and the silenced from within existing limits. Rich writes: "In particular I am concerned with her experience of outsiderhood, closely—though not exclusively—linked with the essential outsiderhood of a lesbian identity; and with how the outsider's eye enables Bishop to perceive other kinds of outsiders to identify, or try to identify, with them" (Rich 1983, p. 16). In her review of Bishop's *Complete Poems,* Rich confronts her reasons for her discomfort with Bishop's reticence. Coming to prominence herself in the 1950s, Rich was asked to "look to 'Miss' Marianne Moore as the paradigm of what a woman poet might accomplish, and, after her, to 'Miss' Bishop." Noting that Bishop's "white, male, and at least ostensibly heterosexual" admirers had "selected and certified" her poetry as authentic verse, Rich admits that for a long time she "felt drawn, but also repelled" by Bishop's poetry (Rich 1986, p. 125). The literary establishment paid attention to Bishop's "triumphs, her perfections, not to her struggles for self-definition and her sense of difference." Rich, whose early poetry was also commended for its radiant finish, knew what it was like to be selected and certified. She may very well have worried about being praised for producing "the best poems . . . written by a woman in this century" and consigned to the same niche "Miss" Bishop had occupied for so long (Lowell 1987, p. 78).

Much of Rich's difficulty with her celebrated predecessor must have stemmed in part from Bishop's refusal to allow her work to appear in women-only anthologies. This controversial decision was consistent with her lifelong aversion to systems of polarization, exclusion, and subordination. As Joanne Diehl suggests, Bishop's poetry blurs metaphysical, ethical, and sexual distinctions, crossing the heavy lines typically drawn between "life/death, right/wrong, male/female" ("Santarém," *CP,* p. 185). Bishop's writings ultimately seek to preserve what Diehl calls "the unyielding fact" of difference in this world and salvage the peripheral perspective at risk of being overlooked or ostracized: the blues vocalist in "Songs for a Colored Singer" (*CP,* pp. 47–51) and the sensitive Brazilian schoolgirl estranged from the plodding, credulous adults around her in *The Diary of Helena Morley.*[8] The understanding that Bishop's poetry offers is the sort of future understanding Jane Gallop (1988) calls for at the end of *Thinking through the Body,* an appreciation of others achieved "not in order to close the divide and reach the space of pure and simple feminine being but in order precisely to 'want this distance between us,' in order better to ask the necessarily double and no less urgent questions of feminism: 'not merely who am I? But who is the other woman?'" (p. 177). In continually directing attention to the differences among people and the otherness of nature, Bishop struggles (with varying degrees of success, as Lorrie Goldensohn suggests in her essay) to adopt an approach to experience that Jeredith Merrin (1990) speaks of as "enabling humility" (p. 144).

Several of the contributors to this volume underscore the revolutionary nature of Bishop's art. For Joanne Diehl, Bishop's poems "aim at nothing short of freedom from the inherently dualistic tradition that lies not only at the foundations of the American Sublime, but at the very heart of the Western literary tradition." Jacqueline Brogan sees Bishop as equally revolutionary in her praxis: "a poet who not only challenges our basic assumptions about the *lyric* [as a genre], but one who does so in such a way that her poetic strategies have ramifications that extend well into the realm of feminist and political concerns." As Diehl argues, Rich and Bishop, "despite their vast differences, both respond to the American tradition's denial of the woman as poet."

A gathering of this kind cannot claim to be comprehensive: Our subject makes it impossible. As Jeredith Merrin observes in *An Enabling Humility,* Bishop persistently countered egocentricity by reminding her readers that "no matter what position we occupy there is always, as Emily Dickinson says, 'Another—way to see'" (p. 139). However diverse in approach, the essays gathered together in this volume play variations on one insistent theme: there is always something more in Bishop's work waiting to be seen. The lens of gender allows us to magnify certain questions, points of view, and possibilities within Bishop's art that might otherwise have been passed over or occluded altogether.

With Bishop's example always before us, each contributor has tried to view his or her own work as simply one among many multiple and juxtaposed perspectives. Indeed, a revisionary project of this kind must be careful to acknowledge the particular danger inherent in reassessment —the risk that one restrictive, normalizing image of the poet will simply be replaced by another. For this reason, each thesis represents what Bishop might call "an active displacement in perspective" (*CP*, p. 36). We hope our readers will revel in a "sense of constant readjustment" as they move from essay to essay (*CP*, p. 10). The critical methodologies represented in this volume are varied, and often in implicit dialogue with one another. The first cluster of essays, by Joanne Diehl, Marilyn May Lombardi, Lorrie Goldensohn, and Lee Edelman, explores issues of "Body, Gender, and Race" by drawing attention to the poet's somatic, erotic, and ethical preoccupations. The second grouping, "Poetry, Perversity, and Pleasure," includes essays by Thomas Travisano, Bonnie Costello, and Jeredith Merrin that challenge an older image of Bishop as a poet of delicacy and pathos by recovering the elements of subversion and gaiety in her verse. In the collection's third section, "Bishop and Literary Tradition," Jacqueline Vaught Brogan focuses on Bishop's "deliberate subversion, or perversion" of dominant artistic decorums, and Barbara Page examines a pair of working diaries in which Bishop "articulates her own aims as a poet and measures herself against her poetic forebears."

The collection concludes with essays by Victoria Harrison and Brett Millier that offer fresh biographical insights into Bishop's relationships with other women and the impact of intimacy on her art.

Elizabeth Bishop: The Geography of Gender begins by examining the psychological, social, and political implications of Bishop's treatment of love and the eroticized female body, subjects that in spite of her guarded approach do make significant appearances in her work. Joanne Diehl's essay introduces us to "Bishop's Sexual Poetics." How, asks Diehl, does Bishop approach the sexual politics of the masculine Romantic tradition with its coupling of virility and poetic power? And in what ways does "her swerve from Emerson and his heirs . . . depend substantially upon her gender, upon the fact of Bishop's being a woman?" Diehl argues that Bishop wins a distance from her precursor poets by interrogating the sexual dialectic at the heart of the Sublime. Tracing Bishop's technique of fusing eroticism with gender crossing in poems like "Crusoe in England," "Santarem," "Brazil, January 1, 1502," "The Moose," and "The End of March," among others, Diehl highlights the ways in which Bishop escapes the limitations of an American poetic based on conventional definitions of sexual identity. In Bishop's alternative sexual poetics, such limitations ultimately "yield before a disengendered, highly eroticized imagination." This erotic imagination in Bishop's poetry is defined, Diehl suggests, "through absence and the unspoken" and emerges "against a psychic background distinguished by a desire for self-protection in a world perceived as irremediably divided between the subjectivity of the self and the threatening possibilities of other persons."

The three contributions that follow Diehl's in this collection amplify this theme by making use of unpublished material to explore Bishop's complex personal and poetic responses towards the eroticized maternal body and her own body's desires and vulnerabilities. Drawing on Bishop's correspondence with her personal physician and on dreams recorded in her private diaries, my essay concentrates on Bishop's chronic, debilitating asthma and allergic inflammations and the rich metaphoric use she makes of them in her art. With their images of suffocation and female intrusiveness, poems like "In the Waiting Room" and "O Breath" explore the tangled relation in the poet's life between asthmatic attacks and deeply ambivalent experiences of the female voice, maternal love, and adult sexuality. Bishop's oblique approach to self-reference is ultimately moored to somatic issues and represents an unflinching attempt to capture the complex and troubling reality of human relationship.

Questions of sexuality and equivocation are also pursued in Lorrie Goldensohn's "The Body's Roses: Race, Sex, and Gender in Elizabeth Bishop's Representations of the Self," which explores the connection in Bishop's mind "between the social and psychological repressions of race and gender." Goldensohn compares Bishop's unpublished and published poetry and asks why Bishop permitted only a handful of love poems to appear in print. Although Bishop wrote poems that focused on the pleasures of the eroticized female body, she would not allow her readers to see them. Instead, her published work stresses the rocky "implacability" of the female breast over its warmth and emphasizes its maternal (and sinister) associations over its erotic possibilities. Tracing Bishop's fascination with the link between blackness and the maternal in works like "Faustina, or Rock-Roses," Goldensohn shows how Bishop "displaces the drama of her deepest fears about love and intimacy onto the more distant terrain of domestic servants and the dark Brazilian other."

Whereas Goldensohn stresses Bishop's fascination with the power of the mother's body to excite longing and evoke fears of abandonment, Lee Edelman calls attention to the terror of being imprisoned within the unempowered female body—the fear experienced by the child-protagonist of "In the Waiting Room." As the shy nine-year-old "Elizabeth" stares with fascination at *National Geographic*'s photographs of naked native women and their "awful hanging breasts," she becomes aware of her destiny as a woman—subject to representation by a "patriarchal culture," subject, like the black mothers and their infants, to disfigurement. In his recovery of the poem's nuances and implications, Edelman argues that Bishop addresses reading itself as a cultural act of placement, mastery, and appropriation in a way that challenges our own attempts to master the poem and position its author. For Edelman, Bishop insists that the cry of pain on which the poem hinges should remain unplaceable in origin, because it is a cry against placement, a cry of displacement, and a cry, therefore, "of female textuality."

The three essays that follow recover the elements of surprise and subversion in Bishop's art. Each author concentrates on Bishop's various revolts against decorum. As Thomas Travisano remarks in " 'The Flicker of Impudence': Delicacy and Indelicacy in the Art of Elizabeth Bishop," Bishop's image as "an all-too-ladylike abstractionist" helped occlude the fact that her bohemian life had left her "open to a variety of sometimes shocking impressions" reflected in her poetry. A tacit dialogue with Travisano's discussion emerges when its principal arguments are set beside those of Bonnie Costello's "Attractive Mortality." Costello recasts traditional assumptions about Bishop by accenting the poet's use of the grotesque in poems like "Cirque d'Hiver," "The Man-Moth," "The Weed," "The Shampoo," "The Armadillo," "Manuelzinho," and "Pink Dog." Through her adaptation of the grotesque style, Bishop blurs the boundaries between generation and decay, and, as a result, Costello argues, the poet maintains a tension between the untamable, aging body—its needs, its desires, its vulnerability to time—and "the culture's wish to control, disguise, or suppress it." In bringing her essay to a close, Costello notes that Bishop "expresses the necessity (though not always the hope) for a less 'barbaric,' more flexible, tolerant culture that can accommodate difference and change without anxiety and remain 'new, tender, quick.'"

Jeredith Merrin's "Gaiety, Gayness, and Change" draws attention away from the "ruefulness" and "poignancy" that have dominated discussions of Bishop's poetry in the past. Merrin retrieves the poet's playfulness and wit by pursuing the question of Bishop's flexible poetic. Focusing on Bishop's evocations of flux and transmogrification, Merrin links the poet's "gaiety or delight in the possibilities of change" with her gayness—her questioning, that is, of gender boundaries through the subtle exploration of same-sex love. Merrin's reading spans the two chronological extremes of Bishop's career, starting with "Pleasure Seas" from 1939 and ending with the posthumously published "Sonnet" (1979). According to Merrin, Bishop's final poem imagines a flight "beyond the confines of the physical body and the world of gendered opposition."

The collection continues with an exploration of Bishop's poetic and personal responses to the prevailing literary tradition. In "Elizabeth Bishop: *Perversity* as Voice," Jacqueline Brogan concentrates on Bishop's "subversions" of "the prevailing assumption that the lyric is defined by a spoken, authentic 'voice,' an assumption that extends from before Wordsworth well into the twentieth century." For Brogan, Wallace Stevens's "Idea of Order at Key West" may be said "to epitomize the assumptions inherent in the 'traditional' lyric context." Brogan argues that "in almost all her lyrics Bishop consistently undermines domination, whether poetically, phallically, or politically conceived," mocking Stevens's "blessed rage for order." In the process, Bishop creates what Brogan names a "white writing" that "dismantles our expectations about the 'authority' of lyric voice." In the next essay, "Off-Beat Claves, Oblique Realities," Barbara Page mines a source of new information on the poet's life and work during her decade in Key West and, in the process, offers a portrait of the artist that complements and extends Brogan's theoretical coupling of Bishop and Wallace Stevens. Page focuses on a series of notebooks that Bishop kept while in Florida in which she considers her literary predecessors. For Stevens's idea of order, Bishop substitutes an "idea of vagrancy" at Key West, finding at the geographical periphery of North America a place "corresponding to her own disposition for the margins" where she could practice the "evasions that gave room to her ambition as a woman poet."

Because so much of our discussion has revolved around Bishop's gendered experience and the ways she managed to touch her art with private meaning, it is fitting that this collection comes to a close with two works that highlight the poet's intimate relations with other women. Victoria Harrison presents an archive of letters between two women writers, Bishop and Ilse Barker. Although Bishop's role as protégée of Marianne Moore is often discussed, it has not been widely appreciated that Bishop went on to play the role of mentor herself in her correspondence with Ilse Barker and May Swenson, often using her letters to both women as a "testing ground for her half-formulated ideas" about herself and her writing. Harrison draws from the Barker letters fresh insights into Bishop's domestic life in Brazil, her feminism, her identification of Sarah Orne Jewett and Emily Dickinson as literary influences, and her complex stance with regard to women's writing.

Finally, in "Elusive Mastery: The Drafts of Elizabeth Bishop's 'One Art,' " Brett Millier follows the development of the poet's elegy through seventeen drafts, from the first draft's "bold, painful catalog" of losses "to the finely honed and privately meaningful final version." Identifying the immediate crisis out of which the villanelle arose, Millier draws connections between the finished poem's discretion and the poet's lifelong deflection of biographical inquiry. An *ars poetica* and, arguably, Bishop's most moving poem, "One Art" is, for Millier, the poet's discrete "elegy for her whole life"—a life lived almost wholly in the company of other women. In her enduring evocation of the lost loved one whose "joking voice" and beloved gesture now seem gone forever, the poet appears determined to survive, to move forward (however haltingly) past the pain of loss and the prison of immediate circumstance. Millier leaves us under the spell of Bishop's "One Art" and the poet's resolve to live with disaster and dream of a time when she is no longer a "creature divided," a body bound, and a spirit trapped—a time when her spirit, like the rainbow-bird of her final poem, breaks free of its prism to fly "wherever / it feels like, gay" ("Sonnet," *CP*, p. 192).

Notes

1. In a 1977 interview with George Starbuck, Bishop examines her unwillingness to be bound by any prescriptive notion of woman's poetry and her wariness about committing to any aesthetic that polarizes the sexes. In a letter to Joan Keefe that same year Bishop declares herself to have been strongly feminist since the age of six but goes on to state emphatically "that art is art, and no matter how great a part these ineluctable facts play in its creation, the ages, races, and sexes should not be segregated" (8 June 1977, VC). Several of this volume's essayists explore the reasons for Bishop's adamant refusal to be grouped with other women writers.

2. The history of Bishop's critical reception is, for the most part, the story of her readers' frustrated attempts to place or inscribe her great subject—strangeness—and to master the perverse and subversive power of her art. Praised as an exquisite miniaturist, she became valued primarily for single stunning poems that were easily anthologized. For many years, poems like "The Fish" or "The Armadillo" floated untethered among the abbreviated work of other artists. The result of this critical patronage, as Kalstone (1977) wryly points out, was "an unusually stunted version of Bishop's variety" (p. 12).

3. In the last year of her life, Bishop complained to her friends U. T. and Joseph Summers that she resented the way reporters would focus on her appearance when she gave a public reading: "apparently lady-poets are supposed to be perennially youthful, or preferably die young" if they want to avoid looking "like anyone's grandmother," but no reporter would think of calling an aging Robert Fitzgerald or an ancient T. S. Eliot "grandfatherly" (Bishop to U. T. and Joseph Summers, 1 March 1979, VC).

4. In "It All Depends [In Response to a Questionnaire]," Bishop writes: "physique, temperament, religion, politics, and immediate circumstances all play their parts in formulating one's theories of verse [and] then they play them again and differently when one is writing it" (in Ciardi 1950, p. 267).

5. Even where sensitive readers like Jerome Mazzaro or William Spiegelman have emphasized the sense of difference, displacement, and ambiguity in Bishop's work, they have made it conform to models that reduce her subversiveness. They place Bishop's concerns over what can be known of ourselves and of others in the context of a Wordsworthian or Emersonian tradition—a tradition that poses essential questions about the way we subjectively experience the world only to ultimately affirm "*our* shared humanity" (Estess 1983, p. 221; my italics). For readings that challenge this identification between Bishop and the Romantic tradition, see essays by Diehl, Goldensohn, Edelman, and Brogan in this volume.

6. The essays in this collection represent a variety of approaches to the question

of Bishop's stylistic indirections and diplomacies. The essays by Diehl, Goldensohn, and myself place Bishop's reticence within the context of historical circumstance and view her "restraint" as well through what Goldensohn calls "the tangling knots of the poet's temperament, gender, and sexual identity." The three essays, each in their own way, come to the conclusion that Bishop's implicative style became a powerful and "enabling" artistic stance. As Diehl senses, "there is an ominous quality to Bishop's restraint more suggestive than confession" and more attuned to the equivocal reality of love and the cultural construction of gender. By clouding the contours of her personal life, by disguising autobiography and complicating our view of intimacy, Bishop stresses the distance and relative impersonality of the relation between poet and reader, deepening by contrast the rare moments of unobstructed relation—and suggesting, far more than would overt confessional, the sheer effort of affection, the ambivalence that is an unyielding fact of human relationship.

7. Any re-reading of Bishop's art that stresses gender considerations inevitably confronts a fundamental controversy in modern poetics and feminist theory: the criteria for defining an autonomous woman's tradition in literature and the authentic subjects of woman's poetry. See Ostriker 1986 for an influential study of contemporary neoconfessional poetry by women that stresses the "imperative of intimacy." For the argument that this imperative only reinforces ancient stereotypes and risks privileging feeling over cerebration, see Bonnie Costello's (1988) review of Ostriker's book in *Contemporary Literature*. For alternative positions, see essays by Diehl, Edelman, Lombardi, Page, Brogan, and Harrison in this volume.

8. In one of her notebooks, the poet writes of "interstitial situations"—"oblique realities that give one pause [and] glance off a larger reality illuminating like light caught in a bevel." This "feeling that everything is unavoidably [interstitial]" directs her gaze to the space that intervenes between people and between things (Box 35A, Folder 2, KWN 2, p. 189). Similarly, Bishop's verbal obliquities remind us of the distance that intervenes between poet and reader.

PART I

Body, Gender, and Race

JOANNE FEIT DIEHL

Bishop's Sexual Poetics

IF CONTEMPORARY POETRY borders on the limits of expressive form, there are, nevertheless, poets who are masters of those limits, who, in creating the poems of our climate, return us to ourselves. Elizabeth Bishop is such a poet. And although she would have resisted being classified with "women poets," her work clearly establishes itself as belonging to that alternative tradition of women poets whose redefinition of the Sublime centers on the interrelation of the imagination and sexual identity. Bishop's poems reveal the complex tensions between women poets and the American Romantic tradition she identified as her own. In response to this tradition, Bishop wrote poems of passionate reserve that fused a capacity for wonder with a descriptive power that makes the Sublime, however provisionally, possible once more. To name the techniques Bishop uses to achieve such verbal moments is itself to recall the strategies practiced by her precursors, those women poets who, like Bishop, experienced the need to conceal as much as to disclose. For Bishop's elusive rhetoric engages her in the complex interactions between women poets and the American Sublime. The impetus of the exile, which paradoxically turned Emily Dickinson into a recluse (her most impassioned form of travel), Bishop converts into the vocation of the traveler, whose powers of observation acquire acuity through estrangement. Yet Bishop's articulate exclusion does not rule out her own poetic indebtedness to the magisterial poets we associate with the American Sublime.

In a wryly discursive letter to Anne Stevenson, her first biographer, Bishop commented directly on her relationship to the American literary tradition. "But I also feel," she writes, "that Cal [Lowell] and I in very different ways are both descendants from the Transcendentalists—but you may not agree" (20 March 1963, WU, in Stevenson 1980, p. 261). Despite the characteristic demurral, Bishop acknowledges that her work derives from that early manifestation of American self-consciousness known as transcendentalism. The particular approach she takes toward American Romanticism, her swerve from Emerson and his heirs (different as it is from Lowell's), depends substantially on her gender, on the fact of Bishop's being a woman. This essay sketches the outlines of a reading of Bishop's work that attempts to account both for the influence of gender and the importance of tradition, her awareness of origins and the origins of her difference. That Bishop defined herself in terms of the American Romantic imagination is perhaps less a conscious decision than an un-avoidable burden affecting all our poets, men and women, who cannot, of course, evade their literary predecessors. Yet a consideration of the relationship between eros and poetics suggests the possibility that the woman poet may win a certain measure of freedom from literary in-debtedness and thus acquire in the very weakening of those traditional ties a restitution born of loss.

If, as Ludwig Wittgenstein writes, "to imagine a language means to imagine a form of life," then contemporary women poets are inventing, through their poems, new forms of constitutive identity; in remaking language, they strive to reinvent themselves. The impetus for this re-invention derives from the woman poet's need to reassert authority over experience, establishing, as I have elsewhere noted, an unmediated rela-tion both with the natural world and with the word. Dickinson is the first woman poet to attempt such a transformation, and although Bishop expresses a certain disdain for the self-pity she perceives in Dickinson's poems, she acknowledges not only her forebear's genius but her his-torical significance. "I particularly admire her having dared to do it all alone," Bishop remarked, and the relationship between Dickinson and Bishop may be closer than the urbanely disingenuous Bishop might have wished to acknowledge (Stevenson 1980, p. 261). Distanced from Dickin-son by both time and temperament, Bishop nevertheless faced an allied, even intensified, version of the Emersonian Sublime, modulated as it is through Walt Whitman's bodily poetics and the various poetic voices of our own century. And even more than Dickinson, Bishop defends against the challenge to her poetic autonomy by usurping the very terms of that challenge; she responds to the coupling of sexual identity and poetic power by interrogating the sexual dialectic on which that coupling de-pends. Bishop's poems may be read as a map of language where sexual identity appears to yield to a fluidity of gender that does away with rigid, heterosexist categories. In this sense, Bishop follows Whitman's poetic coupling of homosexuality with erotic power. Yet, rather than establish the lesbian as an overt erotic position from which to write (Adrienne Rich's choice), Bishop distinguishes between eroticism and sexual identity, a distinction that allows her to deflect sexual identification while simultaneously sustaining a powerful erotic presence. Recollecting how close Bishop's early aesthetic ideals are to Whitman's may remind us how fully his eroticism is translated into her own.

Bishop apparently began reading Whitman very early, and the passages she marked in her copy of *Leaves of Grass* are one indication of what initially impressed her.[1] Bishop was struck by Whitman's emphasis upon precision, the aim of effortlessness, the ideal of a poetry that does not betray the work that produces it. In one such passage, Whitman wrote that poetry should appear "without effort and without exposing in the least how it is done." Along with this apparent effortlessness comes a familiar insistence upon imaginative accuracy and the preeminence of sight. "(What the eyesight does to the rest he does to the rest. Who knows the curious mystery of the eyesight?)" (marked by double line, p. 492). Beyond this allegiance to visual accuracy and the illusion of ease, Bishop learned from Whitman a "prudence suitable for immortality" (underlined, p. 502). Bishop incorporates Whitmanian prudence with sexual radicalism, as prudence assumes the guise of verbal deflection or effacement, the invocation of the magical and displacement of point of view—the definition of erotic pleasure through absence and the unspoken.[2] Such verbal masking allows Bishop to preserve the erotic while deconstructing heterosexist categories. In this reconceptualization, Bishop follows both Dickinson and Whitman; for, although Bishop's admiration for Dickinson may be muted, Dickinson herself practices a similar poetic encoding, employing techniques of gender-crossing, the disguise of authorial displacement, and the substitution of natural tropes for human presence. By eliding the dialectics of heterosexuality, Bishop extends Dickinson's and Whitman's poetic projects to discover an individuating source of renewed poetic authority.

In one of her few public statements on the relation of gender to writing, Bishop commented, "Women's experiences are much more limited, but that does not really matter—there is Emily Dickinson, as one always says. You just have to make do with what you have after all" (1978, p. 1). For Bishop, making do meant a life of daring exploration and an intense dedication to craft—the sustained development of a style of straightforward effacement that coupled indirection with the plainness of speech. The guise of the traveler, the voice of the child, and the testimonies of grotesque, liminal creatures all convey experience profoundly felt and obliquely expressed. Different as these voices are, each carries a quality of existential displacement that restricts as it imagines the possibilities of human relationship.

In "Crusoe in England," Bishop's most extreme poetic instance of gender-crossing fused with eroticism, the practical, stranded voyager with his laconic voice becomes the spokesman for feelings of great intimacy, fear of maternity, and the pain of separation and loss. Here the voice of the isolated man most clearly articulates Bishop's terrain of difference, for Crusoe's hardship is related as much to the claustrophobia of entrapment within an obsessive imagination as it is to the physical conditions of the island.[3] Loneliness finds its projection in a violent, aggressive landscape where volcanoes' heads are "blown off" and the "parched throats" of craters are "hot to touch," an island hissing with aridity and the replication of barren life. It is a place of singleness:

> the same odd sun
> rose from the sea,
> and there was one of it and one of me.
> The island had one kind of everything.[4]

To relieve the tension, Crusoe turns to the imagination's capacity for recollection and for change. But in both efforts, his imagination fails him, for he cannot remember the final word of the Wordsworth he would recite, and the baby goat, whom he dyes red, is rejected by its mother. His most powerful imaginative act is to dream, and his dreams reveal an obsession with procreation, the loss of the mother, and the pain of a subjectivity bereft of relationship.

> Dreams were the worst. Of course I dreamed of food
> And love, but they were pleasant rather
> Than otherwise. But then I'd dream of things
> like slitting a baby's throat, mistaking it
> for a baby goat. I'd have
> nightmares of other islands
> stretching away from mine, infinities
> of islands, islands spawning islands,

like frogs' eggs turning into polliwogs
of islands, knowing that I had to live
on each and every one, eventually,
for ages, registering their flora,
their fauna, their geography.

(*CP*, p. 165)

The hopelessness of a purely biological repetition (or what Alan Williamson in another context has called "desolate accumulation") is broken by the arrival of Friday, whose friendship is mourned both for its future loss and its inherent infertility (Williamson 1983, p. 103):

Just when I thought I couldn't stand it
another minute longer, Friday came.
(Accounts of that have everything all wrong.)
Friday was nice.
Friday was nice, and we were friends.
If only he had been a woman!
I wanted to propagate my kind,
And so did he, I think, poor boy. . . .
—Pretty to watch; he had a pretty body.

(*CP*, pp. 165–66)

Here, "pretty" gestures both toward Crusoe's desire that Friday be a woman and toward the attraction he feels for the boy himself, an expression of homoerotic longing voiced by the speaker, who simultaneously stands in for the poem's author and speaks, in the narrative, for himself. In a unisexual and univocal text, Bishop tells a story rich in allusiveness and human suffering while addressing issues of single-sex friendship and the terrors faced by an intense subjectivity that seeks expression in stark isolation.[5] The themes of this sexual politics emerge through Crusoe's rhetorical guise, enabling the reticent Bishop the veil of prudence that Whitman himself had advocated. Casting her story as Crusoe's enables Bishop to deal with subjects that would otherwise remain unspoken because they were too overtly threatening or simply too overt. Crusoe's "poor old island's still / unrediscovered, unrenamable" because it is both self-created and unique, a terrain of psychic origins known and recognized only by the self. Unlike Defoe's hero, who returns to Brazil and visits his island (bringing with him provisions and women for the men to marry), this Crusoe remains bereft and alone on that other island, England. If, in the end, Defoe's Crusoe learns that providence rewards the believer, Bishop's Crusoe lives in a world without distinctions in a void of meaning.[6]

> Now I live here, another island,
> that doesn't seem like one, but who decides?
> My blood was full of them; my brain
> bred islands. But that archipelago
> has petered out. I'm old.
> I'm bored, too, drinking my real tea,
> surrounded by uninteresting lumber.
> The knife there on the shelf—
> it reeked of meaning, like a crucifix.
> It lived. How many years did I
> beg it, implore it, not to break?
> I knew each nick and scratch by heart,
> the bluish blade, the broken tip,
> the lines of wood-grain on the handle . . .
> Now it won't look at me at all.
> The living soul has dribbled away.
> My eyes rest on it and pass on.

(CP, 166)

In such a world, loss proliferates endlessly, like those "polliwogs of islands" bred of sorrow and despair. Value adheres to externality only through use and former affection as Crusoe enumerates the relics of survival:

> The local museum's asked me to
> leave everything to them:
> the flute, the knife, the shrivelled shoes,
> my shedding goatskin trousers
> (moths have got in the fur),
> the parasol that took me such a time
> remembering the way the ribs should go.
> It still will work but, folded up,
> looks like a plucked and skinny fowl.

How can anyone want such things?
—And Friday, my dear Friday, died of measles
seventeen years ago come March.

(*CP*, p. 166)

The very barrenness of this catalog, with its massive withdrawal of feeling, prepares the way for the recollection of Friday's death, voiced with the quietness characteristic of Bishop's most intimate revelations. Yet that quietness contains insistence, the verbal repetition its own intensity as Friday's memory is kept alive by the repetition of his name and the adjectival "my dear." The last line's plaintive, arcane "come" assures, moreover, that Friday's memory, rather than fading with time, will, in Crusoe's imagination, expand through it.

Adrienne Rich (1983) once noted that "poems examining intimate relationships are almost wholly absent from Bishop's later work" (p. 16). "What takes their place," Rich continues, "is a series of poems examining relationships between people who are, for reasons of difference, distanced: rich and poor, landowner and tenant, white woman and Black woman, invader and native." Intimacy, along with a strong eroticism, exists throughout Bishop's work, yet that intimacy, to extend Rich's observation, is not simply distanced by differences of class and race but is invoked most powerfully in terms of loss. For it is through absence, departure, and death that eroticism in Bishop's poems receives its fullest expression, as if like Dickinson, Bishop believed that "absence makes the present mean."

Bishop's late poem "One Art" (whose title conveys the implicit suggestion that mastery sought over loss in love is closely related to poetic control) articulates the tension between discipline in life and the force of circumstance.[7] The poem speaks in the tones of the survivor:

The art of losing isn't hard to master;
so many things seem filled with the intent
to be lost that their loss is no disaster.

(*CP*, p. 178)

The opening line, with its echo of a folk prescription such as "an apple a day," leads into the specifics of daily loss—of keys, of time—the syntactic parallelism suggesting an evaluative equation of what we immediately recognize as hardly equal realities. Such parallelism, by providing a temporary distraction that draws the reader away from the force building in the poem, functions as a disarming form of humor that undercuts the potential self-pity otherwise latent in the poem's subject.

> Lose something every day. Accept the fluster
> Of lost door keys, the hour badly spent.
> The art of losing isn't hard to master.

"One Art" presents a series of losses as if to reassure both its author and its reader that control is possible—an ironic gesture that forces upon us the tallying of experience cast in the guise of reassurance. By embracing loss as Emerson had Fate (the Beautiful Necessity), Bishop casts the illusion of authority over the inexorable series of losses that she seeks to master.

> Then practice losing farther, losing faster:
> places, and names, and where it was you meant
> to travel. None of these will bring disaster.

The race continues between "disaster" and "master" as the losses include her mother's watch, houses, cities, two rivers, a continent, and, perhaps in the future, an intimate friend whom, breaking out of the pattern of inanimate objects, the poem directly addresses:

> —Even losing you (the joking voice, a gesture
> I love) I shan't have lied. It's evident
> The art of losing's not too hard to master
> though it may look like (*Write* it!) like disaster.[8]

Here conflict explodes as the verbal deviations from previously established word patterns reflect the price of the speaker's remaining true to her initial claim that experience of loss can yield to mastery. With a directness that comes to predominate in Bishop's later work, "One Art" delineates the relationship between the will and the world. Note the split of "a gesture / I love" across two lines: the profession stands by itself as it turns back toward the beloved gesture. Syntax reveals the pain "One Art" has been fighting, since its beginnings, to suppress as the thought of losing "you" awakens an anxiety with which the poem must wrestle down to its close. This last time, the refrain varies its form, assuming an evidentiary structure that challenges as it expresses what has hitherto been taken as a fact recognized from within the poet's consciousness.

Coupled with the addition of "it's evident" is the adverbial "too" (It's evident / the art of losing's not too hard to master") which increases the growing tension within the desire to repeat the poem's refrain while admitting growing doubts as to its accuracy. In the end, the pressure to recapitulate the by-now-threatened refrain betrays itself in the sudden interruption of the closing line by an italicized hand that enforces the completion of the "master" / "disaster" couplet that the poem itself has made, through its formal demands, an inevitable resolution: "the art of losing's not too hard to master / though it may look like (*Write* it!) like disaster." The repetition of "like" postpones, ever so fleetingly, the final word that hurts all the more. "Disaster's" inevitability ironically recalls the fatalism of such childhood rituals as "he loves me; he loves me not"— in which the child's first words, "he loves me," and the number of petals on the flower determine the game's outcome. In its earlier evocation of folk ritual and in the villanelle's rhyme scheme, "One Art" reveals an ironic playfulness that works in collusion with high seriousness, a strategy that proliferates throughout Bishop's work.

Despite the disclaimers, qualifications, and play that mark these poems, Bishop's restraint has an ominous quality more suggestive than confession, a tenuous apprehension of a self moving through a world that is at once alien and mysterious. Her clarity is subjective more than literalizing, an accuracy based on magic and surrealistic surprise. In such a poetics, the Sublime would be what is even more strange, what speaks to us of experiences that carry us beyond our self-reflexive consciousness to what lies unidentified within. Bishop thus articulates an alienated or exiled subjectivity, and, as an outsider, she must observe with all her powers to draw a map, discern a geography.

That geography includes not only the desolate, surreal vitality of Crusoe's unnamed island but an alternative terrain as well. For if Crusoe's unnamed island signifies a terrain of lost invention, "Santarém," the town where the Amazon and Tapajós Rivers meet, is a destination of memory that invites a meditation on singleness and duality. Drawn here and really wanting to go no farther, the speaker admires not only the scene that she discovers but also the idea that informs the scene. Like Crusoe's lost island, Santarém's geography has epistemological conse-quences.

> I liked the place; I liked the idea of the place.
> Two rivers. Hadn't two rivers sprung

From the Garden of Eden? No, that was four
and they'd diverged. Here only two
and coming together. Even if one were tempted
to literary interpretations
such as: life / death, right / wrong, male / female
—such notions would have resolved, dissolved, straight off
in that watery, dazzling dialectic.

(*CP*, p. 185)

This final dialectic deconstructs the dissolution of the binary oppositions that precede it, as if the natural meeting of the two mighty rivers at once washed away all arbitrary distinctions yet held them apart in a single, brilliant, phenomenologically irrefutable suspension. The logical outcome of the conflux of these dialectical opposites would be union; Bishop resolves the division, however, not through a conceptual unity but by preserving the dialectic perceived in nature itself. That Bishop preserves this dialectic may reflect her recognition of a troubling, because naturally derived, dualism that cannot be effaced by linguistic reconceptualization. The presence of difference in the world, whether metaphysical, ethical, or sexual, appears as unyielding fact—the equivocal reality in which her poems strive to create reciprocal meanings. Santarém dazzles because of the singularity of ostensibly exemplary experience, the uniqueness of the place. Yet, singularity here depends upon a merging of dissimilar culture, customs, races. The "mongrel riverboats skittering back and forth / under a sky of gorgeous, underlit clouds" synechdochically reveal the vitality of the exceptional that defines the town. So do the occasional blue eyes, the English names, and the oars, all legacies of the nineteenth-century white southerners who came here because "they could still own slaves." That colonial impulse has been converted through the passage of time and the mixing of race into a reality marked by the exceptional. Finally, the wasps' nest (originally an object of danger) has become an artifact of beauty as well as an occasion to test whether a sense of wonder can survive the medium of exchange. The aesthetics of the singular is always at risk in Bishop's poems, the risk of being misunderstood or simply rejected.

Then—my ship's whistle blew. I couldn't stay.
Back on board, a fellow-passenger, Mr. Swan,
Dutch, the retiring head of Philips Electric,
really a very nice old man,

who wanted to see the Amazon before he died,
asked "What's that ugly thing?"

(*CP*, p. 187)

Unable to recognize the value of the wasps' nest, Mr. Swan, head of an organization that itself controls and so demystifies the lightning bolt that cracked the cathedral tower, remains oblivious to what renders both the gift and Santarém itself sacred. Mr. Swan's utter lack of appreciation speaks to the risk Bishop runs when offering something of value to others. Such moments, however, emerge against a psychic background distinguished by a desire for self-protection in a world perceived as irremediably divided between the subjectivity of the self and the threatening possibilities of other persons. In singling out Santarém and establishing a homeland of the exceptional that incorporates difference, Bishop gestures toward her desire to go beyond the oppositional character of literary and philosophical interpretation (and beyond the conflict between colonizer and colonized as well).

Even more explicitly, "Brazil, January 1, 1502" evokes a sense of place (the particularities of an aestheticized history) and the interworkings of exploration, lust, and greed. The poem's major trope, the interchangeability of nature and tapestry, invites a conflation of epistemological experience and aesthetic representation that, in its very tactility, suggests an elision between the sexual and the aesthetic. The torn tapestry becomes the violated body of nature itself. Bishop approaches her subject as one who simultaneously beholds an aesthetic object and a historic reality.[9] The poem's epigraph, "embroidered nature . . . tapestried landscape" (from Sir Kenneth Clark's *Landscape into Art*) prepares the way for the transformation of text into textile, cloth into life, the explorers into ourselves: "Januaries, Nature greets our eyes / exactly as she must have greeted theirs" (*CP*, p. 91). We are implicated at once, for we see what they see. And yet the poem sustains an aesthetic distance; when sin appears, it is as an allegorical figure.

> Still in the foreground there is Sin:
> five sooty dragons near some mossy rocks.
> The rocks are worked with lichens, gray moonbursts
> splattered and overlapping,
> threatened from underneath by moss
> in lovely hell-green flames,
> attacked above

by scaling-ladder vines, oblique and neat,
"one leaf yes and one leaf no" (in Portuguese).

The hell-green flames, sign of the weaver's wit, are singled out for their loveliness even as the forces of natural power are described in militaristic terms of threat, attack, and scaling-ladders. Any distinction between natural text and tapestry increasingly fades as the observer enters the world described, her eye drawn ever closer to the fabric of things. When that eye settles on the female lizard, there is no turning away.

      all eyes
are on the smaller, female one, back-to,
her wicked tail straight up and over,
red as a red-hot wire.

The inflamed, "wicked" female creature is marked as a sexual, potentially threatening presence and as a sign of evil—an immoral albeit natural presence. Although Bishop preserves her rhetorical distance from this tableau by describing it through the invaders' eyes (note the adjectival "wicked" attached to the lizard's tail), she simultaneously incorporates the invaders' presence into the tapestry and renders her independent judgment of their actions. The army of invaders are not only "hard as nails," but "tiny as nails," for they undergo a miniaturization that effectively symbolizes their meanness of spirit. Like ourselves, they find Brazil "not unfamiliar," for what they recognize is no artificial dissimilarity of culture, rather, the country represents the occasion for sexual and material lust: "wealth, plus a brand-new pleasure." These "hard" men rip through the fabric of nature, each out to snare a native woman for himself:

those maddening little women who kept calling,
calling to each other (or had the birds waked up?)
And retreating, always retreating, behind it.

(CP, p. 92)

With their lovely, birdlike calls and their ease of escape, these women embody a naturalizing freedom and vocal community that eludes the men who must tear the very fabric of nature to assuage their desire.[10]

If those "maddening little women" remain alluringly elusive in the Brazilian jungle, so, in "Roosters," the speaker aligns herself with the voice of the woman whose peaceful pleasure is interrupted by the harsh cries of explicitly phallic birds.[11] For the speaker describes being awakened from an apparently pleasurable sleep by the cocks' cry of "unwanted love, conceit and war." What restores "us" to former harmony is another atmosphere—muted, calm, and transfused with a pink light:

> In the morning
> a low light is floating
> in the backyard, and gilding
>
> from underneath
> the broccoli, leaf by leaf;
> how could the night have come to grief?
>
> gilding the tiny
> gloating swallow's belly
> and lines of pink cloud in the sky.
>
> (*CP*, p. 39)

Like the underlit clouds of Santarém, this "low light" gilds nature, and, like the gilt that rubs off one's fingers when one opens the "big book" in "Over 2,000 Illustrations and a Complete Concordance," this light makes the world (or the text) seem at once protective and secure. Here, the low light signals the distancing of the roosters: the cocks are now almost inaudible, and

> The sun climbs in,
> following "to see the end,"
> faithful as enemy, or friend.

This pink light foreshadows the rising of the sun, a moment described with supreme equivocation. Indeed, the sun may not simply be climbing in the window, but, given the ambiguities of the verb, climbing into bed. Its presence, although signifying the predictability of certain natural phenomena, is itself open to question because it potentially destroys the intimate shades of dawn and with it the sleepers' peace. Yet, despite equivocation, fidelity abides, for the sun climbs in "to see the end" as Peter (Matthew 26:58) follows Christ into the high priest's palace where he sits "with the servants, to see the end." In his earlier betrayal and final act of faithfulness, Peter's actions aptly foreshadow the equivocal question that closes Bishop's poem. The roosters with their pompous, militaristic arrogance, out to prove their "virile presence," usher in a dawn that threatens the alternative intimacy that precedes the day's return.[12] Although the poem will not betray secrets, it nevertheless alludes to a crisis of faith between friends and the possibility of a mutual faithfulness that belies the murderous aggression that surrounds them.

If Bishop identifies patently male images with aggression and violence, traditionally female images may be cast in an equally negative light, for both represent false terms in the dialectic her work seeks to evade. In "The Riverman," for example, the would-be male initiate quests for the acquisition of divine magic and mythic power. What hinders his progress is the normative world of dry land from which he desires to escape. The riverman yearns for a place freed from conventional gender identifications. He laments, "I need a virgin mirror" not spoiled by "the girls" who have used it "to look at their mouths in, / to examine their teeth and smiles" (*CP*, p. 107). This vanity is, in its way, as prurient as the cock's arrogance. In his pursuit of the redemptive, divine river-spirit that would yield magical powers, the riverman must first relinquish a rude domesticity (his snoring wife) and win a singularity that would enable him to aid those he has left behind. It is interesting that the moment of being singled out, of achieving the magical powers that estrange him from his past and the community of others, is celebrated by a maternal union of moon and river; to prove oneself exceptional and alone here signals (as so often in Bishop) a reenactment of maternal bonding that affirms rather than opposes one's isolation.

> You can peer down and down
> or dredge the river bottom
> but never, never catch me.
> When the moon shines and the river
> lies across the earth
> and sucks it like a child,
> then I will go to work
> to get you health and money.
> the Dolphin singled me out;
> Luandinha seconded it.
>
> (*CP*, p. 109)

Singled out at the moment of maternal fusion, the riverman gains his freedom, escaping from earthly realities of wife and home into the waters of mystery, where he seeks a virgin mirror to reenvision and thereby empower the self. For it is only in a world of magic, in the provisional impossibility of things not as they are, that the riverman can discover the power he craves. Indeed, Bishop may welcome isolation as a potential blessing, when, for example, in "Pleasure Seas," she beholds "an acre of cold white spray . . . / Dancing happily by itself" (*CP*, p. 196). But Bishop knows too well the difference between the exuberance of natural isolation and the human need for others, and in her exploration of a poetics rather than a politics of gender, she focuses on the division between self and other, male and female, life and death. Such divisions can be healed only by the imagination's recognition of loss and the ambivalent promise of singularity. Bishop's awareness of the problematic aspects of eros and the cultural construction of gender influences her understanding of her own desire as well as her need to imagine an alternative way of being that counters restrictive, normative definitions.

In an early poem, "Exchanging Hats," Bishop alludes to the conventional ascriptions of gender, teasing out the ontological ambiguities that hide behind costume.

> Unfunny uncles who insist
> in trying on a lady's hat,
> —oh, even if the joke falls flat,
> we share your slight transvestite twist
>
> in spite of our embarrassment.
>
> (*CP*, p. 200)

The acknowledgment of a shared interest in sexual shifts, the "slight transvestite twist," is not unrelated to the plural pronoun, the "we" of the poem which playfully dissociates the speaker from the poet while suggesting her multiple identities. The provisional status of costume becomes an occasion for the fictile imagination: "Costume and custom are complex. / The headgear of the other sex / inspires us to experiment." Mysteries are revealed as much as they are hidden by such awkward experimentation. Tawdry as the "unfunny uncle" seems, he still may be hiding "stars inside" his "black fedora." And the "aunt exemplary and slim," with her "avernal" eyes becomes both male and female: "springlike," embodying the possibilities of change and rebirth, a figure from the ancient underworld.

Aunt exemplary and slim,
with avernal eyes, we wonder
what slow changes they see under
their vast, shady, turned-down brim.

(*CP*, p. 201)

Bishop's play on "avernal" suggests the eyes' deep gaze, with their capacity to witness the "slow changes" of a cosmic panorama beyond any apparent fixity (of gender or of time). The diurnal progression from night to day is analogous to a male-female shift that remains a mystery. The aunt's hat brim, like the uncle's fedora, withholds knowledge from view as it ambiguously shades identity or expression from too intense scrutiny.

Such a blurring of distinctions and the implications of crossing-over through costume reemerge in Bishop's late poem, "Pink Dog."[13] The subject is a rather sickly, depilated bitch, who must disguise herself to avoid becoming an object of scorn: she must don a costume to survive the continuing "celebration" of life known as Carnival. Despite a vast difference in tone, "Pink Dog" recalls Wallace Stevens's "The American Sublime" (Stevens 1954, pp. 130–31), for both Stevens and Bishop address what one needs to survive in a place of deception, a land of danger that requires the individual armor of the imagination. Seeking what will suffice, Stevens asks,

"How does one stand
To behold the sublime? To confront the mockers,
The mickey mockers
and the plated pairs?

His provisional response is a stripping away of the external self until all that remains is "the spirit and space, / The empty spirit / In vacant space." What can such a spirit draw upon for sustenance? Stevens poses the question in sacramental terms: "What wine does one drink? / What bread does one eat?" (lines Bishop will parodically echo at the close of her poem). Like "The American Sublime," "Pink Dog" confronts a world of disguise and advocates a necessary defense, not of stripping away but of costume. This response is associated with the dog's color, her sex, and the perceived embarrassments associated with being a nursing mother with scabies (a disease caused by an insect that gets under the skin and produces intense itching). Her discomfort, then is related to a once external, now internalized agent, a discomfort that can be masked but not cured.

Immediately following the poem's opening, "the Sun is blazing and the sky is blue," with its echo of another Stevens poem about transformation, "The house was quiet, and the world was calm," we meet the hairless dog. Afraid of contagion, the crowds "draw back and stare" with us.

> Of course they're mortally afraid of rabies,
> You are not mad; you have a case of scabies
> but look intelligent. Where are your babies?.
>
> (CP, p. 190)

The dog's raw, pink skin and her hanging teats require a defense that can be achieved only through the use of intelligence operating as disguise. With an apparently effortless, desperado humor, Bishop rhymes "teats" and "wits," an associative verbal gesture so assured that the identification seems to carry all the circumstantiality of truth.

> (A nursing mother, by those hanging teats.)
> In what slum have you hidden them, poor bitch,
> while you go begging, living by your wits?

Unless the poor bitch can redirect her wits towards disguise, she will join those "idiots, parlytics, parasites" thrown into nearby tidal rivers. The practical solution, explains the level-headed, sardonic speaker, is to wear a "*fantasía*," or Carnival costume.

> Carnival is always wonderful!
> A depilated dog would not look well.
> Dress up! Dress up and dance at Carnival!
>
> (CP, p. 191)

The voice that proffers this advice is at once sympathetic and admonitory, as it insists upon the necessity of costume. Woman and dog are related by their gender and, potentially, by their vulnerability. Wit alone can protect each of them—a wit the poet practices so as to preserve her identity. Rarely does Bishop invoke masking so explicitly, although throughout her poems the need for protection is met by the courage of a voice willing to incur the risk of exposure.

Compensation (as Emerson himself came to recognize) is a boon in nature and a significant human activity. In her creation of a poetics that seeks to disrupt the fixities of our inherited understanding, Bishop strives to assign the human map of comprehension a less rigid set of directions, an alternative geography based not on polarities of difference but on the poet-geographer's painterly perception freed of disabling divisions. Such an alternative mapping may create, as in "Santarém," a distinct version of the Sublime, one that develops from a renewed awareness of loss and discontinuity that with dazzling restraint reconstitutes the world according to its and the world's priorities. With an Emersonian audacity tempered by a tact requisite to her radical vision, Bishop's poems aim at nothing short of freedom from the inherently dualistic tradition that lies not only at the foundations of the American Sublime but at the very heart of the Western literary tradition.

Two poems from Bishop's last volume, *Geography III,* approach the Sublime by means of apparently constrasting yet structurally similar experiences. "In the Waiting Room" and "The Moose" both explore the self's relation to others as they articulate a moment that interrupts the continuous act of sublimation that enables us to preserve an ongoing constitutive identity. In each poem, the crisis of that interruption is resolved through a gesture of reunion with life beyond the self that allows identity to reconstitute itself in a recognizable form. These poems delineate an *ecstasis* that recalls the vertiginous psychic shifts of the experiential Sublime. In the waiting room, strangers isolated by anxiety and anonymity come together, their status provisional, for they are on the outside waiting to go in.[14] In "The Moose" the liminal is again invoked as strangers embark on a communal journey only to await their arrival at various destinations. Against these provisional environments, Bishop introduces images of family. The bus passengers in "The Moose" catch a glimpse of a woman shaking out a tablecloth. Anonymous voices float softly from the back of the bus (the recesses of the mind?) to create a soothing lullaby of conversation that retells the history of people's lives. But the family is not the narrator's own; if the recollections draw her back into her past, it is through the aura of remembrance created by others' voices.

In the waiting room, familial forms assume a more terrifying guise. While she waits for her aunt to emerge from the dentist's chair, "Elizabeth" reads an article in the *National Geographic,* where human images assume macabre, distorted forms:

A dead man slung on a pole
—"Long Pig," the caption said.
Babies with pointed heads
Wound round and round with string;
black, naked women with necks
wound round and round with wire
like the necks of light bulbs.
Their breasts were horrifying.

(*CP*, p. 159)

What is meant to pass the time becomes a rite of passage as the seven-year-old Elizabeth is led into the abyss of a self she had not earlier recognized as her own:

Suddenly, from inside,
came an *oh!* of pain
—Aunt Consuelo's voice—
not very loud or long. . . .
What took me
completely by surprise
was that it was *me:*
my voice, in my mouth.
Without thinking at all
I was my foolish aunt,
I—we—were falling, falling,
our eyes glued to the cover
of the *National Geographic,*
February, 1918.

(*CP*, p. 160)

The child counters the vertigo that accompanies her faltering sense of self with facts, information about the external world, and contemporary events. What has threatened her perception of identity can be traced, at least for its proximate cause, to the grotesque pictorial representations of man, woman, and child. What so disturbs Elizabeth that she loses that sense of self one takes for granted in order to live in the world? Lee Edelman addresses this issue: "Though only in the course of reading the magazine does 'Elizabeth' perceive the inadequacy of her positioning as a reader, Bishop's text implies from the outset the insufficiency of any mode of interpretation that claims to release the meaning it locates 'inside' a text by asserting its own ability to speak from a position of mastery 'outside' of it. For this reason everything that 'Elizabeth' encounters in the pages of the *National Geographic* serves to disturb the stability of a binary opposition."[15] This disturbance incorporates, moreover, a questioning of the internalized structures and cultural codes that inform the interpretation of experience. If Bishop's sexual poetics more generally deconstruct the binary oppositions of heterosexist discourse, "In the Waiting Room" addresses a related epistemological concern that arises from Bishop's destabilization of the distinctions by which persons organize information about themselves and their world. Edelman continues: "Though Bishop's text, then, has challenged the stability of distinctions between inside and outside, male and female, literal and figurative, human and bestial, young 'Elizabeth' reads on from her own position of liminality in the waiting room until she confronts, at last, an image of women and their infants" (Edelman 1985, p. 188). By focusing on Elizabeth's vexed response to the horrific image of maternal sexuality, Edelman introduces us to the larger question of female sexuality in Bishop's work as he urges us to hear the "oh!" that "emanates from inside the dentist's office, and from inside the waiting room, and from inside the *National Geographic,* and from inside 'In the Waiting Room' as a cry of the female—that recognizes the attempts to clarify it as attempts to put it in its place" (Edelman 1985, p. 191). That voice of protest, emanating from an epistemological uncertainty, echoes throughout Bishop's work in poems that reengage the mediations between rhetoric and sexual identity. The fall away from awareness of distinctions disrupts the assurance of a constitutive identity. And the restoration of that identity through the intervention of the external is akin to the final stage of the experiential Sublime, where in the poet's identity, momentarily repressed by a power felt to be greater than and external to it, reemerges. That the experiential Sublime should, in this poem, be so closely linked to the voice of female sexuality and the overthrowing of culturally encoded identities reaffirms the alternative aspect of the psychological Sublime for the woman poet. Gender is at the center of any such aesthetic crisis, and the eroticization of literary categories serves the function of deidealizing the work of the human imagination.

"The Moose" describes a related dynamics of the Sublime wherein separation and fusion, the underlying terms of Elizabeth's crisis, are associated with a phenomenon that simultaneously evades and incorporates conventionally disparate categories. For, the appearance of the moose—unknown, mysterious—affirms in the passengers' response the unifying effect of joy. And yet, that joy itself is located in a question that underscores less the sensation experienced than its totalizing impact:

> Why, why do we feel
> (we all feel) this sweet
> sensation of joy?

> (*CP*, p. 173)

Here the issue of communal identity again surfaces only to be called into question as Elizabeth's ontological doubt reappears. In the face of the wondrous, the strange, the otherworldly, these passengers' joy is less compelling than the interrogatory form in which it is cast. Bishop's question, if it does not detract from that joy, certainly redirects the reader's attention to forms of response. That the answer goes without saying provides a clue to the ontological ambiguity of the moment (reflected in the moose's own anomalous status).

> Towering, antlerless,
> high as a church,
> homely as a house
> (or, safe as houses),

the moose combines the domestic with the sacred, female identity with animal nature (Edelman 1985, p. 196). A majestic presence from another world, the moose appears beyond our expectations, an utterly unanticipated presence escaping the predictability of human experience. Her function as surprise (an effect both Bishop and Emerson regarded as among the highest forms of aesthetic achievement) works on another level, for it not only catches us off guard but challenges our notions of a verifiable, ordered universe.[16] The moose thus embodies a female strangeness that constitutes an inherently subversive notion of the Sublime, and the joy "we all" experience is a joy related to the very interruption of the continuum of expectation, hence predictive consciousness. That a female creature is the occasion for a saving disruption of the normative is itself not unexpected: such a gesture participates in the reaffirmation of maternal power that is at once otherworldly and wholly present.

Yet the epistemic displacements of "In the Waiting Room" and "The Moose" create their own anxieties as Bishop pays a price for choosing to work in the liminal space between land and water, the domestic and the strange, eros and art. Against the dangers of exile, Bishop searches for the redemptive possibilities of home. Bishop's late poem, "The End of March," most fully articulates Bishop's understanding of the relationship between the geography of the imagination and the home ground magisterially domesticated by Emerson, Whitman, and Stevens, the major voices of the American Sublime.[17] Here the speaker's footsteps follow the tracks of monumental beachcombers who had sought signs of selfhood on their native shores. The poem opens with the inhospitable character of place and weather; it is not a good day to take a walk.

> It was cold and windy, scarcely the day
> to take a walk on that long beach.
> Everything was withdrawn as far as possible,
> indrawn.
>
> (*CP*, p. 179)

Offering no welcome, the beach grants no access. The bad weather itself, however, makes it possible for the speaker to walk freed from the glaring sun or the night sky's brilliant auroras, so long celebrated as indexes of the American Sublime. In the face of such immediately austere conditions, indeed drawn forward by them, the speaker sees "dog-prints (so big / they were more like lion-prints)," which lead to "lengths and lengths, endless, of wet white string, / looping up to the tide-line, down to the water, / over and over." This "line" lures her to

> a thick white snarl, man-size, awash,
> rising on every wave, a sodden ghost,
> falling back, sodden, giving up the ghost. . . .
> A kite string?—But no kite.
>
> (*CP*, p. 179)

The man who has been there before her has vanished into this snarl; his presence becomes an absence, a ghost who has given up the ghost. Haunted by this absence, the speaker continues her walk, her goal the "crooked box" that would be her "proto-dream-house" where she imagines a bliss of solitude, a place for desultory reading and a "lovely diaphanous blue flame"—"A light to read by—perfect! But—impossible." Having to turn back because "the wind was much too cold / even to get that far, / and of course the house was boarded up," she cannot remain in this place or find her home on this worn shore. The scene belongs to the Whitman of "Out of the Cradle" and "As I Ebb'd," the dream of habitation to the Stevens of "The Auroras of Autumn":

> Farewell to an idea . . . A cabin stands,
> Deserted, on a beach. It is white,
> As by a custom or according to
>
> An ancestral theme or as a consequence
> Of an infinite course.
>
> .   .   .   .
>
> The season changes. A cold wind chills the beach.
> The long lines of it grow longer, emptier,
> A darkness gathers though it does not fall
>
> And the whiteness grows less vivid on the wall.
> The man who is walking turns blankly on the sand.
> He observes how the north is always enlarging the change,
>
> With its frigid brilliances, its blue-red sweeps
> And gusts of great enkindlings, its polar green,
> The color of ice and fire and solitude.

The "Farewell to an Idea," from "Auroras," must be the speaker's rejection as well, for the possibility of domestic warmth remains an illusion. Seeking her "proto-dream house," the speaker is denied entry, prevented from participating in the Stevensian Sublime of solitude, illumination, and terror. Here is Stevens:

> He opens the door of his house
> On flames. The scholar of one candle sees
> An Arctic effulgence flaring on the frame
> Of everything he is. And he feels afraid.

(Stevens 1954, pp. 416–17)

This is the Sublime fear of external power threatening to overwhelm the solitary scholar; it is the fear that lies at the heart of the experiential Sublime as it bears witness to the forces that lie beyond the self.

Barred from that afflatus of terror, the speaker turns back from her journey, never reaching the house that, of course, is already "boarded up." Instead of the auroras that so powerfully move her precursors, she observes the sun's diminishment as the stones throw out "long shadows, / individual shadows, then pull[ed] them in again." Thus, Bishop evades the terror of the Whitmanian Sublime when it becomes, as it will always become for Whitman, an equivalent anxiety of demand: "Dazzling and tremendous, how quick it could kill me, / If I could not now and always send sunrise out of me." [18] Bishop resists Whitman's defiance by herself noting the sun's fall into the western sky. The sun that had formerly walked along the beach trailing his kite string, "making those big, majestic paw-prints, / who perhaps had batted a kite out of the sky to play with," the playful, huge beast of light, fades into the shadows and leaves the poet alone. By abandoning the shore to its ghosts, the poem achieves its own solar flare of momentary brilliance as

> The sun came out for just a minute.
> For just a minute, set in their bezels of sand,
> the drab, damp, scattered stones
> were multi-colored,
> and all those high enough threw out long shadows,
> individual shadows, then pulled them in again.

(*CP*, p. 180)

At the poem's close, the sun reappears as a gigantic playful lion, whose absence leaves a trace of paw prints (and perhaps a bit of lost kite string). This simultaneous expansion and diminution preserves the aura of cosmic power as it calls into play, through its parodic troping, the powers it would cast aside. Thus, "The End of March," like "In the Waiting Room" and "The Moose," presents a moment of experiential discontinuity that questions the reaffirmation following on loss, a reaffirmation that would announce the resolution of the Sublime. Through such a rhetorical subversion of the major trope of American Sublimity, Bishop wins a distance from her precursor poets, and it is within this difference that she inscribes a geography disdaining the radical solipsism that has for so long marked the American poetic enterprise. What distinguishes Bishop's work from the dominant tradition of the American Sublime might be understood as a loss equivalent to restitution, the enactment of Bishop's "I" as the eye of the traveler or the child that only apparently evades issues of sexuality and gender. Bishop's poems inscribe a map of language where the limitations of sexuality yield before a disengendered, highly eroticized imagination. In her revisionary conceptualization of an eros that escapes such categorization, Bishop subtly evades the strife between Emerson and his agonistic disciples. The poems' prevailing absence of overt sexuality, indeed, their very dismissal of binary oppositions, recalls, moreover, Rich's exclusion of the "male" as a way to reestablish women's access to the world and the word. Despite their vast differences, Rich and Bishop both respond to the American tradition's denial of the woman as poet by reasserting their divergence from the scripts of heterosexist culture.

Bishop's poem "Sonnet" (*CP*, p. 192) enacts a rebellion against that script through its rhetorical manipulations of that most traditionally conservative form. The poem engages the tension between sexual freedom and the confines of existing structures.[19]

Caught—the bubble
in the spirit-level,
a creature divided;
and the compass needle
wobbling and wavering,
undecided.
Freed—the broken
thermometer's mercury
running away;
and the rainbow-bird
from the narrow bevel
of the empty mirror,
flying wherever
it feels like, gay![20]

From the opening "caught" to the final "gay," "Sonnet" traces the experience of a "creature divided" (one recalls the tense, bifurcated personae of the early poems: "The Gentleman of Shalott," "Cirque d'Hiver," "From the Country to the City," "The Man-Moth"). "Caught," "wobbling and wavering," "undecided": elements intended to balance are trapped.[21] When, however, the thermometer breaks, its mercury takes flight: for surely, "Sonnet" is as much about the spirit's flight upward into a new freedom as it is about the categories that bifurcate and bind our lives. Formally, the sonnet inverts the Petrarchan paradigm by reversing the positions of the sextet and the octave, a rhetorical shift that mirrors Bishop's play of trope. With the sextet's close, the image changes from the spirit-level to the mercury "running away" as it escapes to a sphere beyond measurement where the false determinacy of empiricism loses its meaning in the exuberance of flight. Such freedom bestows shape on spirit; the conversion of mercury into a "rainbow-bird" transforms the previously entrapped substance into a dazzling presence. If the bird in Shelley's "To a Skylark" sings its ravishing song in a world full of color, the translucent "rainbow bird" in "Sonnet" embodies this array. By breaking the confines of linearity, moreover, the bead of mercury escapes its identity as sign to be read. Thus, like Shelley's skylark soaring among "rainbow clouds," "Sonnet" describes an exuberance beyond mortal limits, a "joy" (Shelley's word) or gaiety that finds its origins in a release not simply from mortality but from the specific, articulable divisions associated with measurement and balance. From the first, Bishop's poems have imagined a world of which the rainbow-bird is only the last, most beautiful synechdoche. Like Santarém, this is a sacred ground where the differences of literary interpretation fall away before the more sublime possibility of a freedom that rises above distinctions, where the mind, escaping the boundaries of preconception, discovers in its sexual, poetic, and epistemic quests an escape from the mirror of history. It is to this region that Bishop's sexual poetics carries us, to an experiential Sublime that assumes a form freed from the ascriptions of gender. The poetic voice that speaks to and from that region is marked by an authoritative clarity that promises not the transcendence of the body but a redefinition of the body's relation to language. Finally, the rainbow-bird's gaiety recalls the power of Bishop's own imagination as it breaks through the inherited codifications of naming to achieve the exuberant stature of an American Counter-Sublime.

Notes

1. Bishop's copy of Walt Whitman's *Leaves of Grass* (edited by Emory Holloway [Garden City, N.Y.: Doubleday, Page and Co., 1926]) is marked and contains some marginalia. Bishop's signature is in a childlike hand. (See the Bishop Collection, HL, for books from Elizabeth Bishop's library.) I indicate Bishop's markings and the pages on which they appear in parentheses within the text.

2. Commenting on Bishop's poem "Florida," David Kalstone (1983a) notes the difference between Bishop's mode of description and Whitman's: "A descriptive poem," Kalstone writes, "which in other hands, say Whitman's, appropriates landscapes and objects, here makes us aware just how, just why we are excluded from such appropriations" (p. 7). Bishop's departure from Whitman depends, as Kalstone suggests, on her sense of exclusion, a subject to which I will turn later in this chapter.

3. As John Hollander (1983) observes, "The very island is an exemplar, a representation; it is a place which stands for the life lived on it as much as it supports that life. Its unique species are emblems of the selfhood that the whole region distills and enforces and on it, life and word and art are one, and the homemade Dionysus is (rather than blesses from without or within) his votary" (p. 250).

4. Marjorie Perloff (1977) notes Bishop's procedures of narrative. Although Perloff is describing the narrative technique of "In the Village," her observations are useful when reading "Crusoe in England." Citing Roman Jakobson's study of Pasternak's early prose, Perloff states that "Jakobson argues that unlike Mayakovsky, whose poetic mode is insistently metaphoric, Pasternak follows the path of contiguous relations, metonymically digressing from the plot to the atmosphere and from the characters to the setting in space and time." Like Pasternak, Perloff concludes, "Bishop digresses from actor to setting, from plot to atmosphere." The narrative of contiguity and metonymic relations characterizes "Crusoe in England" as well as "In the Village" (1977, p. 183).

5. Jerome Mazzaro (1985) comments on Friday's gender: "Friday's being male . . . limits the urge toward futurity that the poem identifies with duty to rude artifacts, since the urge cannot be served in biological propagation. Art thus becomes some kind of adjustment to Necessity" (p. 34). My discussion attempts to consider what kind of adjustment that might be.

6. In a conversation with George Starbuck (1983), Bishop alluded to reading *Robinson Crusoe:*

GS: What got the Crusoe poem started?
EB: I don't know. I reread the book and discovered how really awful Robinson Crusoe was, which I hadn't realized. I hadn't read it in a long time. And then I was remembering a visit to Aruba—long before it was a developed "resort." I took a trip across the island and it's true that there are small volcanoes all over the place.
GS: I forget the end of *Robinson Crusoe.* Does the poem converge on the book?
EB: No. I've forgotten the facts, there, exactly. I reread it all one night. And I had forgotten it was so moral. All that Christianity. So I think I wanted to re-see it with all that left out (p. 319).

7. See McClatchy 1984, p. 39, for a discussion of the sources and formal aspects of Bishop's villanelle.

8. Draft ten of "One Art" conveys a much more specific impression of the "you" who may be lost:

But, losing you (eyes of the Azure Aster)
But-you-if I lose you—(eyes of azure aster)
all that I write is false.

Line two is crossed out in this version and the final "false" is crossed out as well (see the drafts of "One Art," in the Bishop Collection, box 27, folder 410, VC).

9. David Kalstone (1983a) comments on the poem's opening: "Its first word is the generalizing *Januaries.* No longer the 'here' and 'now' of the uninstructed tourist, the poem fans out into the repeating present of the botanist and the anthropologist" (p. 19).

10. Willard Spiegelman (1985) notes Bishop's exploration of "the cliches of masculine conquest in "Brazil, January 1, 1502" and in the first half of "Roosters" (see p. 98). Spiegelman compares Bishop's roosters to Stevens's "Chief Ilfucan" and notes their "lunatic pseudo-heroic fighting swagger" (p. 99).

11. For a sustained reading of "Roosters" and a study of its compositional origins, see Newman 1983. Newman comments on the comparison (in the second part of the poem) between "Magdalen's sin and Peter's—hers of the 'flesh alone,' his of the 'spirit.'" Newman notes that "the male-female comparisons are interesting and add a personal dimension to the poem, but they do not take precedence over the concern for all mankind" (pp. 116–17). Here I would differ, suggesting that the comparison between Magdalen's and Peter's sins underscores the prevailing thematics of the poem of female-to-female intimacy and the dangers of a distinctively masculine betrayal.

12. Focusing on these lines, David Bromwich (1985) writes, "Indeed, there is something like self-reproach in a line that begins the final movement of 'Roosters': 'how could the night have come to grief?' By a trick of context, this phrase opens up an ambiguity in the cliché. It warns us that there has been matter for grieving during the night, before the first rooster crowed, at a scene of passion which is also a betrayal" (p. 166).

13. On the draft labeled 1, Bishop wrote "my good dog" above "Pink Dog," the first phrase emphasizing her proprietary relationship to the animal she describes. On an unnumbered typed draft, Bishop has written and then crossed out the phrase "solution is disguise" (see box 28, folder 418, VC).

14. Of the poems in *Geography III*, David Kalstone (1983a) notes, "her 'questions of travel' modulate now, almost imperceptibly, into questions of memory and loss. Attentive still to landscape where one can feel the sweep and violence of encircling and eroding geological powers, poems such as 'Crusoe in England' and 'The Moose' pose their problems retrospectively" (p. 26).

15. Bonnie Costello (1983) observes, "Most of the enclosed places Bishop describes are waiting rooms in one way or another (the most extreme being a wake). Her ports, islands, bights, are not microcosms of, or escapes from, history; they contain the tides of unity and discontinuity, of presence and absence, with much the same incompleteness as any wider experience of flux" (pp. 114–15).

16. Helen Vendler (1983) draws several interesting distinctions between "The Moose" and Robert Frost's "The Most of It": "There, as in Bishop's poem, a creature emerges from 'the impenetrable wood' and is beheld. But Frost's beast disappoints expectation. The poet had wanted 'counter-love, original response,' but the 'embodiment that crashed' proves to be not 'human,' not 'someone else additional to him,' but rather a large buck which disappears as it came." Vendler concludes, "Frost's beast is male, Bishop's female; Frost's a symbol of brute force, Bishop's a creature 'safe as houses'; Frost's a challenge, Bishop's a reassurance" (p. 46).

17. In an interview with the *Christian Science Monitor,* Bishop commented on the value of surprise:

"A final question: What one quality should every poem have?"
"Surprise. The subject and the language which conveys it should surprise you. You should be surprised at seeing something new and strangely alive" (Alexandra Johnson 1978, pp. 24–25).

18. Harold Bloom (1985) contrasts Stevens's lion with Bishop's:

In Stevens, the lion tends to represent poetry as a destructive force, as the imposition of the poet's will-to-power over reality. . . . Here, I take it, Bishop's affectionate riposte:

They could have been teasing the lion sun,
except that now he was behind them
—a sun who'd walked the beach the last low tide,
making those big, majestic paw-prints,
who perhaps had batted a kite out of the sky to play with.

A somewhat Stevensian lion sun, clearly, but with something better to do than standing potent in itself. The path away from poetry as a destructive force can only be through play, the play of trope. Within her tradition so securely, Bishop profoundly plays at trope. Dickinson, Moore, and Bishop resemble Emerson, Frost, and Stevens in that tradition, with a difference due not to mere nature or mere ideology but to superb art" (pp. 2–3).

Although I share Bloom's conviction that Bishop is secure in her tradition and that she profoundly plays with trope, I would insert between his terms "nature" and "mere ideology" the gender-inflected imagination, for surely to evade the role of sexuality in the life of the mind is to play into the hands of those very idealizers of the imagination that Bloom himself so sharply criticizes.

19. Walt Whitman, "Song of Myself," *Leaves of Grass*, section 25, lines 560–561.

20. Jean Valentine (1984) notes, "This short poem, 'Sonnet,' was to be the last poem she would write: one of her most purely joyful poems about 'the size of our abidance'; a redemptive poem for any particular guests on this earth who start out 'caught' and hope to end up 'freed.' In a published manuscript draft, Bishop tries the first line as 'Oh brain, bubble'; in the finished poem, the bubble itself is freed to be more than brain, to be 'creature.' At the end, the mirror is empty, and the creature is not only freed, but lives to tell the story" (p. 45). Although I share Valentine's interest in the move from "brain" to "creature," I would suggest that what "Sonnet" may redeem is not the self-limiting experience "about the size of our abidance," but the vision of a larger world of unrestricted possibility that breaks through the limitations so often probed in Bishop's earlier work.

21. One recalls Bishop's use of "wavering" in "Love Lies Sleeping" (*CP*, p. 16):

From the window I see
an immense city, carefully revealed,
made delicate by over-workmanship,
    detail upon detail,
    cornice upon façade,

reaching so languidly up into
a weak white sky, it seems to waver there.

MARILYN MAY LOMBARDI

The Closet of Breath: Elizabeth Bishop, Her Body and Her Art

I

IN 1937, when Elizabeth Bishop was only twenty-six, she discovered the wilds of Florida on a fishing expedition and fell in love with the swamps and palm forests of a state that was still a North American wilderness. When the poet and her friend Louise Crane came to live in Key West the following year, their response to the tropical *Cayo Hueso*, known as the Bone Key, was severely colored, however, by the tragic six-month stay in Europe that intervened between Bishop's first visit to Florida and her return.[1] Bishop and her close friends Crane and Margaret Miller had been traveling from Burgundy back to Paris when their car was forced off the road and flipped over. Miller, a painter, was the only one seriously injured. Her arm, partially cut from her body when she was thrown clear of the car, eventually had to be amputated to the elbow.

If we look at Bishop's life and work during her time in Florida, we find that her imagination is understandably haunted by the maiming of her intimate friend and fellow artist. The tragedy brought into terrible focus preoccupations already troubling the young poet—chief among them, the artist's relation to her own body, to its passions and its vulnerabilities. In one of a series of notebooks kept during her years in Key West, Bishop described the automobile accident that severed Miller's arm from her torso: "the arm lay outstretched in the soft brown grass at the side of the road and spoke quietly to itself, 'Oh my poor body! Oh my poor body! I cannot bear to give you up,'" but the detached limb's desire to be quickly reunited with its body soon gives way to other thoughts, "so this is what it means to be really 'alone in the world!'" (KWN 1, p. 59).

Bishop clearly identifies with the lonely arm—the analytic arm of the artist detached from the woman and from the sensual memories that a woman's form retains. Like the acutely conscious arm speaking to itself by the side of the road, Bishop is drawn to and yet alienated from the unconscious life of her own body, which she comes to view with a mixture of fascination, embarrassment, and pity (KWN 2, p. 12).

During the years in Florida, Bishop suffered from almost nightly attacks of debilitating asthma and recorded her dreams and anxieties in a set of small notebooks that have only recently been made available to scholars. In the seclusion of these private journals, she turned with uncharacteristic forthrightness to the subject of the flesh, its pleasures, and its torments. She jotted down plans to develop plays and poems about the bodily afflictions of Job, Jonah, St. Teresa, and St. Anthony and appeared especially preoccupied, for very personal reasons, with the fate of St. Sebastian. Repeatedly referred to in the Key West/Nemer notebooks, he figures prominently again in an unfinished essay entitled *A Little About Brazil* (box 42, folder 643, VC), in which the poet explains her fascination with him: "St. Sebastian protects Rio de Janeiro and perhaps that is the reason why the people are all crazy about hypodermic injections." An asthmatic forced to inject herself with cortisone, Bishop saw Sebastian's martyrdom as a reminder of her own intimate relationship with the hypodermic needle.

The poet's asthma and allergic inflammations—her most chronic physical ailments—are the primary focus of her lengthy letters to her New York doctor during the years in Key West. Dr. Anny Baumann, Bishop's personal physician and a friend as well as a medical adviser, helped the poet trace the tangled relations that existed in her life between psychosomatic illness and early maternal deprivation. Bishop's private correspondence and notebook entries reveal that the poet's early, ambivalent experience of mother love continued to haunt her adult sexual relationships and influence her view of the ambiguous bond between poet and reader.

Bishop's published work rarely speaks about her illnesses directly. In her poetry, she refused to allow herself, her body, and her experience to be contained within any culturally prescribed notion of gender or sexual orientation. She chose, instead, to cloak and recloak her own flesh, to cross-dress, displace, or otherwise project her most intense feelings onto a variety of poetic protagonists to escape stifling categorization and conventional definitions of identity. Still, Bishop's imagination continually pursued the implications of her private battle for breath. As a poet, she transmutes the symptoms of her asthmatic condition into a rich cache of metaphors that help enact her sense of the world: for Bishop, human interaction takes place within a set of smothering categories (a series of waiting rooms) that enforce a kind of artificial intimacy among their occupants—an intimacy that often fails to respect the uniqueness and the privacy of each human soul.[2] Although asthma is not the central subject of poems like "In the Waiting Room," "O Breath," and "The Riverman," knowledge of Bishop's condition opens up new ways to approach crucial images of respiration, suffocation, and constriction in each work—images that draw attention to the equivocal reality of human relationships.

II

For much of Bishop's life, her body registered emotional distress in painful ways. The poet's allergic inflammations were largely responsible for perhaps the most important personal and professional decision of her life—to remain as a permanent resident in Brazil. While visiting friends in Rio de Janeiro, Bishop ate the fruit of the cashew and experienced a violent allergic reaction that left her head and ears swollen. After she recovered, she decided to stay in Brazil. In a series of letters to Baumann from her new home in Petrópolis, she described the onset of her affliction and her distended body: "That night my eyes started stinging, and the next day I started to swell—and swell and swell; I didn't know one *could* swell so much" (8 January 1952, VC).

Taking fifteen cubic centimeters of calcium and seven or eight cubic centimeters of adrenalin each day to bring her swelling down, Bishop was suffering simultaneously from a "very bad" recurrence of her childhood eczema, an inflammatory condition of the skin characterized by oozing lesions that become scaly, crusted, or hardened: "Before this started," she wrote to her doctor, "I had noticed my mouth got sore from eating, I thought, too much pineapple." With the worst case of eczema since childhood, her "ears [swollen] like large red hot mushrooms," and her asthma as bad as ever, Bishop wrote to Baumann with frustration and a hint of justifiable self-pity: "I finally got sick of being stuck with so many things [to reduce the swelling, and felt] like St. Sebastian" (8 January 1952, VC). She proved allergic to the new wonder drug, penicillin and her infected skin glands formed localized inflammations or boils.

Writing about the episode to her favorite relative, Aunt Grace, she remarked, "When someone is allergic like me, you never know what may happen, apparently" (16 July 1956, box 18, folder 252, VC). Even when singing the praises of cortisone, an anti-inflammatory drug that left her in a state of "euphoria" and heightened creativity, she worried about still another form of swelling: "It's amazing how energetic it makes one feel although also I'm afraid it has a tendency to make one get even fatter" (letter to Baumann from Samambaia, 28 December 1952, VC). Weight gain had been a worry for many years; she had been taking two grains a day of thyroid pills to control her weight while in Washington, D.C., in 1949: "If I don't, I just keep getting fat no matter what I eat" (letter to Baumann, 12 December, VC). Like a latter-day St. Teresa, whose *Way of Perfection* became a permanent part of Bishop's private library, Bishop tests her own strength by a "fastidious" disciplining of her wayward, expanding flesh (KWN 2, p. 23).

Of all her inflammatory reactions, however, bronchial asthma was the most chronic. Asthma is an allergic response to foreign substances that generally enter the body by way of the air breathed or the food eaten. In response to the foreign substances the mucus membranes of the respiratory system secrete excessive amounts of mucus, and the smaller bronchial muscles go into spasms. This narrows the passageways, making it difficult to expel air. Bishop's wheezing lungs prevented her from taking up a comfortable and lasting residence in the places she loved, contributing to an already intense feeling of homelessness. To Anny Baumann she confides that asthma had become the single most frustrating impediment to her happiness—"as soon as I get to a place I like best of all it starts again," she wrote from Key West, Florida, on 30 December 1948 (VC). Earlier that year, she wrote to Baumann from Stonington, Maine (5 August 1948, VC), where her asthma and a variety of other acute allergic reactions made it impossible for her to sleep, and the almost hourly injections of adrenalin she took to regulate her breathing left her nauseated and dizzy: "for the past eight or nine years I have had asthma about every day and night." Awarded the first Lucy Martin Donnelly Fellowship from Bryn Mawr College in 1951, Bishop found by February 1952 that the "bounty [from the fellowship] has gone mostly for adrenalin" (letter to Baumann, 10 February 1952, VC).

The period covered by the Key West/Nemer notebooks became a time of psychological investigation for Bishop, who desperately needed to know the cause of her physical misery. Her remarks to Baumann make it clear that she had come to regard her doctor as a psychiatric advisor. From Stonington, Maine, she wrote Baumann that she was concerned with the state of her mind and its impact on her physical condition: "Every magazine or paper I pick up has an article proving that asthma is psychosomatic, everyone now thinks it is almost entirely, if not entirely mental" (5 August 1948, VC). In a letter to Baumann from Yaddo dated 17 January 1951, (VC) Bishop described terrible bouts with asthma that left her emotionally as well as physically exhausted, and she traced her "discouragement, panic, sleeplessness, nightmares" to the realization that she was "exactly the age now at which [her] father died." Her body's seemingly uncontrollable inflammations accorded somehow with what Bishop called in yet another letter to Baumann her "morbid swellings of the conscience"—lasting anxieties rooted in childhood sadness that rose up unpredictably to overwhelm her, like bad dreams. In her notebook she recorded these "dreams that overpowered [her] / ("mugging") from behind" (KWN 2, p. 141). Just above these observations she scribbled three phrases in quick succession: "the fierce odors," "family mortality," "families of mortalities."

The central conditions of Bishop's childhood, her early orphaning and sense of maternal deprivation, left her with an acute sensitivity to the ways in which personal anguish and shame may be hidden from view. Her family corseted their emotions in a futile attempt to tame the brute world of pain and raise themselves out of lassitude. The effort drove them into a den of artificial innocence. Early on she was initiated into strategies of evasion and indirection and a "Puritan outlook" with respect to the body and its "embarrassing" weaknesses that accompanied her on her travels and became the burdensome "inheritance" she carried with her to Brazil—an inheritance that set her apart from that country's more "tolerant" natives (letter to Baumann from Rio de Janeiro, 7 July 1954, VC).[3] Bishop considered herself physically allergic to the atmosphere in which she was raised, the "hypocrisy [that was] so common then, so unrecognized, that it fooled everyone," including the hypocrite himself ("Memories of Uncle Neddy, *CProse*, p. 230). Hypocrisy reminded her of the molds and mildews that made her life so miserable; like the hypocrite, the "gray-green dust" is double in nature, suggesting blooming life and its sooty shadow, "morbidity"—"or perhaps mortality is a better word." In her private notebooks she would call this hypocrisy the "fierce odor" of "family mortality" that surrounded her earliest years.[4]

Though she suffered from bronchitis in the first years of her life in Boston and in her maternal grandparents' home in Nova Scotia, the condition became much worse when her mother succumbed to insanity and was hospitalized for the rest of her life. Bishop was only five years old. Her paternal grandparents took the orphaned girl ("unconsulted and against my wishes," as she later put it) to Worcester, Massachusetts. Bishop was given the impression that her New England relatives were "saving" her from a life of poverty and provincialism in Canada. She was brought to a "gloomy house" where even the pet Boston terrier had a "peculiar Bostonian sense of guilt" (*CProse,* p. 21). Feeling like a "guest" in this airless atmosphere, expected to somehow intuit an "unknown past" that no one ever directly explained to her and held to the strict discipline of behaving as a "little girl" should, Bishop's body rebelled. The combination of severe illnesses that struck her in Worcester—acute asthma, eczema, and even symptoms of St. Vitus's dance—almost killed her in that first winter with her paternal grandparents, and she was moved to the Boston home of her mother's sister, Maud, where she was bedridden and spent most of her time "lying in bed wheezing and reading" (Stevenson 1966, p. 34; Kalstone 1989, p. 27).

Her wheezing seemed to worsen as she felt herself steadily drawn into a conspiracy of evasion concerning her father's death and mother's insanity. The female voices around her—grandmothers and aunts—formed a "skein" in which she was "caught." "In the Village," Bishop's autobiographical account of her mother's final breakdown, describes the inscrutable adult world into which the six-year-old Elizabeth felt herself being pulled "against her will"—a world in which speech is always elliptical and secret shames are guarded even from the child that is most affected by them. Refusing to speak about her mother's "embarrassing" mental illness in anything but oblique terms "in front of the child," Bishop's female relations became associated in her mind with the equivocal: their speech was always subject to two or more interpretations, always generating misleading and confusing double meanings and puns. The young Elizabeth has difficulty with the word "mourning," which she hears as "morning," a confusion that unsettles her: "Why, in the morning, did one put on black" (*CProse,* p. 254). Apparently death—and, in particular, her father's death—had never been explained to the child.

Years later Bishop looked back on this period in her childhood as her initiation into the duplicity of speech and the suffocating constraints that propriety imposes on free expression. In her short memoir, "The Country Mouse," she remembers the hard lessons learned that winter with her paternal grandparents. First among these was the revelation that she was "becoming one of them": rather than tell a playmate the shameful truth about her mother, she lies, saying that her mother has died—a lie born out of a "hideous craving for sympathy." The moment the lie leaves her lips she is gripped by her own capacity to be as "false" as any of her relations, to lie, that is, in the "family voice." In the "family voice"—strongly associated with the garrulousness and duplicity culturally ascribed to women—Bishop finds the tendency towards "morbidity" that she would later attribute to confessional poets (especially women writers like Elizabeth Bowen). The social obligation imposed on the woman to speak in well-modulated tones and corset unseemly emotions exacted a dreadful price on Bishop's own family and especially on her mother, whose "real thrilling beautiful voice," stifled by grief and social convention, became, in the end, a terrifying scream.[5]

Long into adulthood Bishop was haunted by nightmare images of dark, shrouded, caterwauling women whose grating voices threatened to invade and animate her own body and whose intrusive presence she attempted to expel: "In a black sedan with high windows, a tall woman, Aunt Florence, only I knew it wasn't really Aunt Florence, stood outside, wanting to get in talking, talking. I screwed up the window, hurriedly and caught the tips of her gloved fingers in the crack at the top. She kept on talking, talking, begging me to let her in the car, and I felt nauseated. She was dressed all in black, with a large black hat, the gloves were soiled gray" (KWN 1, page 38).

Any reader of the late poem, "In the Waiting Room," will recognize in this Key West nightmare both Aunt Florence (who is concealed behind the name "Aunt Consuelo" in the poem) and the powerful sensations and images that this vision describes. In both dream and poem Aunt Florence's cries of pain induce nausea in her niece and threaten to invade the sanctuary Bishop has provided for herself. The "armored car of dreams," to borrow a phrase from "Sleeping Standing Up" (CP, p. 30), has a window-like "mouth" and seems an extension of the dreamer's own body. Breathing in the fierce odor of her aunt's frantic desperation "to be let in," Bishop responds violently by closing this one avenue of access and figuratively "biting" the hand that reaches out to her. Significantly, Bishop's single most vivid memory of her mother, which she recounts in an interview with Elizabeth Spires (1981), eerily parallels the narrative of her nightmare. Her mother, dressed incongruously in the mourning clothes required of a widow "in those days," sits with the three-year-old

Elizabeth in a swan boat on a Boston lake. A real swan comes up to the boat. Her mother "fed it and it bit her finger," splitting the black kid glove and the skin beneath (p. 74). The mother's gloved hands suggest the extent to which her illness became a barrier to intimacy; the child of such a mother might well harbor an unacknowledgeable desire to bite the hand that failed to feed her.[6] In a recent tribute to Bishop, Elizabeth Spires speaks of having seen the poet's drafts and notes for a poem about the swan boats. It was, as Spires suggests, "a subject fraught with so many explosive associations for her it proved impossible to write" (Bishop 1992, p. 66). And yet tantalizing fragments remain, scattered phrases: "dead water where the live swan paddles," "My mother's hand proferred a peanut from the bag," "Ungracious, terrifying bird!," "the whole pond swayed," "madness and death," "I saw the hole, I saw the blood," "amniotic flood." Approaching these images with her customary sensitivity, Spires writes: "Unconsciously perhaps, there is a pairing and juxtaposition, even in this roughest of drafts, between fearful opposites: life and death, predictability and madness, a white swan and a mother in black. The terror in the memory lies in the child's inability to read the situation, to know if these opposites will cancel one another, and who— swan or mother—is the dark force" (Bishop 1992, p. 66).

The equivocal woman in black reappears in Bishop's nightmare, transposed but still powerfully present in the guise of Aunt Florence. "In the Waiting Room" shows that the peculiar tension between Bishop and her Aunt Florence has a long history, precisely as long a history as Bishop's asthmatic condition. Whether or not a poem like "In the Waiting Room" is intended as a serious attempt to describe the psychogenesis of Bishop's lifelong asthma, it does link a traumatic childhood confrontation with a woman to the onset of intense physical distress: in the poem, as in the dream, Bishop chokes on the "cruel conundrums" of shared female experience (*CP*, p. 73).

It seems right to suggest, as Alicia Ostriker (1986) does, that "In the Waiting Room" is a poem Bishop "waited a lifetime to write" and that "in some sense, [the poet] has never left the room it describes" (p. 72). But if this is the case we should not sanitize the meaning of what takes place there. The child-protagonist of the poem, just shy of seven years old, does not simply become alive for the first time to her identity with others of her gender in the waiting room of a dentist's office; rather, the reality of "womanhood" is rammed down her throat and she chokes on it. The central moment of the poem occurs when Elizabeth hears a cry of pain that disorients her because it seems to come from two places at once—literally from two throats, her Aunt Florence's and her own. In the instant her "timid and foolish" aunt screams, Elizabeth is invaded and possessed from within by what she describes as "the family voice." She feels herself caught in an enmeshed community, a whole "skein" of female voices—voices that seem to rise up out of the pages of the *National Geographic* and shoot straight through her own body. Feeling her own singular sense of herself crowded out by the presence of the collective, Elizabeth drowns under wave after black wave as she falls into "cold, blue-black space"; in other words, she experiences the dizziness that always accompanied one of Bishop's asthmatic attacks.

We have become accustomed of late to certain metaphors drawn from the processes of breathing and speech that are used to celebrate the bond between mother and child and the unconstrained female voice. Hélène Cixous speaks to us of the woman artist who opens herself up to her maternal muse, never defending herself against possession by other "unknown women" but welcoming all the multiple "streams of song" that issue from her ecstatically crowded throat; it is, perhaps, a disappointment to then enter the claustrophobic atmosphere of Bishop's waiting room. When the aunt's cry of pain makes what Cixous might call a "vertiginous crossing" into the body of her young niece, Elizabeth derives no pleasure from the "identificatory embrace" that results. The effect is indeed vertiginous, but only in the worst possible sense; the ground gives way beneath the young girl as her old sense of herself collapses. She is not empowered but emotionally and ontologically battered by the initiation rite. In "The Country Mouse" Bishop is far more explicit about the "great truth" she learned waiting for her aunt to emerge from the dentist's office. Elizabeth feels the full force of being "tricked into a false position" (*CProse*, p. 33). Not only is she trapped forever within her "scabby body and wheezing lungs," but she will grow to resemble the woman who sat opposite her in the dark room, the woman "who smiled at [her] so falsely every once in a while," a disturbingly willing slave to social etiquette and a censorious world.

It is no accident that the child's disorienting experience is triggered by grotesque images that focus her attention on the cruel conundrums of mother love.[7] The multiple and contradictory meanings that seem to attach to the maternal body and the conflicting emotions that the maternal presence evokes in Elizabeth push against each other in the child's throat, swelling up behind her voice and pitching her into a new world without clear dimensions or comforting boundaries. Like the volcanoes that the child finds pictured in her magazine, Bishop's own mother threatened to erupt in unpredictable ways; emotionally numb one moment, she would spill over in rivulets of fiery, hysterical emotion the next. Elizabeth, who we know is feeling the loss of her own mother, studies the pages of the *National Geographic;* her attention is understandably drawn to the photographs of mothers and children as she turns the pages of the magazine: black, naked women, their necks strangled, "wound round and round with wire," hold babies whose malleable heads have been "wound round and round with string." A mother's "awful hanging breasts"—so "horrifying" in their power to excite longing and betray trust—are pictured in unbearable proximity to her infant's distorted head caught in its terrible vise of wire.

The black woman captured by the western photographer's shutter and trapped in the grip of her own culture passes a legacy of submission on to her infant. By manipulating her infant's skull she reinforces the very codes of beauty and sexual attractiveness that have delimited her own life, and we begin to wonder how fully the mother is implicated in her culture's campaign to mute individuality and enforce conformity. This compression of the baby's head also reminds the reader of a scene from Bishop's "In the Village," the extraordinary story of her mother's final breakdown. Elizabeth sits in her grandmother's kitchen in Great Village being force-fed a bowl of porridge by her mother, who struggles to maintain her mental balance by repeating mechanically the primal gestures of maternal love. Then, seeing how tall her child has grown in her absence, the mother impulsively lays her hands on her daughter's head, pushing her down, hoping to bring back the paradisal time of her daughter's infancy and bring the shrill tone of their relationship back down to a safer pitch. The child of "In the Village" quickly "slides out from under" the mother's oppressive hands, but she grows up to be the Elizabeth who cannot escape the lessons of the waiting room—the heavy emotional legacy that may be passed from mother to daughter through the laying on of hands (*CProse*, p. 261). "Sliding beneath a big black wave," the walls of the waiting room seem to dissolve around the child, who experiences the kind of disillusionment that Bishop describes elsewhere in "Hannibal and Napolean," an unpublished poem (KWN 1, p. 199): "the delightful kindergarten, the garden of the world, is shown growing on the hollow soil of a volcano." The acute question of "In the Waiting Room" proliferates helplessly across every Bishop poem concerned, however obliquely, with the dynamics of female connection. But the question is stated most explicitly in "Faustina, or Rock Roses." There, the "sinister kind face" of the black servant tending her white mistress evokes the "cruel black / coincident conundrum" of mother love and female bonding darkened even further by the history of relations between the races: does woman love offer "a dream of protection and rest" or the "very worst, / the unimaginable nightmare?" (*CP*, pp. 73–74).

Whatever happiness Bishop found with other women grew on the hollow soil of a volcano—because, inevitably, she carried her childhood experience of love's instabilities and betrayals into the world of adult relationships. Bishop's mature poetic style, known for its rich ambiguities and oblique approach to love and sexuality, stresses the emotional dislocation and instability in all efforts of affection. Oscillating between self-exposure and concealment, her poetry captures the approaches and withdrawals that mark any human relationship in which an individual's privacy is necessarily placed at risk. Settling on a poetic style that seems to give and take away meaning in the same motion, Bishop captures the quality of circumlocution that, as we have seen, she first found in the conversation of her grandmother and aunts. Irritated with her family's hypocrisy, she nevertheless recognizes that such duplicity is a part of the dynamics of human relation and part of the very language we use as culturally circumscribed human beings.

Bishop's guarded style is attuned to the way parents and their children, poets and their readers, actually appear to one another: the way, that is, that they alternate emotionally between accessibility and obscurity. With the tenacity of the waterspider that stays on the surface of the pool, Bishop holds to a poetry of ripples and verbal feints. But in generally refusing to speak directly about her personal tragedies, she would find herself struggling upstream against the currents of a new post-fifties generation of poets—writers like Anne Sexton who follow the example of Bishop's own dear friend Robert Lowell and plunge headlong into the river of self-reference, making rich use of the sorrow to be found there.

III

In significant ways, Bishop's responses to trends in the poetry of her contemporaries are moored to somatic issues—dependent, that is, on what Bishop considers to be a crisis in the size and scale of personal ambition. Her notebooks show just how closely she tended to relate poetic control and a stoical and disciplined approach to physical discomfort. Indeed, once we fully appreciate the impact of the poet's allergic inflammations on her life—and her private struggle to bring her swollen form back down to the scale of human life—we gain a better understanding of why Bishop published only ninety-five poems in her lifetime, each one a model of leanness and restraint.

Bishop's personal code of ethics demanded such discipline, in art as well as in life. For this reason, her criticism of what she regarded as self-dramatizing confession and easy vulgarity in the work of certain younger poets is far more than the prudish response of a woman raised in an older decorum. The outpourings of Anne Sexton and W. D. Snodgrass raised grave suspicions in Bishop's mind because they struck her as "egocentric—simply that" (Kalstone 1989, p. 209). She considered the general weakening of standards and the failure to discriminate between good poetry and mere self-promotion a peculiarly "American sickness" (letter to Lowell, 5 March 1963, qtd. in Millier 1989, p. 48). Both the art and the culture that produced it had grown bloated, flaccid, infected with unoriginality—and they needed a good lancing. In essence, Bishop objected to the confessional poetry of her peers because its authors "boasted" about their private catastrophes so shamelessly and congratulated themselves so continually on their candor. To speak as though one were always in the throes of some intolerable crisis, Bishop wrote in 1967, was "really something new in the world. There have been diaries that were frank—and generally intended to be read after the poet's death. Now the idea is that we live in a horrible and terrifying world, and the worst moments of horrible and terrifying lives are an allegory of the world. . . . The tendency is to overdo the morbidity. You just wish they'd keep some of these things to themselves" (Bishop 1967).

The key to Bishop's poetic style, its minimalism, deflection, and hard-won moral vision, lies in her battle to rid her work of the excessive morbidity she recognized in the world around her. Morbidity, the body's susceptibility to disease and corruption, becomes Bishop's trope for moral as well as physical "weakness and acquiescence" spreading over the younger generation of poets like the sly growth of mildew. The molds and mildews that make her choke, swell, and violently shake were "just enough to serve as a hint of morbidity" (*CProse*, p. 228), and reminded her of the "great American sickness" she diagnosed in a March 1961 letter to Robert Lowell: "too much of everything—too much painting, too much poetry, too many novels—and much too much money. . . .

And no one really feeling anything much" (qtd. in Millier 1989, p. 47). Bishop believed that her ethical aversion to literary inflation distinguished her in an age that seemed to her to have lost its discrimination and restraint. A deeply reserved and subtle poet, Bishop would apply a cool compress to her poems at the first sign of inflated self-regard or swollen ego.

Objecting to the way confessional art transformed the poet into a diarist and the reader into a confidant or confessor, Bishop insisted that the actual bond between writer and reader was marked, not by genuine intimacy, but by distance and impersonality. Adrienne Rich (1983) once suggested that intimacy was altogether absent in Bishop's later work, in which the poet seems to examine, instead, the way people are distanced from one another by differences of class and race (p. 16). But the effect of distance that Rich observes in Bishop's art may just as easily be seen as the poet's way of expressing her own experience of intimacy: the unyielding reality of loss, separation, even betrayal, that makes erotic and emotional connection "a billion times told lovelier" and "more dangerous," to borrow from Hopkins, one of Bishop's poetic masters.

Finally, Bishop shows us that writer and reader are linked to one another not by imagined intimacy but by the bonds of a common language—a language that is never straightforward in its effects. "In the Village," as we have already seen, describes the poet's early awakening to the fact that language is equivocal, open to two or more possibilities, always hiding something in the process of revealing everything. Donald Hall (1970) was frustrated by this "equivocal" quality in the poetic language of Marianne Moore, which, for him, always appeared teasingly inaccessible—"giving as it takes away, folding back on itself the moment one begins to understand so that an exactly opposite meaning begins to seem plausible" (pp. 84–85). But it would seem that Bishop came to accept an ambiguity that once troubled her, transforming equivocation into a treasured artistic effect. The moments of apparent personal connection between the poet and her reader are enriched by the understanding they share that each must finally remain an unresolvable mystery to the other.

The mystery remains despite the efforts of literary interpreters to, as Bishop put it, "pretty up" the poet's work. "Poetry should have more of the unconscious spots left in," she wrote as she distinguished her own poetry from that of Wallace Stevens: "What I tire of quickly in Wallace Stevens is the self-consciousness—poetry so aware lacks depth" (KWN 2, p. 89). It seems a mild irony that the richly ambiguous Bishop seems to make a model of clarity out of a poet famous for his own brand of obscurity. Once again her criticism of the poet is directed at the way he dissects his own psyche and deprives his reader of a distinct pleasure—the delight of speculation. In a fragment from the same notebook Bishop reminds herself that "art is never altogether pleasing unless one can suspect it of ulterior motive . . . of a 'secret confidence' " that the poet has reserved to herself. A fundamentally shy person, Bishop nevertheless accepts that the reader's pleasure lies in pursuing her maddeningly elusive presence in the poem. She does all she can to enhance the thrill of the chase through subtle indirection.

Bishop obscured the shape of her personal life, of course, for other reasons as well, reasons having to do with the particular social and aesthetic conventions of her day.[8] Love and sexuality were threatening subjects for a woman with poetic ambitions, and doubly so for a woman of Bishop's sexual preference. Even in her late poems, when she no longer cloaks her own sexuality under the guise of animal courtship, her verse still dances around the subject of her homosexuality. Bishop's strategies of concealment resemble those of the female lizard she described on a scrap of paper folded into the back cover of one of her notebooks: the lizard "hides . . . all her tail, all her tiny horny sides" while the males around her "blow out [their] beautiful rose balloon [for all] to see." The poet's imagination during her thirties is distinguished by a desire to protect herself from everything that threatened either the borders of her own body or her uniqueness as a person and an artist, and her poems seem to expand outward in an intimate embrace of the world only to fold back on themselves and on the haven of the sole self.

Bishop's "O Breath" is one of her only published poems about the eroticized female body. At the same time, it is also one of the few poems in which she consciously and conspicuously turns her attention to the "equivocal" nature of her own poetic style. Moreover, here she uses asthma, the disabling condition that afflicted her, to describe the stifling pressures that impinge on her life as a poet. "O Breath" is a captivatingly ambiguous love poem that plays with the narrow passageway for authorized speech permitted a woman of her class and education in 1955. Beneath the poem's surface reticence, we sense something moving invisibly: a faint image of erotic coupling or its aftermath. All we do see clearly is the broken contours of this poem as it appears on the page—as though it were determined to speak though under enormous pressure to hold back. The poem's gasping, halting rhythms and labored caesuras mimic the wheezing lungs of a restless asthmatic trying to expel the suffocating air. In the struggle to breathe, each hard-won phrase wrested from silence arches over the negative troughs, the breaks, the white space left on the page. The poem's structure enables Bishop to "catch her breath" and give the agonies of asthma visible shape—the cradling and containing rib cage of words:

> Beneath that loved   and celebrated breast,
> silent, bored really   blindly veined,
> grieves, maybe   lives and lets
> live, passes   bets,
> something moving   but invisibly,
> and with what clamor   why restrained
> I cannot fathom   even a ripple.
> (See the thin flying   of nine black hairs
> four around one   five the other nipple,
> flying almost intolerably   on your own breath.)
> Equivocal, but what we have in common's   bound to be there,
> whatever we must own   equivalents for,
> something that maybe I   could bargain with
> and make a separate peace   beneath
> within   if never with.
>
> (*CP*, p. 79)

We seem to have entered that ambiguous realm of address where two people have become one yet remain irremediably distant from one another. One lover speaks fitfully between gasps for air as she watches the woman lying beside her "silent bored really." The difficulty and "restraint" associated with breathing and speaking in the poem suggests the ongoing constraints the poet labors under as a woman and a lesbian bound to leading a life of surface conformity and concealed depths.

When the speaker of the poem questions what lies beneath her lover's "celebrated" breast, she does so in a context that extends beyond this single lyric: "O Breath" is the last of Bishop's "Four Poems," a short cycle that concerns itself with the frustrating puzzle of "uninnocent" conversation between lovers—of exchanges that "engage the senses, / only half meaning to" until "there is no choice" and "no sense," or until the tension is relieved with an "unexpected kiss" (*CP*, pp. 76, 77). The poem sequence concentrates on images of the heart's helpless, bewildered imprisonment in miscommunication and its unanticipated release into authentic expression. In "Conversation," lovers obdurately hold to their positions, willfully misunderstanding one another, until the great cage of misconception breaks up in the air around them and they reach a point of understanding when "a name / and all its connotation are the same." In "Rain Towards Morning" an electrical storm suddenly ceases, its "great light cage" releasing a million birds from bondage, and the sky brightens like a face surprised by love. With "While Someone Telephones" the cosmic is brought back down to the personal as the poet shifts from electrically charged "wires" of light to the crossed wires of lovers parted by distance and disconnection waiting tensely for contact and "the heart's release."

Like the protagonists of the other poems, the speaker of "O Breath" regards her lover with tender wariness. She lies awake, watching her lover's breast and the nine thin, black hairs surrounding the nipples—small, flying hairs that stir "almost intolerably" on the woman's "own breath." Aroused by the sight, she nevertheless seems shaken by her lover's apparent insularity, her self-absorption, the regular rise and fall of her breast. Such shallow breathing is "almost intolerable" to the speaker because she herself is forced to gasp for air. The placid lover remains to the poem's end an enigma whose motivations escape the speaker, although she hopes to find in the woman's heart an "equivalent" for her own tumult, her own anxious desire for the unexpected, releasing kiss.

"O Breath," like "Conversation" (the first of the "Four Poems"), gives expression to "the tumult in the heart" that "keeps asking questions" only to "stop and undertake to answer" in the same mystified voice. The speaker of "O Breath," however, seems to talk only with herself or with the reader. Because the true inner workings of her lover are invisible to her, the speaker can only project her own inner turmoil onto her mate by way of analogy, of correspondence. Hoping that boredom is actually a mask for desire, but unable to "fathom even a ripple" of her lover's motivations, the speaker has no recourse but to draw from her own experience of desire in describing what might live and move within the inaccessible woman breathing beside her. She imagines the force of desire within the body lying beside her as "something" moving invisibly—something caged within that body as surely as a clamoring heart or a pair of wheezing lungs. But when she stops and undertakes an answer to the proliferating questions of the heart, the reader cannot tell the difference between inquiry and resolution, and peace is still something to be negotiated once common ground is finally discovered. Like the bond between the two partners, the release obtained at the poem's end is uncertain and "equivocal."

"O Breath" focuses on the "almost intolerable" proximity of the loved one's body, awakening a longing for still deeper contact that may not be achieved. This is no utopic vision of a lesbian continuum where lovers always feel easy in one another's presence, able to, as Cixous would say, "expire without running out of breath." For Bishop, the urge to penetrate the deepest recesses of another person must be resisted for the sake of both people involved. The tactful poet or lover acknowledges the bounds as well as the bonds of love.

IV

Given her equivocal experience of "home" and the "efforts of affection," Bishop had to reinvent her life before she could draw strength from the past and translate her body into song. This reinvention is apparent in a series of dreams Bishop recorded in her private notebooks—dreams that link the poet's own pursuit of "quiet breath" to the figure of the mermaid breathing effortlessly in amniotic seas. These dreams ultimately prepare the poet for her life in Brazil, where she found, for a time, the happiness that had eluded her since childhood. Cradled by an "atmosphere of uncritical affection" in her adopted country, the poet would be able at last to navigate the waters of memory—and explore the remarkable powers of healing that lie within.[9]

The mermaid dreams form an extraordinary sequence that explores the yearnings, imprisonings, and problematic releases of the eroticized female body. Each dream centers on the strange hybrid shape of the sea-creature. In the first of these visions, a dying mermaid washed ashore and gasping for breath becomes an emblem of Bishop's own anxieties. Her estrangement as an artist and a lesbian finds expression in the foundering ocean-woman exiled from her natural element. In a later celebratory dream, the mermaid is returned to the sea, where her body feels exhilaratingly weightless. This vision of liberation prepares the way for the greater personal happiness and freedom of expression Bishop would experience during her first years in Brazil. Although the mermaid begins as a tragic figure, she eventually allows Bishop to navigate the dangerous shoals and eddies of a life spent in the body of a woman.[10]

The mermaid first appeared in a fearful dream Bishop had one night in Stonington, Maine. In a letter to Robert Lowell she confessed that the vision left her shaken: "I've been indulging myself in a nightmare of finding a gasping mermaid under one of these exposed docks—you know, trying to tear the mussels off the piles for something to eat—horrors" (qtd. in Kalstone 1989, p. 180).

Given Bishop's asthma, it is little wonder that she identified so strongly with a mermaid washed ashore or a fish held half out of the water and forced to breathe in "the terrible oxygen." The odd thing, in fact, about the reference to "terrible oxygen" in her most anthologized poem, "The Fish," is that Bishop, the accurate observer and brilliant naturalist, has strategically misspoken. Fish find oxygen no more terrible than we do, because they live on it as well; their gills, however, are equipped to obtain oxygen only from water and not from air. For Bishop to link terror with oxygen, she would have had to first project her own fears onto the sea creature.

What could be worse than to be left "gasping" in an alien atmosphere trying desperately to tear sustenance from a cruelly implacable world? Like the mermaid, the poet feels herself to be unequipped to breathe the same air, to live by the same social strictures, as other beings whose natures are different from her own. The dream suggests that Bishop dreads the "exposure" of her unconventionality—of her body and her homosexuality. In the way it evokes feelings of freakishness and alienation, the nightmare of the dying mermaid ultimately recalls the pathos of "The Little Mermaid," the Hans Christian Andersen fairy tale that Bishop knew and loved so well. In the Andersen tale, the mermaid destroys herself in her futile attempt to cross over into the world of human (heterosexual) union. Seen in this light, Bishop's dream is a poignant reminder of the border-crossings lesbians were forced to make in the forties and fifties—when so many felt compelled to conceal their desires and to publicly embrace the heterosexual erotic ideal.

If we look backwards through even the earliest juvenilia, we see Bishop's struggling to avoid the horror of foundering and hear her yearning for a watery haven. In the 1928 poem "Sonnet," written while Bishop was still a schoolgirl in Massachusetts, she longs for the "subaqueous stillness of the sea" where she might find "a spell of rest, and quiet breath, and cool / Heart" (*CP*, p. 214). At least fifteen years later Bishop had a dream that returned her to the sea, where she enjoyed a rare moment of physical freedom and release. The beauty of the mermaid as an image of the poet is visible in a Key West/Nemer notebook account of this utopian vision:

> The fish was large, about 3 ft. long, large-scaled, metallic gold only a beautiful rose color. I myself seemed slightly smaller than life-size. We met in water the color of the water of the 3rd—clear, green, light (— more like the cut edge of plate glass, or birch leaves in bright sun, than emerald.) He was very kind and said he would be glad to lead me to the fish, but we'd have to overtake them. He led the way through the water, glancing around at me every now and then with his big eyes to see if I was following. I was swimming easily with scarcely any motion. In his mouth he carried a new, galvanized bucket. . . . He was taking them a bucket of air—that's how he'd happened to meet me. I looked in—rough water had got in to make the bucket of air a bucket of large bubbles, seething and shining—hissing, I think, too. I had a vague idea they were to be used as decorations, for some sort of celebration (a "coronation").
> (KWN 1, p. 15)

Like the Stonington nightmare, this dream is intensely interested in air and the mechanics of breathing underwater. In the "inverted" world of sleep, the mortal dreamer seems to breath effortlessly beneath the waves, whereas fish require life-giving oxygen from the surface. The sea, which Bishop once described as a "dark deep . . . element bearable to no mortal" but only "to fish and to seals" (*CP*, p. 65) has become strangely natural to her. In these waters that make mortal bones ache and hands and tongues burn, she is fantastically and utterly free. Like the riverman in a later poem, Bishop communes with speaking underwater spirits, attending a subaqueous "party" where beautiful rose-colored fishes gather to crown one of their number with shining bubbles in "some sort of celebration." The bubbles hiss like a community of whispering voices free to seethe and shine and rejoice.

It is tempting to see the dream as Bishop's way of imagining a time when she could swim the rough waters of intimacy with an ease that had always escaped her. Like the "clear, gray, icy water" of the northern seas she knew so well, the poet-dreamer is "suspended" between air and land, impervious to suffering, poised indifferently above the rocky breasts and cold hard mouth of the world—and the "cruel conundrums" of love (*CP*, pp. 65, 73). Rough water does not disturb the dream's serene mood; instead it turns the air that has troubled Bishop all her life into large shining bubbles—the poet's lifelong metaphor for the buoyant spirit freed from gravity and all physical laws and enabled to rise above all crippling circumstance.

In sleep, Bishop could take on the sexual ambiguity and dazzling versatility of the mermaid, a creature of the sea who breathes with miraculous ease. At the end of her life the true nature of the yearnings expressed in the 1928 "Sonnet" are given fuller, franker expression in a poem to which she gave the same name. In the 1979 "Sonnet," published posthumously, Bishop imagines what it would take to free the bubble-like spirit from the prison of social intolerance, liberate herself from the divided existence. But she cannot conceive of such a possibility, because the very laws of the physical universe would have to be broken. Only in the seclusion of her notebooks and her dreams did she dare to write unguardedly about love and sexuality. As she explains to Anne Stevenson in a letter dated 8 January 1964, Bishop thought of herself as being born into a certain era, situation, decorum, and for that reason she could never truly breath freely—or sing gaily in full-throated ease.

The poet's desire to make a separate peace with her own woman's body by finding some "pure elixir" of *amor matris*—until her arrival in Brazil, a desire reserved for the world of dreams—takes on a pleasing shape in *Questions of Travel,* the volume of poetry she dedicated to her Brazilian lover. There, the poem "The Riverman" seems to resolve or dissolve fear and hope, mother and maid in the "watery, dazzling dialectic" of art. When Bishop was readying her third volume of poetry for publication, she sent off a worried note to Robert Lowell about "The Riverman." Lowell calmed her fears by assuring her that this new book would be her very best and reminding her of a dream she once had: "I wouldn't worry about the Amazon poem—it's the best fairy story in verse I know. It brings back an old dream of yours, you said you felt you were a mermaid scraping barnacles off a wharf-pile. That was Maine, not Brazil" (qtd. in Kalstone 1989, p. 196). Astute as always about the psychic origins and ulterior motives of his friend's work, Lowell had made the connection between Bishop's dream and "The Riverman," the tale of a man who has been "singled out" by the natural spirits of the Amazon, given the power of breathing underwater, and initiated into the rites of the shaman or spiritual healer. Lowell is not deflected by Bishop's use of a male protagonist, recognizing at once that the apprentice shaman is a mask for the poet herself. He remembers Bishop's dream about the mermaid washed ashore and gasping for breath, a dream of extreme dislocation and deprivation, and sees that "The Riverman" is Bishop's transposition of her nightmare into a different key—into a vision of strength. Recognizing the personal origins of the poem, Lowell sees all that the new poem implies about Bishop's emerging poetic—a poetic of healing. Under the cloak of riverman, Bishop tests the waters of her Brazilian life and the haven of "uncritical affection" she had found there—and her capacity to draw from her own heart the remedy for her distress.

"The Riverman" is one of the few of her pieces that Bishop praises for not being literal or accurate—for being entirely a dream salvaged from her own psychic yearnings. At the time when she wrote the poem about a river that "drains the jungle" and "draws from the very heart / of the earth the remedy / for each of the diseases" (*CP*, p. 108), she had never actually seen the Amazon: "When I finally got to the Amazon in February and March [1960] I found I hadn't been too accurate at all, thank goodness." Her Amazon, the river of her imagination, is not drawn from the immediate world that surrounded her as she wrote.

Her Brazilian home is the heart of her experience there and the source of her understanding of the unseen river. As she describes it in "Song for the Rainy Season," the studio her lover built for her away above the main house is bathed in water, cradled by a "private cloud" of vapor, and from this nest the poet can hear the "brook sing loud / from a rib cage / of giant fern" (*CP*, p. 101). Safe in her aerie, the poet, like the riverman beneath the water's surface, can approach the "family of mortalities" that plagued her life, the choking web of voices she left behind in Great Village and Worcester—a "skein of voices" that she can now unravel; like the riverman travelling beneath the waters of the Amazon she glides "right through the wicker traps" of "Godfathers and cousins" who can "never, never catch" her now.

> When the moon burns white
> and the river makes that sound
> like a primus pumped up high—
> that fast, high whispering
> like a hundred people at once—
> I'll be there below.
>
> (CP, p. 108)

The poet who wrote these lines had finally found her element—for as long as she could feel at home in her Brazilian haven. The river she imagines is no more and no less than her own studio, which she describes in a letter to Baumann as "one large room . . . away up in the air" containing a "kitchenette with a pump and a primus stove for tea" (28 December 1952, VC). The stove made the studio resound with the "fast, high whispering" of the hissing kettle. From her aerie Bishop conjured the Amazon deep within her own interior and learned to practice the healing art of remembrance. In *Questions of Travel* Bishop's imagination follows the stream of emotions that link the primus stove beside her as she writes and the "Little Marvel Stove" in her grandmother's kitchen so many years ago. She hears in the Brazilian rain the sound of her grandmother's voice, "talking to hide her tears" ("Sestina," *CP*, p. 123). And so Bishop's travels take her back to herself—through the once threatening but now delightful equivocality of language: with a brilliant pun on her own family name, she escapes her fear of the vocal skein created by the past. Safe in her Brazilian home, Bishop has become the "primus"—a choirmistress who untangles the aural web. From this time forward, she will conjure her haunting family voices and lead them in song.

Notes

1. Bishop and Louise Crane made Key West their home through 1943, while Bishop completed the poems that would make up her first book, *North & South*. Bishop continued to winter there in the home of her friend Marjorie Stevens until 1949.

2. Bishop published only a handful of poems that describe erotic pleasure overtly. As Lorrie Goldensohn (1988) suggests in her consistently illuminating essay on Bishop's erotic imagination, an unequivocal vision of erotic fulfillment may have been blocked in the "rooted sadness of Bishop's childhood" (p. 46). But however it arose, Bishop's characteristic reticence poses problems for her critics. Just when Bishop is beginning to be given her due as a complex poet, the personal directness of much recent woman's poetry has seduced some commentators into underestimating Bishop's talent once again and returning her to the same niche to which she was relegated during her lifetime. Still, some readers are beginning to recognize that Bishop, in her subtle way, explores the same issues that preoccupy the current, bolder generation of women writers. Joanne Diehl, for instance, warns us that Bishop's poetry "only apparently evades issues of sexuality and gender." Diehl (1990) senses an "ominous quality to Bishop's restraint more suggestive than confession" (p. 97) and concludes that a highly erotic imagination is fully present in her poetry: "verbal masking allows Bishop to preserve the erotic while deconstructing heterosexist categories" (p. 93). Similarly, Bonnie Costello (1988) points to the way a woman writer may use

"female vantage point" as "the concrete from which the universal is projected" so as to "unite readers before the shared mystery of embodiment" (p. 309). Costello concludes that Bishop, like many other women poets, resists "labeling [her artistic vision] as female precisely because [she wishes] to make it available to all readers" (p. 310). I argue that Bishop uses her physical ailments to develop a poetic that confronts cultural labels and their stifling impact on personal and erotic expression.

3. This passage from Bishop's 1954 letter to Baumann (VC) is worth quoting in full: "People's attitude about such things [alcoholism and its treatment] is really quite different from that in the U.S. [The Brazilians] are amazingly tolerant, or indifferent, or ignorant. . . . I suspect one thing that made it harder for me in N.Y. and other places was the more Puritanical outlook that I have inherited myself."

4. Bishop's father, grandfather, and three of her uncles succumbed to alcoholism, her own weakness as well. Using a Conradian metaphor, Bishop considers the double lives led by her male relatives, the stealth and guilty secrecy, the lies that gave off an odor of mortality. From her Brazilian studio, Bishop remembers her mother's brother and the "icicle [that formed] in the bottom of her stomach" each time he approached her when she was a child: "I realize only now" that [Uncle Neddy] represented 'the devil' for me, not a violent, active Devil, but a gentle black one, a devil of weakness, acquiescence, tentatively black, like sooty mildew" (*CProse*, p. 228). Trying to understand her repulsion, Bishop focuses on her uncle's "proud and morbid" voice—the voice he used when he spoke of his gory childhood accidents and boasted about his stoical "feats of endurance." The disgust she feels with her uncle's weakness and passivity is closely related to her aesthetic and moral aversion to the morbid, self-congratulatory tone of confessional poetry.

5. In a Key West/Nemer notebook, Bishop records a scrap of verse that describes the false "family voice" as a kind of mutation, a corruption of reality:

> speaking
> It is an adaptation   or
> social obligation of some sort
> the real thrilling   beautiful voice
> is off somewhere else singing loudly
> fully
> in clear choir.
>
> (KWN 2, p. 47)

Throughout her life Bishop grew irritated when she heard the tone of social obligation in the poetry of female contemporaries like Elizabeth Bowen. It was the voice of "old silver" and still older class distinction, of taste in clothes and husbands that she distrusted: "They have to make quite sure that the reader is not going to misplace them socially, first—and that nervousness interferes constantly with what they think they'd like to say" (Bishop to the Barkers, 28 February 1955, PU). Beneath a woman's nervous boasting chatter about being "protected" by her impeccable social standing and taste, Bishop recognizes desperation: "I suppose it is at bottom a flaw in reality that irritates me" because women want to show that they are "nice" and lead beautifully polished lives "even when they aren't" and even when they don't.

6. Bishop's childhood asthma seems to have recurred most violently at points

in her adult life when she is forced to consider the potentially suffocating nature of maternal love. A short time after Margaret Miller's hospitalization, her mother arrived from America, bringing with her a stifling hothouse atmosphere of maternal attentiveness. Mrs. Miller seemed to place an additional strain on the already distraught Bishop, who began to feel her carefully cultivated independence and emotional control breaking down in the presence of the older woman's devotion and solicitude. Significantly, the surge of vulnerability that she experiences when Margaret's mother arrives in Europe to tend her daughter lands Bishop in a hospital herself: the strain of mother love leads to a severe recurrence of Bishop's acute childhood asthma. Writing to Frani Blough, she points to her deep discomfort with disarming flippancy: "Mother-love, isn't it awful. I long for an Arctic climate where no emotions of any sort can possibly grow, always excepting disinterested 'friendship' of course" (quoted in Kalstone 1989, p. 65). For Bishop, whose own mother succumbed to insanity and was permanently hospitalized when the poet was only five years old, mother love would always wear a threatening aspect—and the "imaginary iceberg" of emotional detachment she conjures in her letter to Blough would remain a strongly appealing fantasy throughout her life. That Bishop gradually gravitated away from Arctic climates, choosing instead to make her home in equatorial humidity and cultivate intimate friendships, says much about her intrepid spirit. The tropical life only aggravated her chronic asthma and allergies, those physical signs of emotional distress, and yet when she returned from Europe she moved directly to Florida and embraced all the forms of adventure and hardship that the tropics came to represent for her.

7. As Lee Edelman (1985) argues persuasively, what finally "horrifies" the child is the "fundamental affinity" she shares with monstrously disfigured women—with both the deformed mothers who stare back at her from the pages of the magazine and the women who "smile falsely" at her from the other side of the waiting room, their body shapes distorted by corsets and whalebone. She too will be imprisoned within the "awful hanging breasts" and the unempowered body of a woman. (See Edelman's chapter below in this volume.)

8. For a fascinating discussion of Bishop's indirections on homosexuality and erotic fulfillment, see Goldensohn 1988.

9. From her new home in Samambaia, Brazil, Bishop wrote to her doctor: "But an atmosphere of uncritical affection is just what suits *me*, I'm afraid—kisses and hugs, and endearments and diminutives, flying around" (21 April 1953, VC, Bishop's italics).

10. The body of the mermaid, a siren with her sexuality muted and concealed, lost in the sleek lines of a fish's tail, became a problematic fantasy image for Bishop in more ways than one. Like the late poem "Crusoe in England," the mermaid image speaks to the limitations of homoerotic love and single-sex friendship: Bishop's wish to "propagate [her] kind" is achingly expressed through Crusoe's inherently infertile love for Friday (see *CP*, p. 165) and through the mermaid's eternally maiden status. One can only speculate on how terribly mocked Bishop must have felt by a body that often swelled but never grew large with life.

LORRIE GOLDENSOHN

The Body's Roses: Race, Sex, and Gender in Elizabeth Bishop's Representations of the Self

B ISHOP'S understated and oblique method of self-reference remained directly counter to everything that most of her contemporaries practiced. Yet Robert Lowell, Bishop's poet friend with considerably more confessional manners, is the colleague for whom she herself felt most affinity. She wrote to Anne Stevenson in March 1963: "Cal [Lowell] and I in very different ways are both descendants from the Transcendentalists" (20 March 1963, WU). This may seem surprising. Much that Bishop relies on for original energy in poetry does not appear to come from the prophetic self in quest of the transfigured moment that so much of her understated poetry looks bent on deflating, her coolness and habitual self-possession a compress descending casually but unerringly over any inflammation of the word or deed.

Yet in a 1951 letter to Lowell, Bishop deprecatingly refers to herself as a "minor female Wordsworth." At this stage in her career we are far from the quietly soaring, serenely pastoral transformations of her late poems. Her 1964 estimate of her own work, always without vanity signals a moment of painful self-insight. Writing to Stevenson, Bishop begins to speak, in very general terms, of the braking influences on her work: "Because of my era, sex, situation, education, I have written, so far, what I feel is a rather 'precious' kind of poem, although I am very opposed to the precious. One wishes things were different, that one could begin all over again" (8 January 1964, WU). In these pages I propose to take Bishop's list—"era, sex, situation," and by implication, "education"—and test my sense of how she deployed or evaded deploying sensitive autobiographical material in focusing on race, sex, and gender in her poetry. A large part of this story contrasts Bishop's early and late treatments of these issues in and out of her personal and public life. Her correspondence and her published and unpublished poetry occasionally reveal significantly different preoccupations.

In most of her poems Elizabeth Bishop the person occurs off-page as a body clad in a voice that hovers over the small field of the poem or as a child. In all of her published work, the more volcanic emotions required containment within the vessel of form; overtly autobiographical feeling is poured into sestinas or villanelles, cooled into rhyme, wired into rhetorical figure, or allowed only sotto voce transmission. Her stoical pride, especially to the gossip-loving among us or to those who hunger to touch the naked flesh of the eminent, may be considered in some cases extreme: about confessional poets, Bishop once said, "You just wish they'd kept some of these things to themselves" (Bishop 1983, p. 303). To Wesley Wehr (1981), she is reputed to have said (we wonder how jokingly), "You can never have enough defenses" (p. 326).

Some of Bishop's resistance to self-display must derive from her position as woman and lesbian or, according to some reports, as bisexual. Very gradually, in her last years, it became permissible to speak of herself as a feminist, and in a late interview with George Starbuck (1983) she displays this candid bleakness about the influence of gender on her life: "I wish I had written a great deal more. Sometimes I think if I had been born a man I probably would have written more. Dared more, or been able to spend more time at it. I've wasted a great deal of time" (p. 329). The whole thrust of her early public experience seems to have been to avoid being ghettoized as a woman; she resisted that tenaciously. I think we should not misunderstand or overlook the very quiet bitterness emanating from sentences like these, sifted as they are through Bishop's fair-mindedness: "Most of my life I've been lucky about reviews. But at the very end they often say 'The best poetry by a woman in this decade, or year, or month.' Well, what's that worth? You know? But you get used to it, even expect it, and are amused by it" (Starbuck 1983, p. 324). It's hard not to believe that her "amusement" wasn't a little qualified, especially when the gender confinement that she notes came from close and admired friends like Lowell. She appreciated his review of *North & South;* in fact, early in their friendship, on August 14, 1947, she is "overwhelmed" by it: "It is the first review I've had that attempted to find any general drift or consistency in the individual poems and I was beginning to feel there probably wasn't any at all. It is the only review that goes at things in what I think is the right way" (letter to Lowell, 14 August 1947, HL). Yet in the review in question, Lowell, that inveterate and tireless ranker of poetic reputations, in speaking about "Roosters" and "The Fish" places them as "the best poems that I know of written *by a woman in this century*" (Lowell 1947, p. 78; italics added). And there he was, not even halfway through the century.

If only subliminally, this must have stung even as it complimented. Lowell's review appeared in 1947; it isn't until 1977 that Bishop is heard in a journal interview talking to George Starbuck, a younger poet, about how laurels for women poets are garnered, or, rather, sequestrated. If, then, Bishop believed that her status as poet would have been unfairly colored by her identity as a woman, what must she have felt about her sexual identity, clouded in contour for us even after her death, as more and more discussion enters public notice about her life? During her lifetime her homosexuality surfaced nowhere in print; yet her sexual preference seems an inseparable if mostly puzzling part of the other factors she herself named as limiting: her "era," her "sex," her "situation," and "education."

For Howard Moss (1977), Elizabeth Bishop was "an original" with "the air of having been born civilized, and as at home at a Parisian dinner table as she was traveling into the Brazilian interior" (p. 104). This public persona seems beyond the snares of gender. Yet the poems never entirely excluded sexual phenomena, at least not in the animal kingdom: there is that lizard in "Brazil, January 1, 1502":

> The lizards scarcely breathe; all eyes
> are on the smaller, female one, back-to,
> her wicked tail straight up and over,
> red as a red-hot wire.

(CP, p. 92)

It is interesting to see that folded into a back cover of one of Bishop's notebooks from Brazil is a torn slip of paper with some faint pencilings, dealing more explicitly with that lizard in saurian heat.[1] These observations, a little abortive proto-poem, step in and out of rhyme:

> The male lizard chases the female lizard around the tree
> Blows out his beautiful rose balloon . . . to see—a line of

little ants intercepts, the female hides . . . all her tail, all
her tiny horny sides.

(box 35A, folder 1, unnumbered, VC)

Even a lizard's sexual life requires muffling in Bishop's published poetry;
precise naturalist that she was, Bishop in print still upholds a certain propriety for her animals. The scrap of lizard courtship designed for print
makes us pause, but the moment for sexual contact remains in the fold
of a notebook.

There is a cheerful and casual allusion to a weekend tryst during college at a hotel on Cape Cod with someone she called "my
then-boyfriend," an incident revealed as Elizabeth Bishop, Vassar '34,
chats in an interview comfortably with Elizabeth Spires, Vassar '74 (see
Spires 1981). Bishop's sophistication is flawlessly discreet. In a memoir
essay called "The Country Mouse," which was published posthumously,
Bishop includes a description of her childhood attraction to "a beautiful boy named Royal Something." She says that "once when he helped
me buckle my arctics, as I looked at his long shiny hair, neat starched
collar, and red necktie, I felt a wonderful, powerful thrill go through my
stomach" (*CProse*, p. 24). The eroticism on which Bishop calls is clearly
heterosexual in reference. Even here in late work she is instinctively
building a one-sided picture, omitting the homosexual erotic feelings
that would expose her to the hazards of conventional misjudgment.

In Bishop's poems the only references to homosexuality, whether
hers or anyone else's, are quite oblique or allegorical in nature. As Lee
Edelman has persuasively traced these erotic feelings, the child protagonist of "In the Waiting Room" maintains a fascinated interest in female
parts as well as a terror of being imprisoned within the unempowered
female body appearing within the poem: she is mesmerized by "those
awful hanging breasts" as she stares at a native woman whose naked portrait appears in the copy of *National Geographic* that the seven-year-old
Elizabeth holds in her hands and is "too shy" to stop reading (Edelman
1985, p. 194).

Yet the fascination with the female seems as closely linked to the
theme of the abandoning mother as it does to the seductive, eroticized
female body, whether powerless or not. We could as easily associate the
fear of breasts with a suppressed longing for them and for the monstrous and disturbing power to evoke longing that they retain; negatively
colored feeling could be said to stem from early deprivation. David Kal-

stone supports this reading in his comment on "At the Fishhouses" and the poem's final lines:

It is like what we imagine knowledge to be:
dark, salt, clear, moving, utterly free,
drawn from the cold hard mouth
of the world, derived from the rocky breasts
forever, flowing and drawn, and since
our knowledge is historical, flowing and flown.

(*CP,* p. 66)

Here, according to Kalstone (1985), is "the flicker of human drama, of a vestigial implacable female presence behind the scene" (p. 181). But this is not an unempowered presence. The lines also indicate once again how erotic subjects concerning the female never move very far in Bishop's work from issues of parental abandonment and the subsequent development of an uneasy and orphaned selfhood.

Until *Geography III* there is little material arising openly about either the making of female identity or of erotic attraction and repulsion. Given Bishop's habitual discretion about the topics of gendering and sexuality, her early prose piece, "The Thumb," published in *The Blue Pencil,* the Walnut Hill School's literary magazine, is certainly worth noticing. In this story, as in her other *Blue Pencil* pieces, the protagonist is male; at tea with Sabrina, a woman he has been taken to see, he muses on Sabrina's smallness, lightness, and the underwater glimmer of her dress, qualities that show the nineteen-year-old writer determinedly evoking Milton's nymph, Sabrina. Bishop's narrator is intrigued by Sabrina and says, "Though fortunately unliterary herself she really had quite a little influence—friends among all sorts of artists and writers." Speaking in character, Bishop's stolid male protagonist expresses disdain for blue-stockings.

Yet this experimentation with role-playing in a bohemian world culminates in a discovery. The narrator has been admiring Sabrina's left hand, "small and fine," and now turns to her right hand:

Why did I keep on looking? There was something queer about that hand—I couldn't tell right away what it was. There was no mark, no deformity. Good God!—the woman had a man's thumb! No, not a man's,—a brute's—a heavy, coarse thumb with a rough nail, square at the end, crooked and broken. The knuckle was large. It was a horrible thumb, a prize fighter's thumb, the thumb of some beast, some obscene creature knowing only filth and brutality. . . .

. . . . .

I was horrified. In the midst of that charming, sunny room, that friendly atmosphere, I was frightened. Something mysterious and loathsome had crept out of the night and seized me as I sat there drinking tea. (box 51, folder 764, pp. 6, 9, VC)

After further sprinkling the thumb with "a growth of coarse, black hair," the adolescent Bishop enlarges our understanding of her symbol by poking us with Baudelaire: "What was that phrase? 'Flowers of Evil'— Yes."

There is more than a programmatic and naive flirtation with the postures of Romantic satanism in this exercise. The revulsion that the protagonist feels is directed at more than the thundering menace of a decadent art world; identity is still a fresh, more slippery matter than it will be later, and so the piece opens readily inward to a window of commentary on the writer's own feelings about selfhood.

The protagonist determines to continue seeing Sabrina. "But it wouldn't work. Every time I saw her I felt more and more a peculiar shivering fascination that made me look down at her hand, to those lovely fragile fingers and that horrible misshappen thing that was one of them. Yet I couldn't blame her. She was the most natural thing in the world— the trouble must be with myself." Within the self-conscious transposition of the female writer's imagination into the male there is both the horror and fear of the male bursting out as well as the strong sense of self-transgression in continuing that transposition, with its denial of the female. Yet the parallel horror also seems to be layered into a recognition and fear of the speaker's own developing homosexuality and denial of the male. Sabrina, with a "Madonna" face, both sexes somehow grafted onto her, is "the most natural thing in the world." The choking rage and madness that the ultimately contravened narrator feels is directed at the courtship pattern toward which Sabrina invites him: "I put out my hand slowly and laid my fingers across the back of her hand. It was cool and soft—and then I felt that rough, swollen knuckle, those stiff, coarse hairs against my palm. I looked at Sabrina quickly and I found that she was looking at me with a peculiar tender look in her eyes and what I could only describe as a simper across her mouth. I have never felt the disgust, the profound fear and rage of that moment. She thought— well—she thought I was going to tell her I loved her" (box 51, folder 764,

VC). It is hard to avoid thinking that the underpinning to this encounter is Bishop's own previous experience of a male erotic invitation: the fictive layering allows her sexually transposed Sabrina to meet a sexually transposed narrator and to play out the symmetries of several crucial dilemmas.

Ultimately, however, the narrator's loathing closes with his rejection of all the confusions of Sabrina's sex and gendering, leaving Bishop the writer with the inadequacies of her available models for either loving or imagining; the theater of her story, a kind of salon world in which she tries out the writer's life, ends in untenable relation. Like the adolescent Mary Shelley, whose symbolic fantasies of transposed gender in Frankenstein gave her a brief, free space in which to trace female fears and angers through the opacities of cross-dressing, Bishop did not produce anything for public consumption this concentrated or explicit in her adult life. The very rawness and ardent overstatement of the feeling was never duplicated again.

For all the happiness of the years in Brazil with Lota de Macedo Soares, when same-sex love surfaces pointedly within "Crusoe in England" there is a heart-numbing discouragement, a depleted energy governing its effects. Friday turns up for Crusoe at the end of a vortex of fear and despair; Crusoe names his nightmares of meaningless labor conducted within unending solitude:

> nightmares of other islands
> stretching away from mine, infinities
> of islands, islands spawning islands,
> like frogs' eggs turning into polliwogs
> of islands, knowing that I had to live
> on each and every one, eventually,
> for ages, registering their flora,
> their fauna, their geography.
>
> (*CP*, p. 165)

And at that point, when the voice behind the voice of Crusoe most resembles the tireless describer, the elective sandpiper, who is Bishop herself, Friday enters:

> Just when I thought I couldn't stand it
> another minute longer, Friday came.

(Accounts of that have everything all wrong.)
Friday was nice.
Friday was nice, and we were friends.
If only he had been a woman!
I wanted to propagate my kind,
and so did he, I think, poor boy.
He'd pet the baby goats sometimes,
and race with them, or carry one around.
—Pretty to watch; he had a pretty body.
And then one day they came and took us off.

(*CP*, pp. 165–66)

Friday isn't heard from again in the poem until the closing lines, similarly dashed as in the observation that ends this verse stanza, similarly
echoic in structure: "—And Friday, my dear Friday, died of measles /
seventeen years ago come March" (*CP*, p. 166). "Friday was nice . . .
Friday was nice . . . pretty . . . pretty . . . Friday, my dear Friday." The
muted, deadened, and repetitive baby speech here signs a helpless burden of unacknowledgeable feeling that swells somewhere blackly behind
the voice, choking it.

If in reading this poem we repeat too cautiously to ourselves that we
must not confuse the actor with the role, the poet with the poem, we
will not hear a numbed Elizabeth Bishop after her return to her homeland, reacting to the traumatic death of Lota de Macedo Soares. But
to fail to hear the pressure of particular experience behind and within
the poem (a poem possibly begun in Brazil and finished climactically in
North America) is to deny it its fullest vocal range. There is also a curious moment when a longing for children of one's own also rises from
within the fictive character, Crusoe. At this moment an attentive reader
of Bishop's letters remembers her lighthearted brag to Joseph Summers
that after ten weeks with Lota's grandchildren, they were such experienced hands at child care that they could "give three baths and three
shampoos in half an hour flat" (10 April 1959, VC). The poet is the same
woman who in 1961 eagerly passed on the latest book on painless child-
birth to a pregnant relative, saying that the book "is a wonderful thing—
just about as important, it seems to me, as splitting the atom" (Bishop to
Phyllis Sutherland, 5 January 1961, VC). It is the same Bishop who gave
an Easter egg dyeing party in San Francisco for a mob of children because

she loved dyeing eggs and the same Elizabeth who one afternoon picked a waif off the streets of Ouro Prêto to bathe and care for: All of these episodes come from a life in which the issue of sexual preference may well have made "propagation" a desire to be repressed. To some degree, the desire to have children always clashes with other basic human needs for women or men, but in a lesbian life the problems only intensify. To fail to hear that apparently dry "I wanted to propagate my kind" as a subterranean desire of the "real" shadow speaker performing the poem would be error.

Yet it seems likely that an exact recovery of the subject of her own feelings about love, let alone about the breeding of children, was never Bishop's intention. In an unpublished review, her disapproval of Emily Dickinson's narrowing of poetic subject to "love, human and divine" ("Emily Dickinson's Letters to Dr. & Mrs. Josiah Gilbert Holland," box 27, folder 392, VC) leads one to think that Bishop may have considered a part of her own twentieth-century emancipation from stereotypic womanhood to have been release from that entrapping woman's subject, love.

Her impatience may have been assisted by the same secularization that made older poets like Pound, Eliot, and other High Modernists favor scientific pragmatism over what Pound called in one context the "slither" of Romantic sentimentality (1954, p. 12), and what T. E. Hulme in another called "split religion" (1958, p. 118). Temperamentally, Bishop seems to have joined Eliot in favoring the depersonalization of art. But turning one's back on unacceptable emotionalism, its messiness and supposed lack of precision, in both generations of poets meant a common rejection of what was perceived as a feminizing of the arts, growing out of what modern and contemporary poet-critics, mostly male, could see of the social place for poetry as increasingly marginal and trivial. In certain of Bishop's poems, first in fragmentary, unpublished drafts then more guardedly in published work, the poems turn to renegotiate that rejection as she slips loose from a view of love and the feminine as tethering subjects.

It is certainly our loss as much as hers that for women of her generation a self-description and an inclination toward an analytic and logical mode of discourse or a bent for the scientific could push one to feel that love was a paltry female obsession from which all intellectual ambition and daring were absent. An artist, a poet, was already dangerously close to that slithering in fogs of emotion by the very nature of her trade;

perhaps Bishop found a well-bred repression of the psychosexual and distaste for the traditional female sentimental to be too close in kind to resist evading the too-large presence of either in her work. Moves stressing balance would push her style toward a cool, perhaps on occasion restrictively cool, elegance understanding the too-volcanic, the too-volatile world of feeling.

Adrienne Rich (1983) suggests that we examine how Bishop placed herself within existing limits as a commentator on the unempowered and silenced and that we look at the social, psychological, and political implications of her indirections on love and sexuality, which in spite of her reservations do make their fleeting or subterranean appearances. As a model for such a reading of Bishop's work, Rich offers us "Sonnet" as a cryptic parable of lesbian identity. Two fragmented sets of notes for poems, both of which appear to have been written in the early forties, around the time of "It is marvelous," offer additional insights.

Notations for a poem in the Key West/Nemer notebooks read:

I had a bad dream
towards morning, about you.
You lay unconscious
It was to be
for "24 hrs."
Wrapped in a long blanket
I felt I must hold you
even though a "load of guests"
might come in from the garden
[at] a minute
& see us lying
with my arms around you
& my cheek on yours
but I had to
prevent you
from slipping away

There are other brief lines of description, and then the draft closes:

in the deep of the morning
the day coming
that loneliness like feeling on

the sidewalk in a crowd
that fills with slow, elaborate show
the sidewalk rises, rises
like absolute despair.

(box 35A, folder 2, p. 167, VC)

Another fragmented phrase, "fear and embarrassment," repeats. In the seclusion of a notebook Bishop did head toward direct, candid, and painful autobiographical material in which potential embarrassment itself surfaces as topic.

A draft of another poem appears in a pile of unfinished poem fragments. The reference to rock roses may place it with other Key West material of the early forties, when Bishop wrote the poem entitled "Faustina, or Rock Roses." The question about an army or a navy house bolsters this suggested dating. The draft is headed "Vague Poem (Vaguely Love Poem) and establishes a setting on a trip west: "I think I *dreamed* that trip." An unidentified woman appears at a ramshackle house. The tone of the poem is hesitant, self-questioning. The speaker is looking for rock roses from a woman:

An Army house?—No, a Navy house.
      Yes,
        that far inland
there was nothing by the back door but dirt,
or that same dry monochrome, sepia straw I'd seen every
where.
Oh, she said, the dog has carried them off.
(A big black dog, female, was dancing around us.)

Later, as we drank tea from mugs, she found one,
"a sort of one." "This one is just beginning. See—
you can see here, it's beginning to look like a rose.
It's—well a crystal, crystals form—
I don't know any geology myself . . ."
(Neither did I.)
Faintly, I could make out—perhaps in the dull,
rose-red lump of soil (apparently?)
a rose-like shape; faint glitters . . .
      Yes, perhaps
there was a secret powerful crystal inside.

I *almost* saw it: turning into a rose
without any of the intervening
roots, stem, buds, and so on; just
earth to rose and back again.
Crystallography and its laws:
Something I once wanted badly to study,
until I learned that it would
       involve a lot of arithmetic, that is, mathematics.

Just now, when I saw you naked again,
I thought the same words: rose-rock, rock-rose . . .
Rose, trying, working, to show itself, forming, folding over
unimaginable connections, unseen, shining edges
Rose-rock, unformed, flesh beginning, crystal by crystal
clear pink breasts and darker crystalline nipples,
Rose-rock, rose quartz, roses, roses, roses
exacting roses from the body
and the even darker, accurate rose of sex.

(box 33, folder 532, VC)

Almost like a dream chant, the poem that is groping into being ends as a powerful affirmation of the whole of a woman's body, from center to circumference, without fear, without false shame, and with a full appreciation of beauty and secrecy fused in a primary symbol for women.

Unfinished and sketchy as the poem is, it also lifts a curtain on possibility: if Elizabeth Bishop had been born thirty years later into another public decorum, and if her keen, Moore-trained observer's eye had been released from the Moore prohibitions, the same poet who can see the sexual body as one more interesting object in the world's cupboard might have given us brilliant description, wholly original and incisive in its daring. This tantalizing little proto-poem is in its quiet ambition, and in its penetrating vision of the private body, far more revealing than much writing that later passed for "confessional" by both men and women.

The draft also moves to appropriate, or reconstitute an earlier image, placing it in a less frightening light. We can see clearly Kalstone's "vestigial implacable female presence" existing behind the scenes in "At the Fishhouses"; it is there in "the cold hard mouth" and "the rocky breasts" of the poem's maternal sea world. In "Vague Poem (Vaguely Love Poem)" those rocky breasts become a warm, almost-breathing crystal; while the image is still stiffly mineral, the negative context of the earlier image has been subverted, and turned inside out to represent love, and intimacy; the "implacable" female is in retreat.

Yet where would Bishop have wanted to publish such a poem? It isn't really finished, but she is in total control by that ending; its very hesitance, its tentative groping toward subject have become the drama of the poem's revelation. It seems such an enormous loss that there was no place, either in those years of her life or in any other of them, for such loving or for such a mixture of pride and tenderness to become vocal. One can only wonder, too, at the cost of such a choking off of speech. Still, a partial or at least livable speech forms within the splendid secrecy of that rock crystal at the center, an invisible beauty solidly connected to the visible world, even if only broken out in typescript.

It is a suggestive and enigma-producing linguistic parallel that the public rock roses named in the title of "Faustina, or Rock Roses" should be so stubborn and obtrusive an emblem of the female sinister or of the female unempowered. In the opening of this poem,

> Tended by Faustina
> yes in a crazy house
> upon a crazy bed,
> frail, of chipped enamel,
> blooming above her head
> into four vaguely roselike
> > flower-formations,
>
> the white woman whispers to
> herself.

(*CP*, p. 72)

The sick white woman the protagonist has come to visit lies in "her white disordered sheets / like wilted roses." Above her head, blooming from the bedstead at a level paralleling that of the face of her black attendant, Faustina, Bishop hangs the "four vaguely roselike flower-formations." The poem concludes with a look at Faustina:

> Her sinister kind face
> presents a cruel black
> coincident conundrum.
> > Oh, is it

freedom at last, a lifelong
dream of time and silence,
dream of protection and rest?
Or is it the very worst,
the unimaginable nightmare
that never before dared last
    more than a second?

The acuteness of the question
forks instantly and starts
a snake-tongue flickering;
blurs further, blunts, softens,
separates, falls, our problems
becoming helplessly
    proliferative.

There is no way of telling.
The eyes say only either
At last the visitor rises,
awkwardly proffers her bunch
of rust-perforated roses
and wonders oh, whence come
    all the petals.

(CP, pp. 73–74)

We are back to the female implacable here, made to notice the sinister potential of our bonds to the maternal or surrogate maternal presence; we are not celebrating the erotic, crystalline flower core. Faustina was somebody Bishop actually knew in Key West; she was a local character who sold lottery tickets and whose one preserved letter to Bishop is quite innocuous. But the face in "Faustina, or Rock Roses" is terrifyingly unreadable, moving in and out of protectiveness and malevolence in the flick of a watching eye. The roses framing the poem partake of the "cruel coincident conundrum" and, for our eyes, say only that the nature of the female is a splitting "either."

In this setting, the unpetaling roses that the visitor proffers so awkwardly in the disarray of the poem's ending are actually, metaphorically, and syntactically as disintegrative as the prostrate, invalid female. Roses as a troubling emblem of the female body lingered for Bishop. More than twenty years after the dark rose vision of "Faustina," Bishop made another abortive attempt to represent the female body more tenderly and less equivocally. One of the notebooks contains notes in both prose and poetry for a piece to be entitled "After Bonnard." On a torn piece of onionskin, Bishop typed, "*After Bonnard* The small shell-pink roses have opened so far, after two days in their bottle of water, that they are tired. The pink is fleeing—it is more mauve this afternoon. The centers stick up further and are faded, too, almost brown. Still delicate, but reaching out, out, thinner, vaguer, wearier—like those wide beautiful pale nipples I saw somewhere, on white, white and strong, but tired nevertheless, breasts. Time has smeared them, with a loving, but heavy thumb" (VC).

Time has smeared the breasts; his thumb is loving but heavy. Much of the same material appears in the draft of the poem of the same name, as Bishop tries out the subject in handwritten rhyme. Still tied to associations of death and a disintegrating identity, these flowers too, like Faustina's flowers, emblematize the female body. As in Bishop's juvenile piece, both the breasts in that guarded "somewhere" and the flowers suffer under a phallic thumb.

Beside the roses and women, there are further pairings of interest in "Faustina." Not so faintly etched, a mother-child is subsumed in the master-servant relationship. Bishop suggests the double character of the classic master-servant dilemma by the races of her protagonists in their mutual interdependencies. What happens when one crosses the boundary separating north and south and separating the races? What happens when searching for that "lifelong / dream of time and silence [. . .] of protection and rest," white child and white mistress put themselves at the mercy of the acknowledged black other? Each member of the pair is made to vibrate within the questions raised by union. Although a race-blind child may still, perhaps, rest in helpless innocence on the bosom of her need for a race-blind mother, as soon as we set a needy white in the care of a powerful black servant, age and weakness cannot modify the historically corrupted terms of such an exchange. Bishop is treading here within a dreadful assent, no less potent because implied, to the very old projection throwing white fear onto the figure of the black servant, whose exploited weakness and subjugation is made by a white speaker to grow into a back-lashing vision of frightening power.

In several poems, Bishop projects the problems of trust within love and intimacy onto the more remote arena of the world of servants, where power or control might then have seemed deceptively simpler issues. In the formal distances of that relationship her own doubts about intimacy can be safely tried, their terrors probed. But in her correspondence, her oscillating feelings about intimate relations show themselves directly in images of Lota. A 16 December letter to Ilse Barker in 1959 passes on this acknowledgment of Lota's power (PU). Bishop describes Lota's practical mastery of domestic detail: "She's so good a repairman that once a while ago I held the ladder for her along the road while she climbed up the posts and twiddled with the wires—I thought she'd be electrocuted at any minute, of course—and when we got back to the house we did have both lights and the telephone again." But on 27 January 1965 Bishop sent to the Barkers a darker and differently nuanced picture of Lota and her maid Joanna as mistress and servant: "Lota lay on her bed, in *negligee* . . . barefoot, looking very dark, and Joanna squatted on the floor beside her—the two watching a samba school on a portable tv set . . . everything so absolutely relaxed, tropical, and lush,—exactly like the old prints of Rio interiors, the mistress and the slave" (PU). In the image of Lota as tropical mistress, Bishop shows how in the mythos of this relationship, with its insistence on the outdated perspective of 'old prints,' she moves into a species of pastness to befriend her own dark side, taming and domesticating her vision of the malevolent female. Still, in that "dark," "absolutely relaxed, tropical, and lush" space, the earlier light-bearing Lota now edges closer to Faustina, into an area of projective fantasy, where darkness presents a "cruel black / co-incident conundrum."

In both class and racial terms, Bishop displaces the drama of her deepest fears about love and intimacy onto the more distant terrain of domestic servants and the dark Brazilian other. Through Lota, a dark otherness fuses or alternates attraction and repulsion. In these enactments, the vertical relations of mistress and servant, black and white, loved and feared, implacable mother and vulnerable daughter are, if not canceled, at least qualified. Over and over, in letters far more than in poems, Brazil confronts Bishop with unworkable binaries and provocative social and psychological paradigms in which her own relationships are confusingly set in broader contexts, in which personal urgencies undoubtedly distort her exile's reading of Brazilian realities.

But it is not the complex relation with Lota alone that accounts for the total impact of Bishop's exposure to Brazilian life. The complexities and confusions of these race-haunted relations in Bishop's life are indelibly positioned for any reader and begin with Bishop's own early blending of questions of sexual and racial liberation. Bishop's conflation of liberal attitudes toward race with liberal attitudes on gender goes back to her college years.

As part of a collection of papers that Bishop transferred to Vassar toward the close of her life, she included pages from a 1932 Vassar assignment on "The Noble Savage." In this essay, she imagines a specimen she calls Zubinko, a "natural man" both "free and grand," with "an upright heart" and "a beautiful physique and all the virtues." Bishop's Zubinko takes flesh in a variety of literary representations from Dryden's Alamanzor, to *Oroonoko*, then to an ignominious finish as Mrs. Inchbald's "Amos, a negro slave." In the paper Bishop insists on an important feature: "I can reach only one conclusion: Zubinko was an hermaphrodite. He or she was capable of impersonating either sex upon the stage in a perfectly satisfactory manner, and his or her character, resting always on the bed rock of Freedom, could display either a manly or womanly side. We must not blame or belittle so great an artist for what must after all be considered as merely incidental; rather we must pity him that his private life was thus made even more lonely, and he was denied the great loves he enacted upon the stage" (box 39, folder 605, VC). At twenty-one, Bishop recognized the links between the social and psychological repressions of race and gender. Her own transmutation of these concerns into issues of identity with north and south clearly entered into her personal attachments, even if they were never very clearly articulated in her treatment of either exile or travel motifs in her work. But Bishop's pictures of Lota, held close to her in alternating terms as both a privileged aristocrat and a tropical other, reflect how within metaphors of race that engage our sharpest sense of self and other, we draw the portrait of our conflict-ridden allegiances to love and community.

In the swift sketch of Lota that Bishop presents to her aunt, Grace Bulmer Bowers, in a 1957 letter, we see Lota as a model of integrative affection. Lota is wakened by Betty, the cook's child: "When she was jumping up & down on Lota in her bed the other morning Lota said 'my mother certainly would have been surprised to see me with a little nigger on top of me like this!' " (box 18, folder 253, VC). As patron, Lota gave gifts in an environment less bound by racially restricted behavior than her mother's. Attempting to mitigate the poverty and narrowness of her servants' lives, Lota remained the privileged white benefactress, even as in her final years she labored at enormous physical and mental cost to transform an urban landfill in Rio into a public park. For Bishop, on the mythic map of her southern descent, her Latin American lover, however aristocratic or however correctly *engagée* in upbringing, could still represent in the chain of color her own embrace of a darker, more primitive self and a less disrupted definition of the feminine. For Bishop, Lota could be seen both as a dark and subordinate other *and* as an aristocrat within whose household Bishop herself, habitually attired in jeans, was served by a liveried butler, as she wrote to Ilse Barker (28 March 1963, PU).

Whereas the 1965 letter, written at a time when relations between the two women were beginning to fray, emphasizes Lota's tropical darkness and otherness, in August 1953 Bishop reported to Barker on Lota's aristocratic and leftist background with gleeful pride: "Until Vargas, her father was always in politics—he was exiled several times; they have the straw hat with a bullet hole through the brim he was wearing one day when shot at; Lota says at the convent for a few years the girls whose fathers were in prison—hers was—didn't speak to the socially inferior girls whose fathers were out, etc. . . . all in the best South American tradition."

Both women seem always to have taken free relations with blacks as a necessary consequence of their own political, social, and psychosexual liberation. Writing on 13 March 1965 to Grace Bulmer Bowers, her favorite aunt, Bishop scolds her "severely" for following opinion about Martin Luther King's leadership and points with satisfaction to having recorded for a Brazilian newspaper her own approval of King's Nobel Peace Prize: "You have no idea how the rest of the world feels about how the US treats its colored people—and particularly here, where there is no problem at all. It is one reason I like living here, after ten years or so in the 'south.'" Bishop then tells a story: "Don't forget I did live in the south. My dear old laundress's (black) son was murdered by the Key West police because one of them wanted his wife. Everyone knew this and nothing was done about it. The laundress was given her son's body in a coffin, straight from jail. She said 'I looked at his arm Miss Elizabeth, it wasn't an *arm* any more . . .' etc etc" (box 18, folder 261, VC). More on the subject crops up again on 18 May:

> After living in the south off and on for more than ten years you have no idea what a relief it is to live here and see people of all colors happy and natural together. (All miserably poor together, too, but even so, it is more civilized than what we have in the USA, I'm afraid.) At the grand opening of Lota's "park," a few weeks ago, there was a new outdoor

dance-floor and it was so nice to see all the different colors dancing together, one young couple dancing *with* their baby, about 10 months old, a tall black man, a beautiful dancer. Our mulatto maid went, all dressed to kill, and all Lota's architects, young white men danced away with her and she had the time of her life. Now that is what I call being civilized! It is something I feel very deeply about.
(box 18, folder 261, VC)

Once again, Brazil represents Bishop's world of harmonized opposites, where the "broken-down luxury" of Lota's living quarters in Rio, as she once referred to it in correspondence (24 March 1963, PU) with the Barkers, afforded her a vital and earthy shabbiness within privileged comfort and where one could have the service of maids and still have them watch television with the mistress and dance away with their betters on "civilized" public occasions. (It is worth noting that while Bishop was perennially eager to see the dissolution of racial barriers, her interest in dissolving class barriers was rather less keen.)

Bishop, dependent on Lota for her well-being in Brazil, saw her in their happiest years as the longed-for generously nurturant presence. (Lota's mothering is something both women accepted as defining their relation, although Lota was actually no more than a year older than Bishop.) As their relation grew more strained, a vision obtrudes in which Lota as the dark mistress emerges, perhaps guaranteeing her freedom in an upside-down world of exile ruled by the Southern Cross, in a reverse heaven like that of "Insomnia." Months before Lota's apparent suicide in September 1967 Bishop wrote to the Barkers of one upheaval (13 January 1967, PU). Lota, near mental collapse, was "unconscious most of the time, kept at home. Since I am closest to her of course I am the one she turned against or feels a certain ambivalence for, there have been six months now of this up-and-down, but the last few weeks were by far the worst and it was decided (and I'd already decided myself) that the only thing for me to do was to get out, which I did, in about half an hour, while they took her to the dr. . . . So here I am after fifteen years with a few dirty clothes in a busted suitcase, no home any more, no claims (legally) to anything here, etc."

The women eventually reconciled. Bishop, writing in the days immediately after Lota's death to both the Barkers and the Summerses, tried to make sense of her friend's last days, repeating to each correspondent that her hours in New York with Lota had been free of agitation. To Anny Baumann she reported the events, finding Lota's body with the empty pill bottle in her hand, having to be the official witness. To the

Summers she said: "I was with her for only a few hours, actually, and there was no quarrel or discussion of any sort" (28 September 1967, VC). To the Barkers, she writes:

> I'll never really know whether it was deliberate or a mistake or what, she brought her good clothes, for parties, many presents, pounds & pounds of coffee, etc., so it doesn't look as though she had meant this consciously, but I know she was desperately unhappy. Our few hours were peaceful and affectionate, thank god, but oh oh, if I hadn't gone to sleep, if I had just managed to say the *right* thing, some how—
>   I know now, from Rio, that all her friends and *three* doctors tried to keep her from coming, but I could not seem to resist those pathetic cables, and at least, she did want to be with me, that's my only comfort so far. (3 October 1967, PU)

And to the Summers again, "I just feel worse & worse all the time, but I suppose this will wear away, but don't think for a moment that love does, because it doesn't" (4 October 1967, VC).

For years afterward Bishop tried to make a go of returning to Brazil. Yet the arc of this experience with one woman and one country represented much material accessible in poetry for Bishop in only carefully controlled bits. There is only limited evidence both in letters and in poems for trying to determine what blackness meant by way of symbolic counter to Bishop. Yet neither Bishop, with the instincts of her liberal background, nor Lota seems free of an appropriation in which the wholeness of the black other disappears or is obliterated within the narcissistic back-projections of white fear and white self-congratulation. It seems clear that Bishop's fascination with blackness, in poetry and in her personal life, becomes part of the mechanism by which race comes to stand in for our fears and desire for intimacy: in casting one's lover for a role in the drama of approaching the stranger, fears of intimacy and of being overwhelmed by intimacy are given their ritual place and a kind of valor attaches to overcoming those fears. And yet through whatever clouded personal perceptions, both women, often with courage, generosity, and style, rushed to free themselves from malignant practice and from the recursive dilemmas of race and gender within which we, even in our reflective hindsight, seem still entangled.

Notes

1. The notebooks referred to here are part of a cache of Bishop's papers I examined on a trip to Brazil in 1985. The papers were subsequently transferred to the

Vassar College Library, and they are referred to in this volume as the Key West/Nemer (KWN) notebooks. The notebooks were kept primarily during Bishop's decade in Key West, Florida, and were subsequently entrusted to a legatee, Linda Nemer, in Brazil. All other quotations in this article from Bishop's unpublished work in draft form refer to papers held by the Vassar Library (box 35A, folders 1 and 2, VC).

LEE EDELMAN

The Geography of Gender: Elizabeth Bishop's "In the Waiting Room"

I

I *always* tell the truth in my poems. With *The Fish*, that's *exactly* how it happened. It was in Key West, and I *did* catch it just as the poem says. That was in 1938. Oh, but I did change *one* thing.—Elizabeth Bishop quoted in Wesley Wehr, "Elizabeth Bishop: Conversations and Class Notes."

TIME AND AGAIN in discussing her poetry Elizabeth Bishop insists on its fidelity to literal reality. "It was all true," she affirms of "The Moose," "it was all exactly the way I described it except that I say 'seven relatives.' Well, they weren't really relatives, they were various stepsons and so on, but that's the only thing that isn't quite true" (Spires 1981, p. 62). In her attempts to "place" her poetry by means of such comments, Bishop reproduces a central gesture of the poetry itself. For that poetry, in Bishop's master-trope, takes place beneath the aegis of "geography," a study of places that leads her, invariably, to the question of poetic positioning—a question that converges, in turn, with the quest for, and the questioning of, poetic authority. Even in the casual remarks cited above, Bishop undertakes to authenticate her work, and she does so, tellingly, by fixing its origin on the solid ground of literality—a literality that Bishop repeatedly identifies as "truth."

But what does it mean to assert that a poem is "true," is somehow literal? Is it, in fact, ever possible to read such an assertion literally? Or, to put it another way, for what is such an appeal to literality a figure? Against what does it defend? These questions must color any reading of Bishop's poetry precisely because that poetry insists on the figural subtlety with which it represents the world. "More delicate than the historians' are the map-makers' colors," Bishop writes in "The Map," the poem she placed first in her book of poems (*CP*, p. 3). And that poem provides a key to the landscape of her poetry by directing attention to issues of textuality and trope. The truth that interests Bishop from the outset is not the truth of history or fact per se but the more "delicate" matter of representation, the finely discriminated "colors" that lead back to the functioning of poetic coloration, or trope. If Bishop, as mapmaker, "colors" her world, she has less in common with the sort of Stevensian literalist of the first idea, as which she presents herself at times, than she does with Stevens's sublimely solipsistic Hoon, who calls forth a world from within himself to find himself "more truly and more strange" ("Tea at the Palaz of Hoon," Stevens 1954, p. 65).

To make such a claim about Bishop's work, however, is to displace truth from its relation to literality. To link the ability to see "truly" to the ability to make reality "more strange" is to make truth itself a stranger term—and one more problematic. For truth now comes into alignment with trope, literal and figurative effectively change places. Bishop's remarks about the literal origins of her poetry become significant, in this light, less for their assertions than for their qualifications: "that's *exactly* how it happened. . . . Oh, but I did change *one* thing"; "it was all exactly the way I described it . . . Well, they weren't really relatives." Like the poetry itself, Bishop's characterizations of that poetry question the relationship between literal and figurative, observation and invention, perception and vision. All of which is to say that Bishop's is a poetry conscious of the inevitable mediations of selfhood, the intrusions of the "I," that make direct contact with any literality—with any "truth"—an impossibility.

But critics, for the most part, have refrained from seriously reading Bishop's readings of reading. They have cited her work, instead, as exemplary of precise observation and accurate detail, presenting us with an Elizabeth Bishop who seems startlingly like some latter-day "gentle Jane." David Kalstone (1983a) suggests something of the problem when he notes that "critics have praised her descriptive powers and treated her as something of a miniaturist. As mistakenly as with the work of Marianne Moore, they have sometimes asked if Bishop's is poetry at all" (p. 4). It is indeed significant that Moore and Bishop, two of the most widely praised female American poets of the century, have been championed for their careful observation, their scrupulous particularity, their characteristic restraint. As Sandra Gilbert and Susan Gubar (1979) point out in *The Madwoman in the Attic,* these are qualities less often associated with lyric poetry than with prose fiction (pp. 545–49). They define the skills necessary for success in a genre that historically has been more hospitable to women, perhaps because its conventions, themselves more social and domestic, rely upon powers of perception and narration that coincide with traditional perspectives on women as analysts of emotion, on the one hand, and as busybodies or gossips, on the other. If few would reduce Bishop to the status of a gossip, many have noticed the distinct and engaging quality of the voice that seems to emanate from her work—a voice described by John Ashbery (1977) as speaking in "a pleasant, chatty, vernacular tone . . . calmly and unpoetically" (p. 10). It is this "unpoetic" voice—Robert Lowell (1947) called it "unrhetorical" (p. 496)—in combination with her alert and disciplined eye, that has led critics to read Bishop's poetry, in John Hollander's (1977) words, "almost as if she were a novelist" (p. 359). Viewing it as a species of moral anecdote, even admirers of Bishop's work have tended to ignore the rigor of her intellect, the range of her allusiveness, the complexity of her tropes. Instead, they imply what Anne Stevenson (1966), in her book on Bishop's life and work, asserts: "Whatever ideas emerge have not been arrived at over a period of time but perceived, it would seem, in passing. They are the by-products of her meticulous observations" (p. 31).

Bishop, of course, has encouraged such misreadings by characterizing her poetry as "just description" and by emphasizing its grounding in the literal (see Pinsky 1979, p. 32). I have suggested that this assertion of literality must itself be interpreted as a figure, that it defines for Bishop a strategy of evasion the sources of which this paper will attempt, in part, to trace. But the critical reception of Bishop, with its complicity in her reductive self-definition, with its acceptance of her willful evasions and its misprisions of her irony, exemplifies an interpretative blindness, which is to say, an ideological blindness, that enacts the very problems of reading on which Bishop's poetry frequently dwells. Readings that appropriate Bishop either to the company of poetic observers and reporters or to the ranks of moral fabulists, readings that place her in a clear relation to the literal reality her work is said to register, have the odd effect of seeming, instead, to be already placed or inscribed within that work, within her meditations on the way in which questions of placement and appropriation necessarily inform the very act of reading. No text better demonstrates the intricate connections among these concerns, or better locates the uncanny nature of her poetry's anticipation of its own mis-readings, than does "In the Waiting Room," the poem with which Bishop introduced her last published volume, *Geography III*. A reading of that poem, which is a poem about reading, and a reading that interrogates the various readings of the poem, may suggest something of what is at stake in Bishop's reading of reading and show how "In the Waiting Room" effectively positions itself to read its readers.

II

> First, however, . . . I shall read very carefully (or try to read, since they may be partly obliterated, or in a foreign language) the inscriptions already there. Then I shall adapt my own compositions, in order that they may not conflict with those written by the prisoner before me. The voice of a new in-mate will be noticeable, but there will be no contradictions or criticisms of what has already been laid down, rather a "commentary."—from "In Prison"

Commentaries on "In the Waiting Room" tend to agree that the poem presents a young girl's moment of awakening to the separations and the bonds among human beings, to the forces that shape individual identity through the interrelated recognitions of community and isola-tion. More remarkable than this unaccustomed critical consensus, how-ever, is the degree to which its readers concur in identifying the poem's narrative or "plot" as the locus of the interpretative issues raised by the text. It is significant, in consequence, that critics have felt themselves both able and obliged to summarize the "story," to rehearse the events on which the poem's act of recognition hinges. Helen Vendler (1977), for example, recapitulates the plot as follows: "waiting in a dentist's office, reading the *National Geographic*, feeling horrified at pictures of savages, hearing her aunt cry out in pain from inside the dentist's room, the child feels vertigo" (p. 418). Michael Wood (1977) directs attention to this same central episode when he describes "In the Waiting Room" as a poem in which "an almost-seven-year-old Elizabeth Bishop is hor-rified by the hanging breasts of African women seen in a copy of the *National Geographic,* and hears her own voice when her aunt cries out in pain" (p. 30). Similarly, Sybil Estess (1977) focuses on this narrative relationship when she writes that the child's "encounter with the strange pictures in the *National Geographic* is simultaneous with hearing her aunt's muffled cry of suffering" (p. 853).

These redactions would seem to rule out the possibility of hidden textual complications by the uniformity with which they define the poem's critical events. Yet when I suggest that there is something unusual and telling about the uniformity of these summaries, I anticipate that some will wonder why it should be considered odd that accounts of the same text should focus on the same significant episodes. What, one might ask, is so strange about critical agreement on the literal events that take place within the poem?

One response to such a question might begin by observing that the text itself seems to undermine the stability of the literal. Certainly the poem appears to appropriate—and to ground itself in—the particulars of a literal reality or truth. Bishop takes pains, for instance, to describe the contents of the magazine read by the young girl in the waiting room. Not only does she evoke in detail its pictures of volcanoes and of "black, naked women," but she specifies the particular issue of the magazine, identifying it as the *National Geographic* of February 1918. But Bishop, as Jerome Mazzaro (1985) puts it, "tampers with the actual contents" (p. 46). While that issue of the magazine does indeed contain an article on volcanoes—lavishly titled "The Valley of Ten Thousand Smokes: An Account of the Discovery and Exploration of the Most Wonderful Volcanic Region in the World"—it offers no images of "Babies with pointed heads," no pictures of "black, naked women with necks / wound round and round with wire" (p. 159). In an interview with George Starbuck, Bishop, responding to critics who noticed the factual "error" in her text, declared: "My memory had confused two 1918 issues of the *Geographic*. Not having seen them since then, I checked it out in the New York Public Library. In the February issue there was an article, 'The Valley of Ten Thousand Smokes,' about Alaska that I'd remembered, too. But the African things, it turned out, were in the *next* issue, in March" (Starbuck 1983, p. 318). Bishop's clarification only underscores her insistence on literal origins—and her wariness of her own imaginative powers. For the curious will discover what might have been suspected all along: the "African things" are not to be found in the March issue of the *National Geographic,* either. In fact, that issue has no essay about Africa at all.

With this in mind we are prepared for the warning that Alfred Corn (1977) offers the unsuspecting reader. He notes that, just as the picture essay Bishop describes "is not to be found in the February 1918 *National Geographic,*" so "anyone checking to see whether Miss Bishop's aunt was named Consuelo probably ought to be prepared for a similar thwarting of curiosity." In the face of this, one might well pose the question that Corn then frames: "If the facts are 'wrong,' why did Bishop make such a point of them in the poem?" (p. 535). Or, to put the question another way, toward what end does Bishop attempt to appropriate a literal grounding for her poem if that poem insists on fracturing the literality on which it positions itself? Whatever answer one might posit in response to such a question, the very fact that the poem invites us to ask it, the very fact that the poem revises simplistic conceptions of "fact" or literality, may answer objections to my remark that there is something strange about the critics' agreement on the literal events that take place within the text.

But a new objection will surely be raised, accusing me of conflating two different senses of the "literal," or even of using *literal* in a way that is itself not strictly literal. While there may be questions, the objectors will insist, about the text's fidelity to the facts outside of it—questions, that is, about the literal truth of the text—those questions do not prevent us from articulating literally what happens within the text. Whether or not Bishop had a real Aunt Consuelo, there can be no doubt, they will argue that Vendler and Estess and Wood are correct in asserting that, literally, within the poem, and as one of its crucial events, Aunt Consuelo cries out in pain from inside the dentist's office. And yet I intend not only to cast doubt upon that central event, but to suggest that the poem itself is less interested in the event than in the doubts about it, and that the critics' certainties distort the poem's insistence on confusion.

My own comments, of course, must repeat the error of attempted clarification. So I will approach this episode at the center of the text by way of my own brief summary of what occurs before it. The young girl, sitting outside in the waiting room while her aunt is in the dentist's office, reads the *National Geographic* "straight through," from cover to cover, and then, having closed the magazine, she begins to inspect the cover itself.

> Suddenly, from inside,
> came an *oh!* of pain
> —Aunt Consuelo's voice—
> not very loud or long.
> I wasn't at all surprised;
> even then I knew she was
> a foolish, timid woman.
> I might have been embarrassed,

but wasn't. What took me
completely by surprise
was that it was *me:*
my voice, in my mouth.
Without thinking at all
I was my foolish aunt,
I—we—were falling, falling,
our eyes glued to the cover
of the *National Geographic,*
February, 1918.

(CP, p. 160)

To gloss this passage as the young girl hearing "her aunt cry out in pain" is surely to ignore the real problem that both the girl and the text experience here: the problem of determining the place from which this voice originates. Since the poem asserts that it comes from "inside," the meanings of "inside" and "outside" must be determined, their geographical relation, as it were, must be mapped. The difficulty of making such determinations, however, springs from the overdetermination of meaning in this passage. The voice that cries out and, in so doing, sends the young girl—later identified as "Elizabeth"—plunging into the abyss that constitutes identity, disorients not by any lack of specification but by the undecidable doubleness with which it is specified.[1] The child recognizes the voice at once as Aunt Consuelo's and as her own. Any attempt to fix a clear relationship between these two alternatives, to label one as the ground on which the other appears as figure, must presuppose an ability to penetrate the text, to get inside of it and thereby determine what it signifies by "inside." The critical consensus that attributes the cry of pain to Aunt Consuelo does, of course, precisely that. It refers the literal sense of "inside" to Aunt Consuelo's situation inside the dentist's office and thereby implies an interpretative model that rests upon an ability to distinguish the inside from the outside, the literal from the figurative. It suggests, moreover, that the literal is the textual "inside" on which the figural "outside" depends, and, therefore, that critical understanding must proceed by piercing or reading through the confusions of figuration in order to recover the literal ground that not only enables us to "place" the figural but also allows us, by doing so, to keep the figural in its place.

Bishop's geography, however, persistently refuses the consolations of hierarchy or placement; instead, it defines itself as the questioning of places—a project emblematized by the way in which Bishop tropes upon the volume's epigraph from a geography textbook of 1884. She appends to its confident litany of answers to questions about the world (*"What is the earth?* / The planet or body on which we live. / *What is the shape of the earth?* / Round, like a ball. [*CP*, p. 157]), a series of inquiries that seek to evade the reductive literalism of such an idiot questioner:

> *In what direction is the volcano? The*
> *Cape? The Bay? The Lake? The Strait?*
> *The Mountains? The Isthmus?*
> *What is in the East? In the West? In the*
> *South? In the North? In the Northwest?*
> *In the Southeast? In the Northeast?*
> *In the Southwest?*

Given Bishop's insistent questioning of places, we can say that in a very real sense those commentators who put themselves in a position to identify Aunt Consuelo as the source of the cry of pain in "In the Waiting Room" take the words out of Bishop's mouth in taking the cry out of "Elizabeth's." Their need to locate the place from which the cry or voice originates places the question of the voice's origination at the origin of the textual problem in the poem. That is to say, it locates the poem as an effect of the voice's origination, enabling them to read it as a fable of humanization through identification, a lesson in the sort of Wordsworthian "primal sympathy" that shapes "the human heart by which we live" ("Ode: Intimations of Immortality," ll. 181, 200).

But within the poem itself the voice is contextually located, and since the logic of the poetry allows some truth to *post hoc, ergo propter hoc,* this location determines the voice itself as an effect—as, specifically, a reading effect. The cry that the text tells us comes "Suddenly, from inside," comes, within the text, after "Elizabeth" has finished reading the *National Geographic* and is scrutinizing its cover. To understand that cry, then, and the meaning of its place—or, more precisely, of its displacement—requires a more careful study of the scene of reading that comes before it and, in some sense, calls it forth.

Evoking herself as an almost-seven-year-old child sitting in the dentist's waiting room, the "Elizabeth" whose memory constitutes the poem offers off-handedly, in a parenthetical aside, the assertion that governs the whole of the passage preceding the cry: "(I could read)" (*CP*, p. 159). However casually the parentheses introduce this simple statement, both the statement itself and the simplicity with which it is presented identify a claim to authority. For the child, that authority derives from her mastery of the mystery of written language and from her concomitant access to the documents of culture, the inscriptions of society. Just as she has mastered reading, and as reading allows for a mastery of culture, so reading itself, for the young "Elizabeth," is understood as an exercise of mastery. The child of whose ability to read we are assured implicitly assumes the readability of the texts, since reading for her is a process of perceiving the real and stable relationships that exist between word and image, past and present, cause and effect. The juxtaposition of photographs and captions, therefore, is transparently meaningful for "Elizabeth." From her position as a reader, outside of the text, she can readily decipher the fixed relationships that are delineated within it.

But the critical moment in the poem is precipitated at just the point when this model of reading as mastery comes undone, when the division between inside and outside breaks down and, as a result, the determinacy of textual relationships is called into question. Though only in the course of reading the magazine does "Elizabeth" perceive the inadequacy of her positioning as a reader, Bishop's text implies from the outset the insufficiency of any mode of interpretation that claims to release the meaning it locates "inside" a text by asserting its own ability to speak from a position of mastery "outside" of it. For this reason everything that "Elizabeth" encounters in the pages of the *National Geographic* serves to disturb the stability of a binary opposition. The first photographs that she recalls looking at, for instance, strategically define a sequential process:

> the inside of a volcano,
> black, and full of ashes;
> then it was spilling over
> in rivulets of fire.
>
> (*CP*, p. 159)

Not only do these images undo the central distinction between inside and outside, but they do so by positing an excess of interiority that displaces itself onto the exterior. In other words, the inside here obtrudes upon the outside and thereby asserts its claim to mastery by transforming the landscape and showing how the exterior, how the landscape itself, is composed of interior matter.

The inside/outside dichotomy is reversed and discredited at once, and the effect of this maneuver on the theory of reading is to imply that the textual inside masters the reader outside of it far more than the reader can ever master the text. Or, more precisely, the very distinction between reader and text is untenable: the reader finds herself read by the text in which she is already inscribed and in which she reinscribes herself in the process of performing her reading. Since "Elizabeth" asserts that she "carefully studied" these photographs, it is worth noting, too, that not only do they disrupt the opposition between inside and outside but also, insofar as the "ashes" in the first picture produce the "rivulets of fire" in the second, they disrupt the natural or logical relationship ascribed to cause and effect.

Inasmuch as Bishop's version of the *National Geographic* for February 1918 corresponds to the actual issue of that magazine only in that both include images of volcanoes, her imagined periodical must function as a sort of exemplary text contrived to instruct young "Elizabeth," and us, in the difficulty of reading. Toward this end, the photograph of Osa and Martin Johnson, though it seems less violently subversive than Bishop's Dickinsonian volcanoes, plays a significant part. The Johnsons, in the first decades of this century, achieved fame as a husband and wife team of explorers and naturalists, and in her autobiography, *I Married Adventure*, Osa Johnson provides information that may have inspired, and certainly sheds light on, the rest of the items that Bishop chooses to include in her magazine. But the photograph of the Johnsons themselves does more than allude to one of Bishop's likely sources. Her portrait of husband and wife focuses attention on the particulars of their clothing, and the most significant aspect of their clothing is the fact that it is identical. Both appear "dressed in riding breeches, / laced boots, and pith helmets" (*CP*, p. 159). (I might add that there is a picture of Osa and Martin Johnson in which she appears in such a costume, but her husband, interestingly enough, does not wear an identical outfit.) In terms of Osa's autobiography, this image metonymically represents her transformation from a typical Kansas girl of sixteen, dreaming of weddings and weeping "with all the persecuted little picture heroines of the day" (Johnson 1940, p. 69), into an adventurer able to hold her own in a world of cannibals and headhunters. Osa underscores this transformation precisely in terms of clothing in two passages from *I Married Adventure*. The first time that her future husband calls on her at home, Osa's brother causes her to "burst out crying" by telling her that Mr. Johnson has joined with cannibals in eating missionaries. When her caller arrives, Osa is still upstairs crying, and, as she tells us, "With women's clothes as complicated as they were in that day, even with Mama's help, it was nearly half an hour before I could get downstairs" (p. 78). Later, after they are married and she has agreed to join Martin on expeditions into the realm of the cannibals, he describes to her the sort of clothing that they will need to take along:

> "And some denim overalls and huck shirts," Martin said, following me into the kitchen.
> "For me?" I asked.
> "For both of us," he replied. (p. 103)

The identical outfits in which Bishop envisions the Johnsons in her photograph, then, point emblematically toward the subversion of the hierarchical opposition of male and female, an opposition into the nature of which Osa Johnson will peer when, like Claude Lévi-Strauss, she confronts the role of women in primitive cultures as linguistic and economic objects of circulation and exchange. The structural anthropologist's insight offers a valuable point of reference here because "Elizabeth," after perusing the picture of the Johnsons, encounters in her text disturbing images that illuminate *la pensée sauvage*. (It is important to note, moreover, if only parenthetically, that "Elizabeth," for whom reading is at once a discipline of mastery and a mode of mastering her culture, occupies herself in reading a magazine devoted to geography and ethnology—discourses that imply a troubling relationship between the reading of cultures and the assertion of an ethnocentric form of cultural mastery.)

Bishop now presents the young "Elizabeth" with a textual impasse that resists appropriation by her system of reading as mastery and in so doing challenges her confidence in the very readability of texts: "A dead man slung on a pole / —'Long Pig,' the caption said" (*CP*, p. 159). Dividing image and caption, picture and text, not only by means of the line break but also by the dash—a mark of punctuation that dialectically connects and separates at once—Bishop emphasizes the apparently absolute undecidability of the relationship here. Some element of error seems necessarily to have entered into the working of the text. Has "Elizabeth" mistakenly interpreted the photograph of a pig as that of a human corpse? Has an editor carelessly transposed captions so that the photograph of a corpse has been identified as that of a pig? What "Elizabeth" faces here, of course, is the fundamental "error" of figurative language that creates the difficulty in trying to locate the literal as the ground from which the figural can be construed. The pole on which the dead object—be it corpse or pig—is slung serves as the axis of meaning on which the trope itself seems to turn. Like a dash, or like the slash that marks a fraction or a mathematical ratio, the pole establishes the polarities that it also brings together. For "Elizabeth" only the discrepancy matters, the difference that cannot be mastered or read. But anthropologists—or those familiar with Osa Johnson's autobiography—will be able to read this figural relationship more easily than does "Elizabeth," since they will recognize what the phrase "Long Pig" metaphorically connotes.

Describing her first expedition into a "savage" society, Osa recalls that she and her husband were warned that "those fellows on Vao still bury their old people alive and eat long pig" (Johnson 1940, p. 115). And later, remembering the dismay of the captain who, at their insistence, ferried her husband and herself to Vao despite such admonitions, Osa writes, "If we were reckless enough to risk being served up as 'long pig' by the savages of Malekula, that was our lookout, not his" (p. 115). "Long Pig," then, names man when he ceases to be human, when he enters into a system of signification that he no longer masters from an external position of privileged subjectivity, but within which he himself can be appropriated as an object to be consumed. The metaphoric labeling of a "dead man" as "long pig" has the effect of exposing the metaphoricity of the apparently literal or natural category of humanity itself.[2] Far from being a presence controlling language from without, humanity is understood to be figural, another product of the linguistic system.

Though Bishop's text, then, has challenged the stability of distinctions between inside and outside, male and female, literal and figurative, human and bestial, young "Elizabeth" reads on from her own position of liminality in the waiting room until she confronts, at last, an image of women and their infants:

> Babies with pointed heads
> wound round and round with string;
> black, naked women with necks
> wound round and round with wire
> like the necks of light bulbs.
>
> (*CP*, p. 159)

Osa Johnson may again have provided Bishop with the material that she incorporates here into her imagined magazine. In her autobiography

Mrs. Johnson refers to the Malekulan practice of elongating the head: "This was done by binding soft, oiled coconut fiber around the skulls of infants shortly after birth and leaving them there for something over a year. The narrower and longer the head when the basket contrivance was removed, the greater the pride of the mother. That her baby had cried almost without ceasing during this period of distortion was of no concern whatsoever" (1940, p. 151). The autobiography, however, does not refer to the elongation of women's necks, and in the photograph that Osa Johnson includes of a Malekulan woman and her infant—a photograph in which the child's head is indeed "wound round and round with string"—the mother does not wear the rings of wire that are used to stretch women's necks in some tribal cultures. Bishop willfully introduces the symmetry that characterizes her images of women and children so that both here suffer physical distortion by objects "wound round and round" their bodies. This assimilation of women to the status of children takes place simultaneously with the recognition made by the young "Elizabeth" of her own destined status as a woman, of her own inevitable role, therefore, in the sexual economy of her culture. She reads the burden of female sexuality here as the inescapability of distortion, as the enforced awareness of one's body as a malleable object. Anatomy itself loses the authority of any natural or literal grounding; instead, it becomes one more figure in the language of the culture.

As woman is reduced to a figure trapped in the linguistic circuit, so her body becomes a text in which her figural status is inscribed. The culturally sanctioned—which is to say, the patriarchally determined—markings of female sexuality are thus understood as diacritical marks, and Bishop, significantly, evokes these linguistic markings, these metonyms of woman as erotic signifier, specifically in terms of constraint. Moreover, her particular vision of constriction as the patriarchal writing of woman's sexuality on her body takes the form of a wire wound about the woman's neck, an image that conjures the garrote—an instrument of strangulation that prevents the victim from uttering any cry at all. If the necks of the women in these photographs are bound by these wires "like the necks of light bulbs," then what they illuminate for "Elizabeth" is her fate as a woman, her necessary implication in the system of signs she had thought to master by being able to read. Now, for the first time, she reacts to the text, acknowledging an emotional response to the naked women: "Their breasts," she says, "were horrifying" (*CP*, p. 159).

The horror that "Elizabeth" feels betokens her perception of the monstrosity, the abnormality that informs the given or "norm" of sexuality. Sexuality itself, she has discovered, is always constituted as a system of signs that must operate through the substitution of figures; consequently, it is neither a "natural" system nor an inevitable one. Yet within the patriarchal order the "normal" figurations of female sexuality take the form of literal disfigurations. Woman herself becomes a creation of man since, as Simone de Beauvoir recognized years ago, one is not born a woman: as a linguistic construct who figures through disfiguration, woman is the monstrous creation of the patriarchy. And what most horrifies "Elizabeth" as she focuses on the breasts of these monstrous or disfigured women is her recognition of the fundamental affinity she shares with them. In a sense they speak to her in the words that Mary Shelley gave to the monster that she imagined as the product of a wholly masculine gestation: "My form is a filthy type of yours, more horrid even from the very resemblance" (Shelley 1965, p. 125). It is finally this resemblance, which is to say, the relationship of metaphoric interchangeability, that horrifies "Elizabeth." At last she must recognize fully what is at stake in the dismantling of binary oppositions, for the reader and what she reads collapse into one another as "Elizabeth" finds herself located *by* the text, *inside* the text, and *as* a text.

Yet in neutral, uninflected tones she continues:

I read it right straight through.
I was too shy to stop.
And then I looked at the cover:
the yellow margins, the date.

(*CP,* p. 159)

The very blandness of this account, following her admission of horror, testifies to an effort of denial or repression as "Elizabeth" seeks to master herself by affirming her difference from the text and, thus, her ability to master *it* through reading. She studies the cover, the margins, and the date in order to construct a frame for her reading experience that will circumscribe or contain it. The burden of her task here is the desperate need to contextualize the text so as to prevent her suffocation, her strangulation within it. The "yellow margins" that she focuses on represent her margin of security to the extent that they define a border, a yellow or cautionary zone distinguishing the inside from the outside. But the security of such a reading of the margin falls within the margin of error as soon as one recognizes the complex dynamic involved in the positing of such a frame. In a brilliant analysis of these problems in her essay "The Frame of Reference: Poe, Lacan, Derrida," Barbara Johnson (1980) cites Derrida's contention that "frames are always framed" (p. 128). What this means in terms of "Elizabeth" and her reading of the *National Geographic* is that the act of framing arises as a response to her disturbing recognition that the text refuses to be delimited or framed. Thus her framing of the text is itself framed by her terrifying awareness of the text's unframeability. As Johnson observes in her analysis of Derrida, therefore, "the frame thus becomes not the borderline between the inside and the outside, but precisely what subverts the applicability of the inside / outside polarity to the act of interpretation" (p. 128).

One subversive aspect of "Elizabeth's" response to the photograph of the women remains to be considered. The breasts that "Elizabeth" describes as horrifying may horrify not only because they link her to the disfigurations and constraint that mark female sexuality in patriarchal cultures; they may horrify as well because they evoke an eroticism that undermines the institution of heterosexuality—the institution that determines sexual difference as well as its inscriptions (see Wenzel 1981, p. 278). Adrienne Rich (1983) has recently discussed Bishop in terms of "the lesbian writing under the false universal of heterosexuality" (p. 16), but here in "In the Waiting Room" and at the other crucial points throughout her career, Bishop covertly discredits that "false universal" and its ideology. After acknowledging her emotional reaction to the breasts of the naked women—in an earlier draft (box 30, folder 447, VC) they are said not to horrify her but rather to fill her with awe— "Elizabeth" explains that she continued reading because she was "too shy to stop."[3] This shyness surely corresponds to the fearful embarrassment that expresses desire in the very act of trying to veil it. Too shy, then—which is to say, too inhibited or constrained—to stop or to linger over these pictures, "Elizabeth" reads the magazine "straight through" because doing so, in a sense, marks her reading as "straight." It prevents the embarrassing discovery of her emotional investment in the "naked women" and of her unsettling response to their breasts—a response that shifts between horror and awe.[4]

But by silencing the voice of her own sexuality, by succumbing to the constraint of shyness and framing the text in order to distance herself from the desire that it unleashes, she locates herself, paradoxically, inside the text once more. For her constraining shyness merely reenacts the cultural inscriptions of female sexuality that the magazine has presented to her in terms of silencing and constraint. Because her reading has alerted her to the patriarchal and heterosexual foundation on which the ideology of binary oppositions rests and because it has suggested to her the inevitability of her reduction to the status of a figure in that cultural system or text, "Elizabeth" directs her attention to the magazine's cover in an obvious effort to cover up, to deny or suppress the insights that her reading has uncovered. In the act of foregrounding the cover she undertakes to frame the text as a literary object, to reduce its provenance by underscoring the literary status of its discourse. Such a framing has the same effect as the framing achieved by the bracketing of a word or phrase by quotation marks: it produces the detachment of irony. But the irony of "Elizabeth's" attempt here to position herself ironically with relation to the text is that irony introduces once more the elements of subversion and indeterminacy that are precisely the elements of the text that she fears and from which she seeks to detach herself.

This, then, is "Elizabeth's" situation after her exercise in reading: sitting in a dentist's office while her aunt receives treatment inside, she looks at the cover of the *National Geographic* and tries to hold on to the solid ground of literality outside the abyss of textuality she has discovered within it. In doing so, she silences the voice of her own internal desire and conforms to the socially determined role that her shyness forces her to play. At the same time, however, she recognizes, as a result of her reading, the inadequacy of the inside/outside polarity that underlies each of her tensions—tensions that mount until they no longer admit of repression or constraint: "Suddenly, from inside, / came an *oh!* of pain."

With this we come back to where we began—back to the question of the voice and the question of the place from which the voice originates. But we return with a difference to the extent that the critical desire to locate or to define or to frame any literal inside for that voice to emerge from has been discredited as an ideological blindness, a hierarchical gesture. There is no inside in this poem that can be distinguished from its outside: the cry emanates from inside the dentist's office, and from inside the waiting room, and from inside the *National Geographic,* and from inside "In the Waiting Room." It is a cry that cries out against any attempt to clarify its confusions because it is a female cry—a cry of the female—that recognizes the attempts to clarify it as attempts to put it in its place. It is an "*oh!*" that refuses to be readily deciphered because it knows that if it is read it must always be read as a cipher—as a zero, a void, or a figure in some predetermined social text. Those critics, then, who read the poem by trying to place the cry, effect, instead, a denial of that cry, which is a cry of displacement—a cry of the female refusal of position in favor of dis-position. As a figural subversion, it wages war against the reduction of woman to the status of a literal figure, an oxymoronic entity constrained to be interpreted within the patriarchal text. It is against that text that the cry wages war, becomes a war cry to unleash the textuality that rips the fabric of the cultural text. To conclude, then, is only to urge a beginning, to urge that we attend to this cry as a cry of female textuality, a cry that links "Elizabeth" to her "foolish" aunt and to the tormented mother in Bishop's story, "In the Village." In this way we can approach the poem's cry, in Stevens's words, as the "cry of its occasion" (1954, p. 473) and begin to engage the issues of gender and constraint that are so deeply involved in Bishop's story of "*oh!*"

Notes

1. The name of the young girl Elizabeth will be placed within quotation marks throughout the essay so as to work against the tendency on the part of too many critics to conflate this "Elizabeth" with the author of the poem. There is, of course, an autobiographical element here. But the autobiographical element is not a simple correspondence and must not be used to reduce the complexities of Bishop's poetic argument by authorizing a naive translation of "Elizabeth" as Elizabeth Bishop herself.

2. The *National Geographic* of October 1919 includes an article by John Church entitled "A Vanishing People of the South Seas" that discusses "long pig" as "the Marquesan's somewhat startling description of the human victim intended to grace his feast" (p. 277). Although there is no photograph of a dead man slung on a pole, there is a picture captioned "A Scene Posed by Marquesan Natives Showing the Killing of a Victim to be Used for Sacrifice and 'Long Pig.'"

3. For a more detailed reading of the inscriptions of lesbianism in Bishop's work, see Procopiow 1981.

4. In the context of repressed sexuality it is appropriate to point out that the perusal of the *National Geographic* constitutes, particularly in literature of the period between the second decade of the century and the nineteen sixties, a topos of sexual curiosity. As one of the few socially sanctioned periodicals that included pictures of naked people, it played a significant role in the satisfaction of voyeuristic desires (primarily of men). An important instance of this topos occurs in William Carlos Williams's *Paterson I*. Bishop's poem responds to Williams's very different reading of the *National Geographic*—and of woman—in his work.

PART II

Poetry, Perversity, and Pleasure

THOMAS TRAVISANO

"The Flicker of Impudence": Delicacy and Indelicacy in the Art of Elizabeth Bishop

bright green leaves edged neatly with bird-droppings
like illumination in silver
—from "Seascape"

M Y EPIGRAPH, taken from one of Elizabeth Bishop's dazzling Florida poems, illustrates one of her most important and least recognized artistic strategies. Bishop proffers a delicate image ("bright green leaves edged neatly . . . / like illumination in silver") while dropping in a factually precise—but incongruously indelicate—detail ("green leaves *edged neatly with bird droppings*") (CP, p. 40). It is this detail that brings the picture alive, achieving a witty and almost surreal disjunction and surprise. A similar effect was termed "the flicker of impudence" in Marianne Moore's prescient introduction to five early poems by her young protégée in the anthology *Trial Balances* (1935), the first critical piece ever written about Bishop. Moore's whole observation is worth recalling: "The rational considering quality in her work is its strength—assisted by unwordiness, uncontorted intentionalness, the flicker of impudence, the natural unforced ending" (Moore 1983a, p. 82). Moore had only a handful of early poems to go on, but she put her finger on more than one signature characteristic of Bishop's style. The others have by now received appropriate recognition, but the quality I am attempting to isolate has not fared so well. Bishop's reputation for modesty and delicacy goes back a long way. For example, Moore titled her second piece on Bishop "A Modest Expert" (1946). But Bishop's skillful and frequent exploitation of indelicacy, resulting for Moore in that "flicker of impudence," has never been widely appreciated. Indeed, Bishop's famous modesty is often associated with both the primary meaning of that word, humility, and with a secondary meaning, prudishness. The former association is well deserved, but the latter is not. More than one early critic felt sure that Bishop had expressed a decided preference for delicate abstraction in that oft-quoted final line from her first mature poem, "The Map" (1935): "More delicate than the historians' are the map-makers' colors" (*CP*, p. 3). This imputed preference for delicacy, voiced in a line that has always seemed to me brilliantly equivocal, was linked to the view (once widely held) that Bishop was an elegant but minor poet.

Bishop's image as all-too-ladylike abstractionist helped to defer recognition of her achievement, encouraging early literary historians to assign Bishop a liminal status as a talented outsider, plowing an obscure furrow of her own. Stephen Stepanchev (1965), alluding to "The Map," wrote in an overview of contemporary American verse that "unlike many of her Auden-influenced contemporaries, she distrusts history, with its melodramatic blacks and whites, and prefers geography, with its subtle gradations of color" (p. 69)—showing that he must have overlooked the finely graded, subtly colored reading of domestic and cultural history that forms the subtext of so many Bishop poems. Charles Elliott (1969) spoke confidently from a similar mind-set in a review of *The Complete Poems* entitled "Minor Poet with a Major Fund of Love." Elliott said of that famous final line from "The Map," "There is no doubt which colors she prefers, or about her own predilection for the map-maker's role. Her world is at once like and startlingly unlike the real world." Elliott concedes that "A historian—or a more literal-minded poet—would never grant us such perceptions," but there is no mistaking the condescension that underlines this conception of Bishop's femininity and of her approach to history. Elliott hears in Bishop's work, "the voice of a much-prized, plain-spoken, pleasantly idiosyncratic maiden aunt, one who has traveled, observed, considered and savored, for the most part alone" (Elliott 1969, p. 13). Elliott's remarks provide a remarkably clear and unvarnished statement of a view of Bishop as female writer that was widely prevalent among critics while she was working and that influenced a generation of readers. Of course, for most of her adult life Bishop was by no means alone in the personal sense, as Elliott implies—although her long-term intimate relationships were always with women. In casting Bishop in the role of pleasantly eccentric maiden aunt, Elliott either did not know or chose to ignore just how cosmopolitan, even bohemian, was Bishop's life. And this life, which left Bishop open to a variety of sometimes shocking impressions, was reflected frequently, although not always directly, in her published work.[1]

Bishop often encountered slighting references to her age and single status, even as late as 1979, the last year of her life, and she resented these not a little, as she made clear in a letter written to her friends U. T. and Joseph Summers in March of that year: "I balked a bit at being told I looked 'like anyone's grandmother' but let me tell you the latest & perhaps you'll understand my feelings. . . . My reading in New Jersey was written up in a N.J. newspaper; favorably, on the whole, but *it* said I looked 'like somebody's great-aunt.'! Apparently lady-poets are supposed to be perennially youthful, or preferably, die young. . . . Because can you imagine reporters writing that Robert Fitzgerald (older than me) looks like a grandfather (he is one) or a great-uncle? (Or the same of *T.S. Eliot?* who was even older the last time I heard him read.) It has brought my feminist facet uppermost" (1 March 1979, VC). James Merrill (1988) showed how he understood Bishop's unique public persona when he remarked in a television interview, "She gave herself no airs. If there was anything the least bit artificial about her character and her behavior it was the wonderful way in which she impersonated an ordinary woman. Underneath, of course, was this incredible fresh genius who wrote the poems." This appearance of ordinariness seems to have been an important form of protective coloration for a writer who was at once subtle, daring, and very private, but it lulled many early reviewers and readers into displaying a mistaken sense of security, even superiority, toward Bishop's feminine posture. To return once more to Elliott's review: "Plainly there are limits to what a poet with this approach is likely to achieve, or attempt. Her translation of a superb poem called *The Table* by the contemporary Brazilian writer Carlos Drummond de Andrade, a swashbuckling, wholly *involved* account of a heroic family dinner, makes Miss Bishop's *observations*, keen though they always are, look slightly bloodless by contrast" (Elliott 1969, p. 13). Bishop's poetry could never be called swashbuckling, of course, but neither was it uninvolved, bloodless, or merely delicate, as a more alert reading of the texture of her published verse might have shown Elliott.

Though few would now espouse a view like Elliott's so openly, some recent critics may perpetuate the image of Bishop as an exceedingly "modest" poet in the very process of defending her right to be different. For example, in an otherwise excellent recent article entitled "Modesty and Morality: George Herbert, Gerard Manley Hopkins, and Elizabeth Bishop," Brett Candlish Millier (1989) wrote that, "As one might suspect, Bishop . . . felt alienated by the easy vulgarity of some writers of the 1960s, which she saw as at best 'a defence against the great American sickness.'" Millier concludes: "Perhaps, for Bishop, the sexual frankness, moral laxity, and unrefined confessions of her sixties contemporaries were just too easy" (p. 48). True as far as it goes, Millier's assessment makes no mention of Bishop's distinctive, pervasive, and by no means easy way of working vulgarity into the fabric of her verse. Millier thus implies, perhaps unintentionally, that Bishop's work was more precious and more removed from the gritty materials that absorbed her contemporaries than it actually was. Vulgar detail abounds in Bishop's work, reflecting both her natural instincts as an observer and a conscious method of achieving depth and complexity of tone. But these details are harder to observe than in the verse of her contemporaries because Bishop refused to grant them featured status or to cry "Woe!" over them. Instead, she wove vulgar detailing so skillfully into the fabric of her verse that most casual readers and many not-so-casual ones have failed to notice them, although they will not have failed to feel their effects. That fabric metaphor comes alive in a poem like "Brazil, January 1, 1502," in which landscape is tapestry and in which the European dream of conquering and enclosing nature comes face to face with the vulgar fecundity of the tropics. And this points to another feature of Bishop's approach: in her work, indelicacy only sometimes emblematizes sickness; just as often it emblematizes health, vitality, or humor, that force within nature or people that refuses enclosure or constraint. Indelicate details frequently contribute, in her work, to the liberating quality of surprise that Bishop felt was the most vital attribute of a good poem.

Once one starts noticing indelicate details in Bishop, they emerge vividly from poem after poem. I'm thinking of the "open, bloody eyes" of the dead fighting cock spread-eagled on a dung heap in "Roosters" (*CP*, p. 37); of the barnacles growing on her great catch in "The Fish": "fine rosettes of lime, / . . . infested with tiny white sea lice" (*CP*, p. 42); of the "big fish tubs" in "At the Fishhouses" with their "layers of beautiful herring scales / and the wheelbarrows similarly plastered / with creamy iridescent coats of mail, / with small iridescent flies crawling on them" (*CP*, p. 64); of the white hen, found "run over / on West 4th Street" in "Trouvée," which is "red-and-white now, of course" (*CP*, p. 150); of the "little pockmarked prostitutes" from "the brothels of Marrakesh" and the Muslim inscriptions "yellow / as scattered cattle-teeth" in "Over 2,000 Illustrations" (*CP*, p. 57); of the "naked" dog suffering from "scabies" in "Pink Dog" (*CP*, p. 190); and of "all the untidy activity" in "The Bight" that "continues / awful but cheerful" (*CP*, p. 60). Once clued to Bishop's method of embedding indelicate details inside a delicate frame, any reader can find similar examples in dozens of other poems. These subtle but altogether pervasive indelicacies emerging, as they do, from a prevailingly delicate context bring realism, comedy, bawdiness, local color, and (to use Bishop's own phrase) "violence of tone" into a verbal field that might otherwise seem just pretty. In poems like "Over 2,000 Illustrations" or "The Prodigal," indelicacy works on a deeper level, suggesting psychological disturbance while underlining the disjunction between a desired decorum and an actuality that may be sordid, disorderly, even brutal.

Her poems often suggest how the "awful" can make life "cheerful," but Bishop did prize delicacy as well. Her delicate aspect seems at times to insist on traditionally feminine values—decorum, beauty, order, elegance—but the vulgar aspect challenges these values, suggesting how difficult decorum can be to establish and maintain and even how dull existence might be if it always prevailed. Bishop called the Aunt Consuelo of "In the Waiting Room," who is modeled on her Aunt Florence, "a foolish, timid woman" (*CP*, p. 160). As a young adult Bishop struck out on her own to live a life more physically adventurous and more diverse in what it offered to the eye than the lives of her mostly professorial (and male) poetic colleagues. Displaced from the power centers of contemporary poetry by her sex, avocations, and geographical location, she was positioned by this displacement to see things outside the range of her contemporaries. Bishop rarely claimed anything for these adventures, but they inform her visual field in extraordinary ways. Displaced as she was, John Ashbery (1983) could describe Bishop with ironic accuracy as "somehow an establishment poet herself, and the establishment ought to give thanks; she is proof it can't be all bad" (p. 201). Her vivid, tonally complex treatment of geographical, cultural, and sexual diversity from a perspective that never surrenders to easy point-making accounts in part for her ever-mounting posthumous reputation.

Another major contemporary, Robert Lowell (1983), called Bishop an "unerring Muse who makes the casual perfect" (p. 207). One way to read Bishop's work is as a contest between the "perfect" domestic values absorbed from a "delicate" establishment upbringing—one thinks of the subtly ironic "Manners," with its all-important subtitle, "For a Child of 1918"—and the values she derived from the risky and quietly bohemian life she actually chose to lead. Bishop's casual or vulgar details often draw attention to creatures or objects that are unpretty, indelicate, somehow "minor," or otherwise marginalized but that make subtle but insistent claims on a viewer's attention and empathy. These figures speak of displacement within a cosmos whose order is more wished for than achieved, and through them Bishop questions a smugly "establishment" worldview while refusing necessarily to decry all established cultural norms.

From the very start, Bishop's writing dramatized the contesting claims of the delicate and the indelicate. The revealing juvenile story "The Thumb" (1930), published in Bishop's school literary magazine when she was a nineteen-year-old high school senior boarding at Walnut Hill School in Natick, Massachusetts, portrays a beautiful, charming, and intelligent young woman, Sabrina, who lives in "one of those silk-hung apartments, with sunlight coming in at the windows through pale lime-colored curtains." Sabrina's domicile is delicate, and her physical delicacy is also stressed: "She was quite a small woman, very little and light. 'Small bones', you would say; or 'Light as a feather.' In the first moment I realized vaguely that her face was extraordinarily beautiful, and that she wore a dress colored like dim gold—gold under water, maybe" (Bishop 1930, p. 6). But Sabrina has on her left hand "a man's thumb! No, not a man's,—a brute's,—a heavy coarse thumb with a rough nail, square at the end, crooked and broken." Here, long before Bishop had begun reading Marianne Moore, is a juxtaposition of indelicacy against a background of delicacy that would arrest any reader. As the story unfolds, the psychological disturbance of the first-person narrator becomes clear; he continues to fall in love with Sabrina even as his revolted fascination with the grotesque thumb increases. I have elsewhere explored the psychosexual implications of this story, particularly the mingled attraction and repulsion expressed by the narrator for a beautiful woman. Here I want only to stress how close to Bishop's mature working method the story comes: a vulgar detail stands at its center and gains force and mystery from the delicate setting. Bishop explores a conflict between traditionally feminine values and impulses that are darker, more vital, more disorderly, and harder to understand. In her later work, however, Bishop would handle such indelicacies with less melodrama.

With the exception of two newly discovered juvenile poems, "The Ballad of the Subway Train" (1927) and "Dead" (1928), most of Bishop's boarding school verse may really be too delicate. It is certainly less fresh and less surprising than her juvenile prose. But a different image of Bishop's early imagination emerges from these recent discoveries. "The Ballad" evokes a world far from the melancholy, late-Victorian loveliness of poems like "Behind Stowe," or "Sonnet," or "Imber Nocturnus," conjuring up a surreal light-and-shadow world that is at once funny and psychologically ambiguous. "Dead," on the other hand, is perhaps the single early poem that offers a clear suggestion of the tentative and troubled nature of her emerging sexuality.[2] Later, in her Vassar College poems of the early 1930s, Bishop experimented with a violence of tone that is often quite out of proportion to its apparent cause. The most flagrant yet touching example of this is her Hopkins-influenced "Hymn to the Virgin" (1933). The poem, "awful" in a way possible only to a talented writer who has not quite found her voice, is addressed to a figure of the Virgin Mother discovered in a dusty attic: an emblem, apparently, for the sacred object in the modern world. But here the Virgin is spoken to with an angry comedy, a worshipful belligerence, that seems curiously at odds with the Hopkins-derived style.

> Ah! wouldst not, wax-faced, wooden-bodied one, have us to
>   worship us-wise?
> Turn not aside Thy pretty-painted face, parade and meet our
>   audience-eyes you must.
> Long-hardened candle-grease about Thy feet, and tarnished
>   dimes and nickles, thus-wise
> Did previous paltry penny-clinkers come, but we bear ark-like
>   our great trust.
> What, take it not? Oh petulant and cranky princess, shall we
>   force it on Thee lust-wise?
> We cannot bear to draw the curtains back, leave Thee to
>   barrenness and rouging rust.

(*CP*, p. 222)

Until I began to notice the pervasiveness of indelicacy in Bishop's work, I had great difficulty reconciling this poem with my image of the master. I had to write it off as a curious anomaly. But now its significance seems clear enough—it is an important experiment on the path to a more mature deployment of indelicacy, one that could balance the indelicate against humor or seriousness while placing it in a setting of elegance and grace. One can similarly understand Bishop's impulse, at this time, to translate Aristophanes's *The Birds,* a classical play in whose frequent scatological indecencies she found a good deal to relish, judging by the draft translation in the collection of the Vassar College Library. One can hardly imagine Marianne Moore choosing a similar translation project. For Moore the shrewd neoclassical ironies of La Fontaine went just far enough.

Indeed, while Bishop was working on her version of Aristophanes, Moore was expressing concern in her introduction to Bishop in *Trial Balances* about the (mild) indelicacy of Bishop's "Three Valentines" (1934)—the last poems she wrote before she found her authentic voice. Moore worried to the point of ignoring the far better "The Map" (1935), also anthologized there, in which Bishop's authentic voice emerged for the first time. In "Valentines (I)" Bishop's quaint observations on the sexual habits of English sparrows "who languish for each other in the dust / While from their bosoms, puffed with hopeless lust, / the red drops fall" (*CP,* p. 225), Moore found "not revolting, merely disaffecting." It was here, too, of course, that Moore discovered words for that quality in Bishop's work that I have been trying to articulate: "the flicker of impudence." I have drawn attention to Bishop's use of indelicacy in her juvenilia to suggest how deeply ingrained this trait was in her style and to trace to its beginnings the process by which she learned to control indelicate detail by placing it within a prevailing delicate texture.

During Bishop's earliest mature period (1935–39), the years after Vassar when she centered in New York City (and for two longish periods, Paris) Bishop was preoccupied with what I have called "fables of enclosure" (1988). In her poems and stories of this period, Bishop explored allegorically her deep-seated uncertainties about the limits and powers of the imagination. She tended not to include details of the kind of that I have termed indelicate—in the sense of being tinged by the vulgar. This was not, I think, because she feared Moore's censorship but because she was concerned with describing inner terrain rather than the sometimes crude realities she witnessed with her eye. The prevailing tone is dark, but, if I may make the distinction, these pieces are more often grotesque than vulgar. There is nothing sordid, for example, about her Man-Moth's strange plight or the equally peculiar situations of her Gentleman of Shallot or her Unbeliever, although there is much that is odd, displaced, or pathetic. A fine poem like "Love Lies Sleeping" often borders upon the indelicate and the object described in "The Monument" is quaint and homely, but when Bishop turned her eyes to the subtropical fecundity of Florida, as she did decisively starting in 1940, unambiguously indelicate details returned to the texture of her verse with frequency and telling effect.

If Bishop's aura as a merely delicate master still lingers, it is in part because she remains closely identified for many readers with her mentor, that genius of delicacy, Marianne Moore. Moore initiated their now-famous (and oh-so-courteously conducted) dispute in 1940 by largely rewriting "Roosters," a poem, submitted to Moore for her customary critique, that Bishop rightly called "the most ambitious I had up to then attempted" (*CProse*, p. 145). In it, Bishop allegorizes roosters, who brutally awaken one and who fight each other still more brutally, in terms of two related phenomena: facistic militarism and what would now be called male chauvinism. Moore completely rewrote Bishop's poem, dispensing with numerous indelicate details and with the poem's scheme of triple-rhymed stanzas; this rhyme-scheme is technically challenging and the results are at times cheerfully (even impudently) "awful," as in the deliberately grating triplet "making sallies / muddy alleys / Rand McNally's," though at other moments Bishop achieves effects of uncanny delicacy. Moore's letter makes the case for her proposed changes through a long discourse on the word "water closet"—really the least of Bishop's vulgarisms. Moore apparently could not bear even to speak of, say, the poem's decomposing roosters lying face up on dung heaps with "open, bloody eyes / while those metallic feathers oxidize." Bishop's response to Moore highlights her awareness of crucial differences, not just with Moore's temperament but with Moore's more abstract aesthetic. "I cherish my 'water closet' and the other sordidities because I want to emphasize the essential baseness of militarism. . . . I can't bring myself to sacrifice what (I think) is a very important violence of tone—which I feel to be helped by what *you* must feel like just a bad case of the *threes*" (17 October 1940, quoted in Kalstone 1989, p. 81).

Bishop's "cherish," a delicate word, sets off not just the allegedly indelicate "water closet" but the shrewdly uncomfortable coinage "sordidities." David Kalstone (1989) asserts: "The rewriting insistently purges the poem of a Bishop that Moore clearly doesn't recognize" (p. 81). But, judging by Moore's shrewd early remarks in *Trial Balances* (Kalstone 1983b), it might be more accurate to say that Moore was wishing away a Bishop she recognized much better than most but who made her distinctly uncomfortable. Moore continued to reflect this recognition in her review of *North & South* when she observed, "Miss Bishop does not avoid 'fearful pleasantries,' and in 'The Fish' . . . one is not glad of the creature's every perquisite; but the poem dominates recollection" (see Moore 1983b, p. 178). To crudely paraphrase, Moore is confessing that despite its indelicate details, a poem like "The Fish" is unforgettable.

Perhaps the dispute over "Roosters" was less of a watershed in Bishop's development than has been suggested. The differences between Bishop and Moore were already obvious to both before the encounter took place, and although Bishop respected Moore's artistic judgment and shared many interests with the elder poet, she never shared Moore's distaste for the indelicate, as a reading of Bishop's amusing and penetrating memoir of Moore, "Efforts of Affection," will make clear. The dispute over "Roosters" merely made these differences explicit. At any rate, although Moore once dropped the acquaintance of a well-known and admiring writer because "He *contradicted* Mother," she was unwilling to forfeit Bishop's friendship, and she never tried to censor Bishop again (see *CProse*, p. 137).

In 1963 Bishop wrote to her first biographer, Anne Stevenson, "I am rather weary of always being compared to, or coupled with, Marianne—and I think she is utterly weary of it, too! We have been very good friends for thirty years now—but except for 1 or 2 early poems of mine and perhaps some early preferences in subject matter, neither she nor I can see why reviewers always drag her in with me! For one thing—I've always been an umpty-umpty poet with a traditional 'ear.' Perhaps it is just another proof that reviewers really very rarely pay much attention to what they're reading & just repeat each other" (18 March 1963, WU). Of course, despite their differences, Moore and Bishop did share the determination to achieve directness, immediacy, and surprise. Moore, though decorous in matters sexual and scatological, consistently achieved something like a "flicker of impudence" in her own work through daring exploitation of form, deploying unsettling juxtapositions, unconventional prosody, and startling syntax—the techniques of modernism—to startle and alert her readers. Bishop's "sordidities" were part of her own individual method, a technique influenced by modernism—although on the surface more conventional—that works surprising juxtapositions into an apparently straightforward narrative or descriptive surface. Such sordidities pervade the work of her middle period. In "Jerónimo's House," for example, a poem contemporaneous with "Roosters," the impoverished speaker describes his home as "my gray wasps' nest / of chewed-up paper / glued with spit," but only after setting it in a delicate context: "my house, my fairy / palace, is / of perishable clapboards" (CP, p. 34). A similar pattern is evident in this passage from "Florida":

> Enormous turtles, helpless and mild,
> die and leave their barnacled shells on the beaches,
> and their large white skulls with round eye-sockets
> twice the size of a man's.
>
> (CP, p. 32)

Such tropically indelicate details are laid on with vivid strokes against a background of empathetic appreciation. Similarly, her mildly indelicate but wholly inimitable description from "A Cold Spring" of "Greenish-white dog-wood" that "infiltrated the wood, / each petal burned, apparently, by a cigarette-butt" (CP, p. 55) brings together two unlikely frames of reference in a startling way and undercuts any impression that this is a conventional nature poem. Moore (1983b) said of "The Weed" that "it has so somber an authority, surrealism should take a course in it" (p. 177). The authority of "A Cold Spring" is far from somber, of course, but it offers surrealism a postgraduate course in the art of achieving dreamlike surprise while describing everyday things.

In "Over 2,000 Illustrations and a Complete Concordance" and "The Prodigal," poems central to Bishop's achievement, sordid details are indispensable and point toward profound psychological and teleological disturbance. For example, the prodigal's attempt to elude the claims and risks of love is set in a physically repellant barn whose sordid details are rendered with curious delicacy: "The floor was rotten; the sty / was plastered halfway up with glass-smooth dung" (CP, p. 71). The prodigal apparently wants to believe his world more proper and domesticated and less appalling than it can ever really be. If Bishop did, in Millier's words, feel "alienated by the easy vulgarity of some writers of the 1960s" (1989, p. 48), it was not because they employed vulgarity as such, but because that vulgarity was often handled with less art, and less psychological subtlety, than Bishop demanded of herself.

Bishop's Brazilian poems from *Questions of Travel* continued to exploit vulgar detail. One instance may stand for many. "Squatter's Children" concludes of a brother and sister playing near their home, a shack perched on a mountain just above the rising storm clouds:

> Children, the threshold of the storm
> has slid beneath your muddy shoes;
> wet and beguiled, you stand among
> the mansions you may choose
> out of a bigger house than yours,
> whose lawfulness endures.
> Its soggy documents retain
> your rights in rooms of falling rain.
>
> (*CP*, p. 95)

Here delicacy and indelicacy are hard to separate in lines that fuse legalism and whimsy, hope and despair, Christian charity and a shrug of the shoulders. In a scene in which a more conventional poet could have found plenty of easy vulgarity, Bishop's indelicate figures blossom on the canvas against a ground of suggestive syntactic ambiguity.

In her later work, indelicacy continued to play a vital role. "Crusoe in England," for example, one of the finest poems from Bishop's masterful last book, *Geography III* (1976), evokes a world saturated by sordidities yet rendered with an extraordinary blend of affection and desperation. Even after Crusoe's island is left behind, he brings with him—he doesn't quite know why—vulgar-looking souvenirs of his past struggle to survive his isolation and domesticate his island:

> the flute, the knife, the shrivelled shoes,
> my shedding goatskin trousers
> (moths have got in the fur),
> the parasol that took me such a time
> remembering the way the ribs should go.
> It still will work but, folded up,
> looks like a plucked and skinny fowl.
> How can anyone want such things?
>
> (*CP*, p. 166)

Bishop titled her memoir of Moore "Efforts of Affection." Affection born of effort is ingrained in Crusoe's feeling for these tattered objects, however much he might try to deny it.

In "Crusoe," sordid details point inward, toward the emotional disturbance, the sense of isolation, and the yearning for connectedness of the isolated speaker. In perhaps Bishop's most disquietingly indelicate poem, "Pink Dog" (1979), written in her last year, the focus is external, but here too she suggests a yearning for connectedness, in this case underlined by one's responsibility to others. To reflect the appalling urban poverty of Rio, Bishop shrewdly exploits the "awful." She remained a master of the expressive stanza: the poem's triple rhymes—quite exact through the poem's first three stanzas—create a discomfort reminiscent of "Roosters." The perfectly rhymed "rabies / scabies / babies" is surely one triplet that has never before appeared in the history of the language; the discomfort it causes is essential to its effect. Bishop plays with both one's sympathies and one's instinctive abhorrence. She knows that she can get a reader to accept a poem in which she speaks directly to a suffering and homeless dog more easily than one addressed to a similarly bereft human. But she also knows that a dog denuded by a skin disease is less likely to evoke a sympathetic response than an impoverished man or woman who is somehow picturesque and hopeful—say, Wordsworth's Old Leach Gatherer. Bishop is, of course, suggesting that the sick and homeless cannot help looking indelicate, and she gradually leads us through the initial shock toward something like empathy. This is a female dog, "a nursing mother by those hanging teats" and many phrases hint at a human subtext, in which a violated domesticity is examined with grisly humor. As the poem brings this human subtext to the surface, the rhymes relax at times into the inexact; paradoxically, this makes the poem more comfortable on the ear just as the human dimension becomes most unsettling.

> Didn't you know? It's been in all the papers,
> to solve this problem, how they deal with beggars?
> They take and throw them in the tidal rivers.
>
> Yes, idiots, paralytics, parasites
> go bobbing in the ebbing sewage, nights
> out in the suburbs, where there are no lights.
>
> If they do this to anyone who begs,
> drugged, drunk, or sober, with or without legs,
> what would they do to sick, four-leggèd dogs?
>
> (CP, p. 190)

Bishop hardly comes across as someone's "pleasantly idiosyncratic maiden aunt" as she sets slashing ironies against a light-verse rhythm that is, in context, curiously unnerving. The poem's tough satiric edge, its clear-eyed, anguished comedy, recalls the Aristophanes of *Lysistrata:* "In the cafés and on the sidewalk corners / the joke is going round that all the beggars / who can afford them now wear life preservers." This is a bleak joke indeed; the poem directs irony at a culture that could make— let alone circulate—such a piece of waggery and still more irony at what Mark Twain called "the damned human race" (1935, p. 346) for allowing such conditions to exist and persist. More painful irony emerges in the speaker's concluding advice that the dog hide its nakedness in a *fantasía,* a Carnival costume: "A depilated dog would not look well. / Dress up! Dress up and dance at Carnival!" (*CP*, p. 191). Carnival's gaiety emerges here as a desperate deferral strategy, an attempt to deny, postpone, or dance away life's most unsettling problems. Yet one feels that Bishop really means it when she says in the previous line "Carnival is always wonderful!" The simultaneous and parallel existence of loveliness and squalor, of gaiety and tragedy, of acceptance and irony was something Bishop attempted neither to justify nor to deny.

Bishop delicately proffered the indelicate, the sordid, the pathetic, and even the tragic to a reader's attention. Widely recognized at last for her championing of the small and overlooked, she also championed the vitality of the indelicate—that pink dog still persists, for example, in spite of her disadvantages. Bishop found fresh ways of seeing and of making her readers see creatures and objects that many would consider beneath civilized attention. Helen Vendler (1983) initiated one field of inquiry with her splendid essay "Domestication, Domesticity, and the Otherworldly." Vendler rightly stressed the domestic in Bishop's work and argued that for Bishop the otherworldly stands just to one side of the homely and homey. But the vulgar and the grotesque stand just to the other side. Bishop is the major American woman poet whose work is most closely in touch with values traditionally thought of as feminine— that is, with delicacy, with domesticity, with an accepting warmth. But there is another wilder side to her poetry that explores aspects of life that are cruder, more visceral, and, frequently, more disturbing. She was in all things a dualist, and, although it remains important to recognize Bishop's delicate and domestic side, her affinity for the indelicate must also be recognized if we are to appreciate her work's full vitality and complexity. Frank Bidart (1983) makes a related point when he says, "I want to emphasize the pain and tremendous struggle beneath this 'perfection.' For I'm scared to imagine *observing* as much as Miss Bishop does" (p. 214). Bishop responded to the life inherent in the things she saw—their energy, their surprising movement, their diversity, and, ultimately, their freedom. The word "free" appears over and over at crucial moments in her verse. Her work explores the right of creatures and things to exist, whether crudely or delicately, outside the observing self and the cultural norms that self might wish to impose. The flicker of impudence in her verse registers not just a personal relish for the indelicate; it also celebrates the impudent and individual life of each created object and each living thing.

Notes

1. Delicately erotic poems, unpublished in Bishop's lifetime and brought to our attention by Lorrie Goldensohn (1991) and Lloyd Schwartz (1991), have enriched and complicated the picture of Bishop's literary response to her sexuality, an aspect of her work that Bishop had no wish to make public while she lived. A forthcoming biography by Gary Fountain is likely to add considerably to our understanding of many aspects of the life and work of this discreetly daring writer. Brett Candlish Millier's biography of the poet, *Elizabeth Bishop: Life and the Memory of It* (1993), appeared just as this book went to press. My present concern, however, is neither with Bishop's eroticism as such nor with the rich trove of unpublished Bishop material currently being investigated by scholars but with the pervasive use of carefully encoded vulgar detail in the work Bishop chose to publish.

2. "The Ballad of the Subway Train" was discovered by Gary Fountain in the 1927 issue of the student magazine, *The Owl* (North Shore Country Day School). It was reprinted in the winter 1991 issue of the *Western Humanities Review* (p. 25) with my essay "Heavenly Dragons: A Newly Discovered Poem by Elizabeth Bishop." "Dead," which is not included in *CP*, appeared in the winter 1992 *Gettysburg Review* (p. 15) for the first time since its publication in the December 1928 issue of *The Blue Pencil.*

BONNIE COSTELLO

Attractive Mortality

NOTHING DISARMS US like the violation of categories we assume are secure ("life/death, right/wrong, male/female"—CP, 185). Bishop's poems are full of little revolts against decorum, images and associations that cross conventional boundaries to challenge complacent or repressive thought. These reveal her thoughts about organic process, about the body, and about our ambivalence toward it. Bishop presents objects undergoing convergence and mutation in a way that is disturbing, even frightening, but that can also be exhilarating. She further presents the forces—psychological, social, political—that work to suppress such a process. Throughout she reveals an effort to connect her resistance to gender conventions with a larger sense of nature's fluidity and mutability.

Bishop objected, in a letter to Robert Lowell, to the overemphasis of her contemporaries (Lowell in particular) on "this suffering business."[1] Her own way is not to deny suffering or one's distaste for a brutal world but to locate it in terms of the larger world of change. In a letter to Anne Stevenson Bishop wrote, alluding to George Herbert: "My outlook is pessimistic. I think we are still barbarians. . . . But I think we should be gay in spite of it, sometimes even giddy,—to make life endurable and to keep ourselves 'new, tender, quick'" (8 January 1964, WU). It is this effort to remain "new, tender, quick" (and perhaps, as a consequence, to relinquish mastery) that accounts for much of Bishop's use of the grotesque. We tend to associate this style with Edgar Allen Poe or Mary Shelley, with nightmares of uncontrollable, unnatural, demonic power, whether from inside or outside the human soul. Bishop's style is more deeply ambivalent and undecidable than this tradition of morbidity and horror.[2] There is certainly a subversive element in her violations of decorum, an effort to undermine social and conceptual norms, but most often it is tied to a representational aim, an effort to find aesthetic equivalents to a fluent reality. She emphasizes the betweenness of seeing form against conflicting form, the perceptual challenge of the world as process. The grotesque style brings together (without resolution) the categories that our minds and our culture like to keep apart but that constantly converge in nature and experience. Gender is by no means the only example in which Bishop finds experience and nature resisting convention, but it becomes, in many poems, the angle of vision by which she reveals our ambivalence about the body. Her effort is to connect deviance and organicism, hence to reimagine what is "natural." Bishop herself expresses mixed feelings of attraction and revulsion toward the organic world's resistance to icons, form, and cultural convention and to her own emotional deviance and iconoclasm. Her appeal as a poet includes this honest expression of mixed feelings, a matter both of tone and representation.

With disarming nonchalance Bishop confesses in "Memories of Uncle Neddy," "I am very fond of molds and mildews" (*CProse*, p. 228). Like anyone else she does what she can to keep them back, wiping off the portraits often to preserve them for posterity, yet she admits to a certain delight in the advance of these transmogrifying growths over the domestic protections of walls, furniture, clothing:

> I love the dry-looking, gray-green dust, like bloom on fruit, to begin with, that suddenly appears here on the soles of shoes in the closet, on the backs of all the black books, or the darkest ones, in the bookcase. And I love the black shadow, like the finest soot, that suddenly shows up, slyly, on white bread, or white walls. The molds on food go wild in just a day or two, and in a hot, wet spell like this, a tiny jungle, green, chartreuse, and magenta, may start up in a corner of the bathroom. The gray-green bloom, or that shadow of fine soot, is just enough to serve as a hint of morbidity, attractive morbidity—although perhaps mortality is a better word. The gray-green suggests life, the sooty shadow— although living, too—death and dying. (*CProse*, p. 228)

That complex hint of mortality is everywhere in Bishop's poetry, intruding with its gray-green bloom and black soot on the white world that the mind and the culture set up against it. Unruly life, which includes death and dying, asserts itself despite our efforts to contain it. Bishop's grotesque style reveals her ambivalence about opening protective forms to life's processes: repellent and attractive, awful and cheerful, frightening and beautiful at once. Pain often accompanies this openness, yet the rewards are amply displayed. If Bishop expresses the inevitable shock and resistance before that which challenges fixed perceptions, she also expresses an exuberance and freedom in that challenge. Her attention rests on the margins and thresholds that designate the limits of the known and the burgeoning of new orders from contradictory ones.

Bishop's earliest poems are not concerned with organic process as such. Instead, they tend to take natural images as symbols of the human spirit asserting itself against fixed forms and forces of mechanization. Yet issues of gender and the body remain prominent. "Cirque d'Hiver," "The Man-Moth," and "The Weed" form a sequence toward the increased identification of the human spirit with natural flux. In "The Fish" and "Roosters" Bishop confronts the patriarchal urge to master nature; together these poems contrast the consequences of relinquishing or asserting power. Bishop is better known as a descriptive poet, but her mimetic surfaces are similarly full of contradictions. Her observations—in "A Cold Spring," "Faustina, or Rock Roses," "The Shampoo," "The Armadillo," and others—represent a variety of responses to the mutable body, particularly the female body. In each poem Bishop juxtaposes the beautiful with the awful, the morbid with the vital, aesthetic pleasure with moral indignation, in ways that challenge our conventional responses to life. Through Manuelzinho, the Pink Dog, and other misfits she confronts her own ambivalence about spiritual and corporeal deviance. She can write with sympathy about the desire to order or transcend the mess of life, but she writes with even more passion about the terrible, "barbaric" implications of our efforts to deny life or suppress it. In contrasting an ideal, autonomous, timeless, and totalizing mode of thought to a temporal, mortal, pluralistic existence Bishop often draws implicitly on gender distinctions. Her "fleshed, fair, erected indivisible" "imaginary icebergs" and "stiff and idle" "final thoughts" are clearly phallic, and in many poems plurality, metamorphosis, and decenteredness are associated with female experience. One can argue that Bishop's grotesques, open to change and contradiction, resisting dualities of mind and body, self and world, reflect female consciousness. Bishop does not idealize, abhor, or attempt to master the body; instead, she confronts the challenge our corporeal, historical being makes to all fixed and totalizing forms, all illusions of immortality. But although the poet sometimes invokes gender distinctions, she is by no means consistent in her use of them. Women as well as men in her poems express the fear of life, the longing for cultural mastery or aesthetic and conceptual transcendence. Male as well as female beholders confront an elusive, contradictory, mutable, and recalcitrant reality. Bishop's misfits are of both sexes. The will to autonomy, to transcendence, includes but is not explained by gender.

In the early poems of *North & South* the grotesque style arises, rather conventionally, to describe an inner being asserting itself against material and social limits. The mechanical toy of "Cirque d'Hiver" suggests Bishop's early sense of dichotomies in human experience that are uncomfortably joined. The toy grimly mimics a horse and dancer from the Paris Winter Circus:

> Across the floor flits the mechanical toy,
> fit for a king of several centuries back.
> A little circus horse with real white hair.
> His eyes are glossy black.
> He bears a little dancer on his back.
>
> She stands upon her toes and turns and turns.
> A slanting spray of artificial roses
> is stitched across her skirt and tinsel bodice.
> Above her head she poses
> another spray of artificial roses.
>
> His mane and tail are straight from Chirico.
> He has a formal, melancholy soul.
> He feels her pink toes dangle toward his back
> along the little pole
> that pierces both her body and her soul
>
> and goes through his, and reappears below,
> under his belly, as a big tin key.
> He canters three steps, then he makes a bow,
> canters again, bows on one knee,
> canters, then clicks and stops, and looks at me.
>
> The dancer, by this time, has turned her back.
> He is the more intelligent by far.
> Facing each other rather desperately—
> his eye is like a star—
> we stare and say, "Well, we have come this far."

(*CP*, p. 31)

The yearning marionette and the mechanical dancer are stock figures of Romantic and symbolist imagination, suggesting the captivity of an infinite human spirit in deterministic being. Hoffman and Kleist come to mind as well as De Chirico. Here, more specifically, Bishop depicts the problem of the artist, who can perhaps achieve a gleam of the genuine but whose aspirations exceed his formal means. She hobbles her form with monosyllables and identical rhymes as if to turn the poem itself into a clumsy machine that winds down at the end. "I think the title referred more to the mood than anything else," Bishop wrote to Anne Stevenson (20 March 1963, WU). This is indeed a wintry poem. The little horse seems doomed, even if he is more comic than tragic.

The poem turns to include the speaker at the end and to suggest a mutuality between herself and the horse, whose "glossy black" eye is now "like a star," a symbol, perhaps, of the speaker's aspirations.[3] "We have come this far," remarks the little horse at the end of the poem. The "we" may refer to the horse and the speaker, in which case they are collaborating intelligences. Or perhaps the "we" refers to the artist and the shadow of himself and his aspirations that gleams through the artifice of the work and exceeds the performance of its formal devices, symbolized in the dancer. The little horse has "real white hair," here marking his authenticity rather than his corporeality. He is controlled by a "big tin key," perhaps symbolizing forces that also bind him to the duller and entirely artificial dancer, his burden and his pride. Thus his look is "desperate," implying that he has come this far but may go no farther in realizing his sublime ambition. The beholder shares his desperation, suggesting that the big tin key runs through the artist as well as her work. Hers is no more a position of mastery than is the horse's. This opposition, of a transcendent ambition desperately curtailed by a mechanical universe, will be considerably altered in Bishop's later work, in which natural flux is associated with freedom.

The split that Bishop imagines in "Cirque d'Hiver" between the artist's aspirations and his burden of form is also a gender dichotomy and reveals Bishop's discomfort with the gender identity available to her. Her communion is with the male consciousness against the female body. The mechanical dancer is, of course, the conventional female performative role complete with roses, an image to which Bishop often returns. The more authentic, inward part of the self she here represents as male and nonhuman yet bound to the dancer. Bishop explores this sense of self-division throughout her work, often in terms of gender, but the gender alignments of the conformative and the deviant constantly change, as if to resist a static dichotomy.

In "The Weed" the experience of being divided is the narrative focus, and although questions of gender are suppressed (the weed is an "it," the poet's gender evaded through the first-person pronoun), the symbolic site of psychic division is the body, and its evolution suggests a movement from male to female orientations. The experience of being divided effects the poem's tone and representational style. Indeed, there is almost no aspect of the poem that does not involve some form of convergence or division. Although nature still symbolizes a timeless, inner landscape, the details of the poem pressure its boundaries.

The poem describes a dream of death-like composure suddenly disrupted by inner turmoil. In the dream, a mental state of resolve and finality is represented as bodily stasis, even entombment. But the relationship between mind and body (here tenor and vehicle) is highly unstable.

> I dreamed that dead, and meditating,
> I lay upon a grave, or bed,
> (at least, some cold and close-built bower).
> In the cold heart, its final thought
> stood frozen, drawn immense and clear,
> stiff and idle as I was there;
> and we remained unchanged together
> for a year, a minute, an hour.

(CP, p. 20)

The spark of conflicting frames of meaning arises in the first two lines of the poem: "I dreamed that dead, and meditating / I lay upon a grave or bed." Such ambiguities of inner/outer, conscious/unconscious, dreaming/waking states continue throughout the poem. The tension is temporarily suspended here by the motionless self, who contemplates a "final thought" in a timeless dream. The uncertainty of "a year, a minute, an hour" seems only to emphasize the measureless quality of eternity. But the ambiguity of "grave or bed" and the contradiction in "dead and meditating" plants the seed of active division without a clear Christian context to resolve the paradox. As though to reinforce the effect of the words, Bishop introduces incidental rhymes into the much halted tetrameter lines, making readers uncertain of what they will hear next.

Bishop represents the agency of the turmoil as a weed that springs up from the dreamer's breast:

> Suddenly there was a motion,
> as startling, there, to every sense

as an explosion. Then it dropped
to insistent, cautious creeping
in the region of the heart,
prodding me from desperate sleep.
I raised my head. A slight young weed
had pushed up through the heart and its
green head was nodding on the breast.

Although remaining a symbolic, abstract space of "final thought," the scene's disruption is felt "to every sense." The weed introduces narrative sequence into this eternal space. The dead self then raises her head without reviving (the heart changes but does not beat). These insistent contradictions express the ambiguity and ambivalence of the dream life, but Bishop repeatedly breaks the dream frame that tolerates them with parenthetical remarks of the conscious, remembering subject who struggles to resolve them. The weed releases two rivers ("with my own thoughts?") and ultimately divides the dreamer's previously frozen heart. The symbolic underground spring, expressed into "one tear" in "The Man-Moth," becomes a cascading river of thoughts that washes over the dreamed body and threatens to wash away the very weed-self that released it. Bishop controls the high drama of the dream with a matter-of-fact observer's voice (the wakened speaker's), chillingly detached from her own inner turmoil. That voice also suggests another line of division in this divisive poem.

"The Weed" still posits an inner region of perspectiveless selfhood, designated by the darkness of the dream space. But that region quickly becomes subject to penetration, flux, and even illumination. Bishop vaguely suggests gender distinctions here. In "The Weed" the male space of the icon, of mental finality, of "stiff and idle" thoughts is transformed to an iconoclastic female space of "the heart," its broken membranes and cascading streams associating the heart with the womb ("it split apart / and from it broke a flood of water"—an image foreshadowing her later volcanoes). She treats the weed as a newborn baby or a poem from the heart. The very dynamic, contradictory, and open nature of that psychological space denies static oppositions, of male/female, inner/outer, feeling/thought, body/mind, pain/pleasure, any rigid alignments of its images. Although the natural imagery remains symbolic, its detail and emphasis predict the complex continuum of inner and outer geography that will characterize Bishop's mature work. At this point the natural imagery serves to emphasize the idea that inwardness is no retreat from mutability.

The most discomforting contradictions in the poem arise as Bishop details the physical features of the psychological space. Although mind and body meet on a third, metamorphic plane of geology, they converge rather than synthesize. Two arterial or amniotic rivers flow into the externalized "black grains of earth," but they also shower the weed with "thoughts." They "glance" off the sides as if they were eyes, and the drops on the dreamer's eyes empower her with sight, even in the dark. Sight cannot simply be made a trope of insight; the dream is "in the dark" yet intensely visual.

The images continue to divide, as do the emotions they evoke. These streams also provide a sudden illumination within the darkness. "Assuredly, smooth as glass" they turn out to be mirrors and are themselves racing images.

> (As if a river should carry all
> the scenes that it had once reflected
> shut in its waters, and not floating
> on momentary surfaces.)

Having adjusted from the retentive "final thought" to the cascading streams, we discover within that flux a principle of retention. The weed is an unwelcome intruder on the heart enclosed in antivital permanence, in "a close-built bower." But while the violation of this spiritual stasis is unwanted, the untidy, tormenting weed is associated with refreshment and fertility. ("A few drops fell upon my face / and in my eyes, so I could see.") The bower is a grave, and the sleep in it is desperate. A tenderness develops for the "slight young weed," with its "graceful head" "nodding on the breast," almost washed away by the powerful stream. The stream, in turn, is attractive as it makes its way toward the equally "fine black grains of earth." Yet if a certain exhilaration develops over this inward mutability, it never entirely supplants the original feeling of invasion. A shudder accompanies the thought that this process will be endlessly repeated, that the weed grows "but to divide your heart again."

"The Weed" remains ambiguous in its representation. By contrast, George Herbert's "Love Unknown," which Bishop acknowledged as the inspiration for this poem, depends on an immutable force that controls the transformations of the heart. For Herbert, bodily torments remain symbols of the soul's torments, explainable within a specific tradition of

Christian redemption. In Bishop, the inner life is defined by and inclusive of corporeal life; they are not simply parallel. No immutable force controls either. Herbert's imagery is violent (the heart is plucked from a bowl of fruit and thrown into a bloody font, then immersed in a boiling cauldron, then forced to lie on a bed of thorns). Bishop retains a landscape of flowers, streams, and cascades. Yet without the confidence in a higher authority, an ulterior system of meaning and value, this landscape is more disturbing than Herbert's. The weed moves "like a semaphore" whose meanings cannot be decoded:

> The nervous roots
> reached to each side; the graceful head
> changed its position mysteriously,
> since there was neither sun nor moon
> to catch its young attention.

The baptism does not revitalize anything, so that we cannot make the easy choice of life over death but can only witness a transition from stasis to change. Whereas Herbert's antagonistic God provides a context of righteous purpose (his apparent aggressions "all strive to mend, what you had marred"), Bishop's weed has no other motive than division. Behind that division may be Herbert's message, though, that change makes us "new, tender, quick."

Near the time Bishop wrote "The Weed" she recorded a vision in her diary that, although it pursues a different narrative from that in "The Weed," includes some of the same imagery of memory and self-reflection within the larger flux of the world: "The windows this evening were covered with hundreds of large, shining drops of rain, laid on the glass which was covered with steam on the inside. I went to look out, but could not. Instead I realized I could look into the drops, like so many crystal balls. Each bore traces of a relation or friend: several weeping faces slid away from mine, water plants and fish floated within other drops; watery jewels, leaves and insects magnified, and strangest of all, horrible enough to make me step quickly away, was one large drop containing a lonely, magnificent human eye, wrapped in its own tear." ("Recorded Observations: 1934–37," box 40, folder 624, VC)

The image of the windows from which she cannot look out parallels the dream space of "The Weed." The self is projected into the world and, conversely, the mutable world enters the domain of the self. Bishop sees at the threshold, along the pane of glass. Each drop, while it falls, retains an image of some particular lost friend or object. The "crystal ball" rain-drops reveal lost human connections, which fall along with vegetation and insect and animal life, in a general course of loss which neutralizes it. The vision returns to the human center, in the most surreal manner, at the end. The human eye metaphysically "wrapped in its own tear" causes a shudder, for that organ of perception turns back to reflect the "lonely" perceiver, suddenly conscious of the passage of her own life yet isolated by her grief from all the "watery jewels" she contemplates. Moments of self-reflection such as this send Bishop to "that self-forgetful, perfectly useless concentration" on the physical world. But just as the self, even in these early meditations, is conceived as but another space of mutability and metamorphosis, so also her most outward gaze is subjective; it bears the image of the eye as an organ of grief as well as of sight.

Bishop's early work is insistently symbolic, yet it makes a link, which will become more overt later on, between the internal resistance to fixed forms and nature's organic processes, between deviance and mutability. This gives her a grounding on which to defend her resistance to cultural norms.

"The Weed" demonstrates how even within a symbolist aesthetic Bishop binds the mental to the corporeal that it cannot master. The parallel imagery of the last poem in "Songs of a Colored Singer" (*CP*, pp. 47–51) reinforces this interpretation with a more explicit movement across the boundaries of internal and external reality. In this case the weed emerges as a consequence of "dew or tears" that have become "black seeds" and form a "conspiring root." What emerges is the "flower or fruit" of a face.

The ambiguity of equating tears and dew goes beyond a pathetic fallacy to link grief to natural metamorphosis. This association of dew and tears, of personal grief and nature's processes, persists throughout Bishop's career (in "Sestina," "Song for the Rainy Season," and several others). The analogy resists self-absorbing sorrow and suggests a more inclusive vision of loss as natural change, a *lacrimae rerum* imaged as rain. The "face" here emerges not as a source of the tears, not as some original realm of feeling, but as its fruit or flower. This face itself becomes quickly plural, "Like an army in a dream / the faces seem," connecting individual grief with the collective suffering of World War II. Thus, although the poem remains, like "The Weed," highly figurative, it insists on locating feeling and identity within the world, not within the isolate self. The consequence is a tonal tension—a delight and a terror. As dew, seed, and flower, as natural process, the vision is lovely. As tear, conspiring root and face, it is frightening. The poem insists on this balance to the end, just as it insists on moving freely between human and natural forces and insists that the vision is not securely internal but rather is (like the weed in the other poem) "too real to be a dream."

In "Roosters" Bishop abandons psychological questions and internalized vision in favor of a hard look at realities of patriarchal aggression and public acquiescence such as are hinted at in "Songs of a Colored Singer." The poem remains concerned, in this new framework, with questions of the body, mortality, and our repressive impulses toward the organic, issues that martial power brings to a focus.

Bishop employs her iconic imagination most dramatically in "Roosters" (*CP*, pp. 35–39). The roosters, traditional symbols of patriarchal power, stand, at first, for masters of war. The poem was inspired by the Nazi invasion of Norway; there can be little ambiguity in the poet's feelings toward that subject. She relishes the demise of the roosters, ironically "flung / on the gray ash-heap," where their prowess means nothing. "Those metallic feathers oxidize" along with all that is mortal, including the "courted and despised" hens. But the roosters come, in the end, to represent Christian forgiveness as well. Thus, questions of mastery apply not only to subjects within the referential world of the poem but also to poet and reader as they attempt to absorb the political and spiritual significance of that world. Through the initial image of a barnyard scene in Key West, Bishop deals not only with World War II but also with the nature of aggression and the failure to resist it. Male arrogance and female submission become a subtheme of militarism. But the greatest challenge of the poem arises as the symbolic context and the moral import of the roosters reverses, from war in modern Europe to Peter's betrayal of Christ. The result is an icon that resists idolatry to provide an open, dynamic response to the world.

The iconic nature of the image emerges indirectly, through description. Bishop directs her meanings through a controlled palette—here the "gun-metal blue dark" of four o'clock in the morning suggests the grimness of military occupation. Later the metallic glitter of the roosters' iridescent feathers suggests "green-gold medals," and "glass-headed pins, / oil-golds and copper greens, / anthracite blues, alizarins," the arrogance of military glory, "the vulgar beauty of iridescence." The tendency of roosters to perch high and their emblematization on weather vanes "over our little wooden northern houses" connects them in Bishop's mind with militarists "marking out maps." They divide up the world into domains of power, each seeing the world in terms of his own interest and authority, "each one an active / displacement in perspective" rather than a tolerance of many perspectives. The metallic glitter of the rhymed "medals" also combines with the brilliant synesthesia of the rooster's inflammatory crow, which "grates like a wet match. . . . / flares, and all over town begins to catch." A slow-burning fire of oxidation ironically destroys him later.

The roosters serve not only to parody evil, however. They remind us that a terrible evil can "wake us" from indifference and dream-indolence, "here" (in America, away from Europe) "where are / unwanted love, conceit and war." The sleepers are implicated by the incongruous sequence "love, conceit and war" in denying mortality. No one wants conceit and war (although perhaps we should be criticized for our indifference to their force in the world). But surely a place where "love" is "unwanted" must awake to human compassion. For Bishop, indifference to violence goes hand in hand with indifference to love (summing up married love for women as "hen's lives" of "being courted and despised"). The indictment not only of the combatants but of those who tolerate their violence and those who would sleep through brutality and love permits the abrupt reversal in the symbol of the roosters. Bishop recollects an "Old holy sculpture" (likely of northern derivation) that depicts St. Peter.

> St. Peter's sin
> was worse that that of Magdalen
> whose sin was of the flesh alone;
> of spirit, Peter's,
> falling, beneath the flares,
> among the "servants and officers."
>
> (CP, p. 37)

Magdalen's sin arises here to contrast with both the loveless populace and the scene of the decomposing bodies that precedes it. Her indulgence of the flesh (her acknowledgment of the weakness of the flesh) is nothing against the merciless, arrogant denials and hatred of the flesh displayed by both sleepers and patriarchal roosters. Indeed, Bishop associates spiritual sin with indifference to or denial of the body.

Bishop subtly links the two scenes of her poem and the two emblematic meanings of the roosters. The heavy, irregular trimeter triplets that suggested the grim force of militarism now take on the sacred meaning of the trinity. The flares of the "servants and officers" (in quotation marks to denote the official mask that evil wears) remind us of the flame-feathers of the barnyard roosters. But the rooster himself is now not the perpetrator of sin but a "pivot" between denial and the remorse that brings on forgiveness. Although Bishop links the two parts of her poem both imagistically and thematically, she makes this pivot deliberately shocking and never resolves the two versions of the symbol. Its contradictory force remains to pressure our understanding within aesthetic, moral, and conceptual frames. Thus, Peter, figured on the sculpture, "still cannot guess" the full meaning of "his dreadful rooster."

Bishop's reader must accommodate yet another turn in the description, back to the barnyard where the light of day is appearing. The iconic roosters are "now almost audible." The poet brings the vision down from its heraldic "pillar" to meet the iconoclastic sun, symbol of mutability. Its light is "low" and comes "from underneath / the broccoli," "gilding the tiny / floating swallow's belly." The sun is, like Peter, like the sleepers, "faithful as enemy, or friend," yet different in lying outside the moral sphere of the icon, challenging its boundaries. The Christian meaning, which supplanted the military meaning of the poem, is now in turn supplanted by the noniconic force of nature.

That predominance of nature over our symbolic and iconic defenses informs many poems after *North & South*. Bishop confronts organic processes more directly in these poems. Yet the tension of frames continues. Through various antimimetic devices Bishop expresses the force of nature against perceptual norms. Her constant conjunction of life and death within a single image disturbs our will to separate them. "Nature" is a central concern of Bishop's poetry now, not only a detached, observed environment but also the growth and degeneration of the body.

By imagining organic processes in the landscape, where they can be confronted and affirmed, Bishop reduces the fear of life, the horror of the body; this is part of her attempt to associate deviant, iconoclastic impulses with nature. The most personal anxieties are released into visual awareness. "A Cold Spring" exemplifies Bishop's grotesque realism within the pastoral mode. This is indeed pastoral poetry, not because it idealizes the landscape but because it provides, through the landscape, a way of accepting human change and loss. Bishop's later, more direct confrontations are less emotionally resolved.

It is tempting to read the epigraph from Hopkins, "Nothing is so beautiful as spring," ironically, given the title and the series of inauspicious beginnings that follow it.

A cold spring:
the violet was flawed on the lawn.
For two weeks or more the trees hesitated;
the little leaves waited,
carefully indicating their characteristics.
Finally a grave green dust
settled over your big and aimless hills.
One day, in a chill white blast of sunshine,
on the side of one a calf was born.
The mother stopped lowing
and took a long time eating the after-birth,
a wretched flag,
but the calf got up promptly
and seemed inclined to feel gay.

(CP, p. 55)

The poem—because it has no social referent other than its dedication—completely evades gender questions. Even the distinctly female imagery of birth and afterbirth is absorbed into a larger asexual organicism, and I am certain there is no double meaning in the calf's inclination to feel gay (unlike Bishop's own in "Sonnet"). But the turn toward nature (in exchange between female poet and female friend) provides a pastoral background against which the poet can go on to confront the social repression of the mutable body, especially the female body, in "Faustina, or Rock Roses."

All the images in "A Cold Spring" arise in precarious balance of life and death. The calf and mother intensify the grotesque conjunction as the birth occurs within a "chill white blast." Yet this is a blast of sunshine, not the blast of winter wind that lingers in memory. Similarly, the afterbirth signifies both the beginning and the end of a process. But this tension is already apparent in the flawed violet and the "grave green dust" of budding spring, which settles over the "big and aimless hills" like a mold over the dead. In the next stanza, which describes the next day, it is clear that nature is not dead, only sleeping, and the vague personification of the landscape becomes explicit; the sleeper awakens, "stretching miles of green limbs from the south." Yet the poem continues to resist a one-directional conception of this seasonal sequence. "In his cap the lilacs whitened, / then one day they fell like snow." The landscape continues to present the conjunction of birth and death, growth and decay, although without reversing the onward process. The lilacs do fall, but they are only "like" snow. Yet the dogwood that redemptively (as a traditional symbol of Christ's wounded body) "infiltrated the wood" has itself suffered, been "burned, apparently, by a cigarette-butt" and "the infant oak-leaves swung through the sober oak." Although in the first stanza the "little leaves" were "carefully indicating their characteristics," the beholder does not sustain this vision of definition and distinction. The "blurred redbud," though motionless, is paradoxically "almost more / like movement than any placeable color." The unframable force of change overwhelms the distinct outlines of objects. Bishop does for spring what Keats did for autumn, resisting the monolithic association with birth as he resisted the monolithic association with death. Her poem is as affirmative as Keats's; indeed, "nothing is so beautiful" to her as this metamorphic life of nature in which no object or being can remain "stiff and idle."

Against this seasonal instability and temporal advance the beholder possesses the stabilizing power of recollection and anticipation. The poem makes a successful transition from spring to summer through the shifting attention of the beholder, from the past, to the present, to the future. The present and future are imagined in the evening and the pastures are shadowy, thus countering the sense of seasonal beginnings with the brief passing of a single day. Bishop presents the dark and light negative of the passing landscape at the end, against the burgeoning color of oncoming summer. This summer evening landscape is strikingly different from that of spring. The directives are now vertical, in contrast to the shifts from foreground to background that characterize the earlier sections of description. The coloring is now luminous rather than pastel; the hesitant spring gaiety has become a wild party with sexual bullfrogs playing bass, moths as Chinese fans, and fireflies like bubbles in champagne. Yet even these "glowing tributes" are uncertain and metamorphic, so the poem reaches no stable destination.

It is easy to pass over this poem, just as Keats's "To Autumn" was once passed over, as "mere description." But it is feeling and thought perfectly realized in sensation. I have mentioned its visual complexity: its shuttle from foreground to background, its shifts to verticals, its carefully constructed coloring in which bright colors and lights set off the seasonal pastels and the nocturnal shadows to resist a static conception of the landscape. Through visual details Bishop registers a temporal awareness. Equally impressive are the aural images and effects, from the synesthetic "blast" of sunshine and whip-cracking red (or sharp call?) of the cardinal to the invisible but aurally blatant bullfrogs. Within the open form of the free verse the poem is densely alliterative, assonant, and rhythmic, allowing an undersong to persist within the casual voice.

In "A Cold Spring" Bishop achieves a vision of generation and decay that is indeed beautiful. This is not a beauty of symmetry but of convergence and mutation, the beauty that Darwin beheld and through which he developed new concepts of nature's evolution. But when our eye is turned to the processes of our own bodies it is less easy to embrace metamorphosis. Indeed, our instinct is to resist, as Bishop shows in the dying woman in "Faustina, or Rock Roses," one of several poems in which Bishop explores the cultural disgust at female aging, at the valuation of a narrow image of the female body (the rose-adorned mechanical dancer) as an expression of the culture's larger fear of mortality. Bishop shows, in contrast, the hideousness in the repression of the mutable body and the beauty to be found in its changes.

In the world of "Faustina, or Rock Roses," the rose—classic symbol of life, female beauty, and erotic love—has become calcified in the effort to stay its passing. Our culture values the female as youthful object and suppresses mutability. Bishop shows us a nameless, even faceless, old woman surrounded by pills and powders and attended by her mildly complaining black maid. As an ungendered, unidentified visitor brings roses to the dying woman, we are reminded of how futile, even grotesque, the efforts to resist the aging process can be. In this fetid, airless indoor world, nature makes a bizarre appearance. Bishop employs a reduced palette of inorganic colors: white on white, black, and metallic, offset only by "rust-perforated roses" at the end. The tacks in the wallpaper have an eerie intensity, "glistening / with mica flakes." A "dew glint on the screen" and "glow worms / burning a drowned green" ("drowned" like corpses) offset an "undazzling" white on white to create an uncanny effect of imminent death.

It is not nakedness but its opposite, disguise, that is embarrassing here: the enamel, the "towel-covered table" that

> bears a can of talcum
> and five pasteboard boxes
>   of little pills,
> most half-crystallized.

The poem barely acknowledges the humanity of the old woman, which has no outlet, focusing instead on inhuman surfaces and the coverings of flesh: white hair, undershirt, fan. The poem moves to the attending Faustina only two-thirds of the way through, making her "sinister kind face" the funnel of uncertainty into which the other details flow as the petrified becomes petrifying. Oddly, Faustina, the only named figure in the scene, presents the "coincident conundrum." Her kindness as the poet reads it includes, emblematically figured in her black face, an acknowledgment of death as an enigma. Her face generates the question at the heart of the poem, the question all the whiteness of the scene is designed to evade, a question embedded in the racial subplot of several of Bishop's poems.

> Oh, is it
>
> freedom at last, a lifelong
> dream of time and silence,
> dream of protection and rest?
> Or is it the very worst,
> the unimaginable nightmare
> that never before dared last
>   more than a second?
>
> (*CP*, pp. 73–74)

When the beholder looks at eyes for an answer to her question, she does not designate whose, as though the servant and master had become one. Faustina is at home in this scene of suffering. This is not Herman Melville's Benito Cereno. It may even be that the "sinister" face of Faustina, as it discloses the mystery of death, provides an alternative affection to that of the rose-bearing visitor, who would preserve the false hopes of the beauty myth.

The visual tensions and ambiguities of the poem return us to the gaze of the visitor, a distancing surrogate of the narrator (whose discomfort and anxiety in this scene are registered in the tense trimeter stanzas, each closing with an indrawn, shuddering dimeter). "Meanwhile the eighty-watt bulb / betrays us all." What it betrays are all the disguises and denials—talcums, gowns, and fans—leaving exposed the paralyzing enigma of death. Uneasy in this enigma (which is detached from the dying lady and floats, becoming "helplessly / proliferative" as vegetation), the visitor "proffers her bunch / of rust-perforated roses." The roses have been there from the beginning, in the "vaguely roselike / flower-formations" on the chipped enamel, in the pattern of the disordered sheets, "like wilted roses." They remind us of mutability even when they are inorganic (make them of enamel, they will chip; of metal, they will rust). They remind us, too, that life is "proliferative," not something to be hoarded or mastered. The final query of the poem—"whence come / all the petals" (a whence now rather than a what or why)—is much gentler and less demonic than the first, "snake-tongue" question. Rock roses are, after all, not roses made of rock but rather a shrub that grows in rocky soil, something vital and mutable, defying the barren whiteness of the scene.

These roses do not emerge again in Bishop's published poetry, but unpublished manuscripts reveal her preoccupation with the image and her unconventional use of it. They also make much more explicit her association of roses with the mutable female body and her challenge to the sad sentence women receive under the carpe diem tradition. These are poems of homoerotic desire in which beauty and mortality are juxtaposed. The detail and tenderness with which they describe the aging human body provide an alternative to the sinister vision of "Faustina" and suggest that Bishop was able to sustain an open, realistic vision not only of the changing landscape but also of the human body.

In the unpublished prose piece "After Bonnard," Bishop sustains a visual and aesthetic disinterestedness toward the aging body, displacing her own desire to touch onto a personified "Time": "The small shell-pink roses have opened so far, after two days in their bottle of water, that they are tired. The pink is fleeing—it is more mauve this afternoon.—The centers stick up further and are faded, too, almost brown. Still delicate, but reaching out, out, thinner vaguer, wearier—like those wide beautiful pale nipples I saw somewhere, on white, white and strong, but tired nevertheless, breasts.—Time smeared them, with a loving but heavy thumb" (box 41, folder 635, VC). Ostensibly modifying roses, the breasts become the real focus of this piece, their erotic immediacy buffered by the emphasized roses. The tired breast is attractive and time's thumb is loving, as the beholder would like to be. The image remains ambivalent—the attraction to the delicacy of flesh combines with a fascination in its decay; the gesture is both loving and wounding. But in this impressionistic world, the ambivalence is light and the desire is tranquil. In another unpublished piece, "Vaguely Love Poem," Bishop attempted a more hard-edged, cubistic vision (as in William Carlos Williams's "The Rose") to describe a less mediated, not at all "vague" passion. But this is a "vaguely love poem" in the sense that love and harshness uncomfortably converge. The roses here are "rock roses" because they proliferate toward some intense erotic center both physical and emotional, rapturous and exacting.

> Just now, when I saw you naked again,
> I thought the same words: rose-rock; rock-rose. . .
> Rose, trying, working, to show itself,
> Unimaginable connections, unseen, shining edges,
> (forming, folding over,)
> Rose-rock, unformed, flesh beginning, crystal by crystal,
> Clear pink breasts and darker, crystalline nipples,
> rose-rock, rose-quartz, roses, roses, roses,
> exacting roses from the body,
> and even darker, accurate, rose of sex.
>
> (box 33, folder 532, VC)

Although there is a grotesque effect in the convergence of hard and soft images, the hard images do not suggest an antivital ideal but rather strong sensation at once pleasurable and violent. The symbolic nature of the rose icon implies a unity of sensation rather than of emotion. This is not an image of petrification or of Bonnard-like gentleness but of rose and rock modifying each other in a momentary bodily coalescence.

Among the published poems of this period, only "The Shampoo" offers a real counterpoint to the anxious vision of the mutable female body presented in "Faustina, or Rock Roses." Although the focus is on "hair" rather than on sexual "breasts," the washing becomes a loving ritual. In the first two stanzas the lover is compared to nature. This nature is not idealized or timeless but metamorphic. As in "A Cold Spring," Bishop finds spatial registers of imperceptible processes.

The still explosions on the rocks,
the lichens, grow
by spreading, gray, concentric shocks.
They have arranged
to meet the rings around the moon, although
within our memories they have not changed.

(*CP*, p. 84)

The association of the lover's hair with the lichens in the next stanza
has a grotesque effect, but again there is no revulsion. The shocks in the
visually accurate oxymoron "still explosions" turn out to be imperceptible and harmless, making the aging process more acceptable. But the
sense of alarm remains. The temporal sequence is not abrupt, but the
revelation of change may shock us. The grotesque is not a register of
ugliness but a challenge to fixed ways of associating beauty and nature.
In an inverse of the courtly trope the lover surpasses nature, not by being
more ideal, but the reverse. Though the lichens seem not to have changed
and are slow in their ascendancy to the moon, the lover has been "pre-
cipitate and pragmatical" in her aging process. But this is a backhanded
compliment. Her gray hair, now "shooting stars," will reach the moon
faster than the lichen. But the moon itself is "battered and shiny," not
a transcendent object but part of a cosmic metamorphosis, a symbol of
mutability. This simile works inversely, just as the lichen metaphor does.
The moon ostensibly modifies "the big tin basin" (with rings around
it?). But the simile serves to bring the moon (associated with lovers) into
the domain of time, with the easy swing of the rhyme that sustains the
relaxed, variant line lengths of the poem. There is none of the cramped
rhythm of "Faustina" here. "The Shampoo," which ends *A Cold Spring*,
is Bishop's earliest study of the body in time. It challenges the courtly
convention (as "Insomnia" does, but now more positively) that recognizes as lovable only what is youthful or immutable. Bishop endows the
carpe diem rose with many days, many moments in its changing life, but
she does not evade the shock we feel in the awareness of our mutability.

In "Faustina," "The Shampoo," and many other poems, Bishop takes
a fairly clear position against repression, embracing mutability and resisting static norms of beauty. But Bishop was hardly naive or optimistic
about the implications—social and psychological—of such an embrace.
Many of her poems look hard not only at the consequences of repression
but also at the consequences of deviance. They participate in the am-

bivalence about the mutable body and about social marginality that they explore. To abandon cultural norms may be, as she suggests in "In the Waiting Room," to fall off the turning world into blue-black space. In such poems Bishop takes on the perspective of someone who feels herself part of a cultural framework yet is attracted to or empathetic toward those marginal elements it cannot accommodate and tries to suppress. In such poems deviance is defined not as an escape from the body but rather as an alternative relationship to the body that reminds us of its uncontrollability. In particular, Bishop turns to carnivalesque images of the misfit, who resists the social and cultural norms through which nature is disciplined and controlled.

"Manuelzinho" represents Bishop's most joyous, although still ambivalent, view of the misfit, and as such she can, at the end of that poem, take off her hat to him. The poet's surrogate self, the landowner, remains within her own world, ambivalently open to new potentialities and freed from cliché by her unruly, Cain-like gardener. But "Exchanging Hats" (which Bishop published in *New World Writing* in 1956 but did not include in any collection) describes an anxiety about social roles as well as about creative deviance. The "hats" we wear, the social identities we take on, are inherently insecure. Bishop describes a world of sexual anxiety, where men become effeminate and women become the captains. The sportive Carnival atmosphere of "Manuelzinho," in which alternative, even mystical, orders are tolerated, is here replaced with a more sinister humor and leads to a darker vision at the end. Here the exchange is "unfunny," because it exposes "a slight transvestite twist" in us all, which we suppress. The insistent, end-stopped rhymes and processional tetrameter build to a reeling rhythm that expresses the "madness" acknowledged in the sixth stanza.

> Anandrous aunts, who, at the beach
> with paper plates upon your laps,
> keep putting on the yachtsmen's caps
> with exhibitionistic screech,
>
> the visors hanging o'er the ear
> so that the golden anchors drag,
> —the tides of fashion never lag.
> Such caps may not be worn next year.

Or you who don the paper plate
itself, and put some grapes upon it,
or sport the Indian's feather bonnet,
—perversities may aggravate

the natural madness of the hatter.
And if the opera hats collapse
And crowns grow draughty, then, perhaps,
he thinks what might a miter matter?

(*CP*, p. 200)

Bishop employs a deliberately grating diction and punning sarcasm that cuts through the civilized, mock-poetic voice ("visors hanging o'er the ear / . . . the tides of fashion never lag"). The anandrous aunts who pretend to be at the helm are screeching orders. Bishop's own marginality as lesbian and poet becomes normal in this family in which men become effeminate and women become captains. This inherited "natural madness of the hatter" is exacerbated in the fifth stanza as an unnamed "you" (the poet's uncle and perhaps the poet herself) tropes further, putting on "the paper plate / itself." This "you" at least acknowledges the arbitrariness of the hats and can enjoy their array. At this point the hats become endlessly exchangeable and the outlandish roles accelerate. Bishop speaks from inside a culture that cannot sustain the norms of gender identity but perceives their instability as "abnormal," perverse, or experimental. In this sense the openly deviant poet who converts role-playing into troping becomes the only potentially joyous member of the family. Her subversion of various forms of masculine power (metonymically shown as Indian's headdress, monarch's crown, bishop's miter) can be heard in the alliteration ("what might a miter [meter] matter?").

The Carnival hysteria reaches a pitch in stanza six and turns somber as it moves toward the singular, personal perspective. Uncle Neddy and Aunt "Hat," remembered as devils in "Memories of Uncle Neddy," are alluded to here: the man who could never establish a successful identity but with whom the poet feels a strong affinity, the "exemplary" woman who dominated, scowled, and disapproved. These dead now wear the figurative hats of darkness ("black fedora" and "shady, turned-down brim"). The poet wonders about the uncle's aspiration ("are there any / stars inside your black fedora?") and about the aunt's judgment of history ("what slow changes"). These stanzas, like the dream of the grandparents in Eternity in "The Moose," take Bishop outside the anxious experimentations of the world she lives in, but they do so without providing any solace. She is not sure that there are any stars under the uncle's black fedora or that the aunt has seen any genuine changes, however slow, within the unlagging tides of sexual and social fashion. The creative deviance of Manuelzinho, whose hat signified the sportive alternative to the conventional world of the speaker, has been displaced by a world of relentless "costume and custom," where roles are exchanged rather than made flexible. The divine, creative madness of the gardener is now the perverse madness of the hatter who has lost all connection with nature. Instead of expressing the freedom from fixed order and identity, the grotesque here expresses the radical instability and inauthenticity of all cultural roles.

This same decadent Carnival world of "costume and custom" defines "Pink Dog," one of Bishop's last poems. What makes this exploration of social and physical anxiety so powerful is that she both abhors the enforcement of "costume" and sees its necessity. We are embarrassed here by nakedness and by its opposite. In "Exchanging Hats" the poet may share the "transvestite twist" of the unfunny uncles, may feel inspired to experiment with unstable identities. In "Pink Dog" she urges a costume on a naked dog (a dehumanized image of the body) for the sake of its survival in a culture that wishes to deny the mortal body. The poet writes from the margin, on the divide between culture and nature, a creature of both. It is her empathy for the pink dog, her own sense of marginality, that provokes her terrible advice. In a culture that abhors the body's mutability, disguise is the only alternative to expulsion or annihilation. The dog in us must be dressed up and taught to dance if it is to be tolerated at all. Carnival is now the expression not of freedom but of repression.

In Carnival time, when everyone is disguised, the poet sees a naked pink diseased female dog. It is not easy for Bishop to embrace the reality of the pink dog. Her impulse is to hide it, not just from herself but from the forces that threaten it (which she has internalized). In "Pink Dog" Bishop makes her most complete and successful use of the grotesque; its style, its imagery, and its tone are all intensely ambivalent. Whereas other poems explore grotesque images but collapse them in thematic reduction, "Pink Dog" sustains its uneasy vision of marginality. In "The

Armadillo" Bishop depended on a dramatic shift of sympathy from the desire for spiritual and aesthetic transcendence in the fire balloons to the will to survive and the rage against oppression. In this poem the two impulses are in more immediate competition. The beholder is herself ambivalent—horrified by and concerned for the grotesque figure, participating in the repressive forces even while she wishes to save the dog. The poem is not simply responding to the depilated dog, an image of disorder and mutability; Bishop also turns the techniques of the grotesque against the culture that the dog offends. If a depilated dog does not look attractive, one in mascara, dressed up and dancing, is truly obscene.

There are two parts to the grotesque in this poem. One part represents the decay and regeneration of the body, to which the poet responds in shock; the other represents the attempt to disguise that process. The opening of the poem introduces both responses:

> The sun is blazing and the sky is blue.
> Umbrellas clothe the beach in every hue.
> Naked, you trot across the avenue.
>
> Oh, never have I seen a dog so bare!
> Naked and pink, without a single hair . . .
> Startled, the passersby draw back and stare.
>
> (*CP*, p. 190)

Nature, including the beach where nakedness is supposed to be displayed, must be clothed. Color here is a sign of disguise rather than of festive deviance. The idiots, paralytics, and beggars all exacerbate a body anxiety by exhibiting their vulnerabilities. The pink dog combines degeneration and regeneration, displays ongoing metamorphosis. But the poet does not sustain the neutral descriptiveness of "A Cold Spring" toward this coincidence. The engaged voice makes this a far more powerful, far more troubling poem. "You have a case of scabies / but look intelligent. Where are your babies? / (A nursing mother by those hanging teats)." Bishop herself suffered from eczema and other skin ailments and as a schoolgirl was sent home for open sores. She had the constant sense, then, of physical betrayal. Yet a dog without hair is a reductive image of any human form. The dog is female to express woman's greater identification with the body, male culture's symbolization of the body as woman.

Whatever combination of compassion and horror we may feel toward the nurturing, festering body, these feelings are increased as we imagine the impersonal violence wielded against it by society.

> Yes, idiots, paralytics, parasites
> go bobbing in the ebbing sewage, nights
> out in the suburbs, where there are no lights.
>
> If they do this to anyone who begs,
> drugged, drunk, or sober, with or without legs,
> what would they do to sick, four-legged dogs?
>
> In the cafés and on the sidewalk corners
> the joke is going round that all the beggars
> who can afford them now wear life preservers.
>
> (*CP*, p. 190)

The black humor of the passage heightens the grotesque effect of the brutal actions it describes. The drowned bodies "go bobbing," forms of suffering are hurled together in the syntax as "with or without legs." Whose crass language is this? The poet does not seem to participate in the brutality beneath the veneer of culture (she exposes the fringes, "out in the suburbs, where there are no lights"). But her own alternative, she knows, is equally grotesque, if more complex.

> Now look, the practical, the sensible
> solution is to wear a *fantasía*
> Tonight you simply can't afford to be a-
> n eyesore. But no one will ever see a
>
> dog in *máscara* this time of year.
>
> (*CP*, pp. 190–91)

The poem clearly parodies this proposal. But it also suggests that, in a culture as hysterically repressive as this one has become, the logic of survival leads this way. The contorted language of the poem emphasizes the strain of this logic, however. The awkward enjambments and forced triple rhymes form Bishop's commentary on her earlier attempts to disguise personal dread in elegant patterns and tropes. They are also a comment on the fundamental lack of grace inherent in our repression of the body.

This poem offers no clear answer to the public fear of the mutable body, yet that fear and the repressive behavior it provokes are obviously criticized. We are left suspended between sympathy and judgment toward this speaker. Pink dog and speaker appear as two rival aspects of the self—one that would parade its nakedness, whatever the consequences, and one that would cover and protect, because it cannot or does not wish to expel the body. The pink dog has none of the alterity of the fish or other iconic figures in Bishop's poetry. She lives among us, in our element, as the aspect of ourselves we cannot tame. But by making her central figure a dog rather than a human, Bishop reminds us that the animal does not represent, in her naked, diseased state, a viable human option. The poet is not the dog but the troubled speaker who must somehow reconcile her culture to the dog it despises.

Bishop's late poetry, with its greater realism in treating biological and social themes, is pessimistic about our ability to remain open to difference and change. The tension that produces her grotesque style is no longer between a beautiful, transcendent, or inwardly infinite self and a mechanistic environment, or, as in the middle period, in the strangely beautiful coincidence of generation and decay in nature. In the end she focused on the untamable body, its needs, desires, processes in time, and the culture's wish to control, disguise, or suppress it. In the landscape we are able to experience joy in the vision of mortality in a solacing way. But when nature parades naked within the boundaries of culture, when "nature" includes our own untamable desires and processes that threaten its stability, the society responds with fear and loathing. Nature, when it intrudes on culture, is an "eyesore"; nor are the forms of culture (the *fantasía*, the *máscara*, rhyme and meter) beautiful when they are designed to disguise or suppress nature. Yet in bringing nature and culture together in the confrontational style of the grotesque, Bishop reminds us that they are not discrete or dichotomous realms, that our imaginations need form and order but must remain open to mutable, deviant life. She expresses the necessity (though not always the hope) for a less "barbaric," more flexible, tolerant culture that can accommodate difference and change without anxiety and remain "new, tender, quick."

Notes

1. Bishop to Robert Lowell, 8 September 1948, HL. "Sometimes I wish we could have a more sensible conversation about this suffering business, anyway. I imag-

ine we actually agree fairly well—it is just that I guess I think it is so inevitable & unavoidable there's no use talking about it, & that in itself it has no value, anyway."

2. I differ particularly with Robert Dale Parker (1988), who, in response to early emphasis on the pastoral pleasures of Bishop's work, reads her as a poet of terrors. Bishop's work insists on an emotional and conceptual openness to the contradictions in life. She is not her unbeliever who, with his eyes closed, projects a malevolent will on the sea. She is the clear-eyed poet who sees a rusted capstan as a blood-stained crucifix but also sees the hirsute begonia brightening the black translucency, the luminous rocks in their bezels of sand despite bleak March winds. Bishop's poetry is not merely gay in the presence of barbarities, of course. The humor is often black. But her imagination resists tonal as well as conceptual stasis; it acknowledges a perpetually dividing heart.

3. As a young poet, Bishop took up almost obsessively the metaphysical conceit of the eyes as expressions of the heart and windows of the soul. But the eyes increasingly became symbols of problematical or elusive identity. What continues and develops, to displace the essentialist conceit of the eyes gazing inward or heavenward, is a narrative of looking, staring, glimpsing that is often, as in "Brazil, January 1, 1502" (*CP*, pp. 91–92), directly related to gender.

JEREDITH MERRIN

Elizabeth Bishop:
Gaiety, Gayness, and Change

"Sad friend, you cannot change."
—from "North Haven"

"I feel my colors changing now"
—from "Rainy Season; Sub-Tropics"

"Without surprise,
The world might change to something quite different,
As the air changes or the lightning comes without our blinking,
Change as our kisses are changing without our thinking."
—from "It is marvellous to wake up together"

I

THE STORY OF Bishop's poetry is larger and finally less lugubrious than much previous criticism leads us to believe. Full of humor and color and wit, her writing is, as Harold Bloom (1983) points out, playful—sometimes profoundly playful (p. xi). Her poetry opens up, too, the tantalizing option of seemingly endless transmogrification: by overt simile or by more subtle suggestion, everything is always turning into something else. And metamorphosis translates, for both poet and reader, into refreshment, buoyancy, gaiety. In shifting critical attention from Bishop's frequently cited "ruefulness" or "poignancy" to her playfulness and wit, I would like to bring into focus a new, more complex, image of the poet. Two poems, from the beginning and from the very end of her career, "Pleasure Seas" (1939) and "Sonnet" (1979), are particularly useful for bringing into relief the neglected and interconnected issues of poetic pleasure and gayness in her work.

An obsession with transmogrification and changeability is inextricable from Bishop's gaiety or lighthearted whimsy; even as she muses obliquely on painful personal experience, she cheerfully indulges in and offers us the diversion of the surprising and unexpected. In the second section, I suggest that Bishop's gaiety or delight in the possibilities of change is in turn inextricable from her gayness: her questioning of gender boundaries, for example, and the exploration (however oblique and shrouded) of the pleasures and anxieties of same-sex love. Bishop relies throughout her career, as I argue, on specific organizing tropes identified here as "inversion" and "thirdness"—powerful patterns of mind or psychological gestalts that convey her multivalent response to her sexual disposition. Finally, I consider Bishop's abandonment in "Sonnet," her final poem, of these tropes of inversion and thirdness for a double-edged evocation, at once cheerful and poignant, of flight beyond the confines of the physical body and the world of gendered opposition.

II

First then, in her early "Pleasure Seas," how does this poet play, moving from entrapment to freedom, from (to borrow Bishop's own phrasing in other poems) Despair to Espoir, from the "awful" to the "cheerful"?

> In the walled off swimming-pool the water is perfectly flat.
> The pink Seurat bathers are dipping themselves in and out
> Through a pane of bluish glass.
> The cloud reflections pass
> Huge amoeba-motions directly through
> The beds of bathing caps: white, lavender, and blue.
> If the sky turns gray, the water turns opaque,
> Pistachio green and Mermaid Milk.
> But out among the keys
> Where the water goes its own way, the shallow pleasure seas
> Drift this way and that mingling currents and tides
> In most of the colors that swarm around the sides
> Of soap-bubbles, poisonous and fabulous.
> And the keys float lightly like rolls of green dust.

From an airplane the water's heavy sheet
Of glass above a bas-relief:
Clay-yellow coral and purple dulces
And long, leaning, submerged green grass.
Across it a wide shadow pulses.
The water is a burning-glass
Turned to the sun
That blues and cools as the afternoon wears on,
And liquidly
Floats weeds, surrounds fish, supports a violently red bell-buoy
Whose neon-color vibrates over it, whose bells vibrate
Through it. It glitters rhythmically
To shock after shock of electricity.
The sea is delight. The sea means *room*.
It is a dance-floor, a well ventilated ballroom.
From the swimming-pool or from the deck of a ship
Pleasures strike off humming, and skip
Over the tinsel surface: a Grief floats off
Spreading out thin like oil. And Love
Sets out determinedly in a straight line,
One of his burning ideas in mind,
Keeping his eyes on
The bright horizon,
But shatters immediately, suffers refraction,
And comes back in shoals of distraction.
Happy the people in the swimming-pool and on the yacht,
Happy the man in that airplane, likely as not—
And out there where the coral reef is a shelf
The water runs at it, leaps, throws itself
Lightly, lightly, whitening in the air:
An acre of cold white spray is there
Dancing happily by itself.

(CP, pp. 195–96)

The first line here suggests both "walled-off" entrapment and lassitude or dullness. But then the picture is immediately made "gay" with color (the word "gay," from the Medieval French "gai," meaning both "merry" and "brightly colored"): "pink Seurat bathers," "bluish glass," and "white, lavender, and blue" bathing caps. The overcast gray sky is transformed by its reflection in the pool—the swimming pool, like the mind of the poet, performing an egregiously fanciful metamorphosis of the drabness collected: "Pistachio green and Mermaid Milk."

Now the poem expands spatially from the contained water of the pool to the freer water surrounding the ship: "But out among the keys / Where the water goes its own way." If we extend the water/mind analogy, this other, unconfined water evokes a mind unconstrained—a good thing, surely. This going one's own way suggests the young poet's artistic independence as well as possibly hinting at her sense of social and sexual difference. But of course at this point in Bishop's drifting, tentative poem it is not entirely clear whether we are meant to see the water in the Florida keys that "goes its own way" as likened to or contrasted with the speaker's mind. "The shallow pleasure seas / Drift this way and that," Bishop writes, in a way describing her own poetic procedure. Even the irregular couplet form of this poem—with jagged line-lengths and frequent slant rhymes—may remind us of the sea's lapping waves, while it evokes both freedom and constraint, singularity and sameness. A wavelike recurrent blending and separation or braiding and unbraiding of scenery and mental state: that is the strategy of "Pleasure Seas," how this early poem works.

The pleasure seas are "shallow," because Bishop is as usual being scrupulously accurate in her physical description but perhaps also because the pleasure this particular voyager takes in the view is not very deep or covers a deeper sadness. And when next the poet describes the colors of the water in the keys—"most of the colors that swarm the sides / Of soap-bubbles, poisonous and fabulous"—the mind/water metaphor is delicately reactivated: the speaker's mind is threatened by something "poisonous," we may suppose, by some unhappiness, at the same time that it is capable of manufacturing its colorful fictions that are "fabulous." (Bishop, who in the thirties wrote short stories—"The Baptism," "The Sea and Its Shore," and "In Prison"—would at the time of this poem's composition have thought of herself very much as a writer of fiction or of fables.)

The word "poisonous," though, in the playful, emotionally reticent context of this early poem, is so emphatic, so dire, that we are provoked into wondering about its cause. Rather than supplying some explanation, the poet, perhaps reacting to the word as too painful or self-dramatizing, quickly swerves away from emotion with an arresting simile—"The keys float *lightly* like rolls of green dust"—the adverb here hinting at a buoyant change of mood. And then in the next line Bishop switches to another, more distant and presumably dispassionate perspective, that of the airplane above her. This is one of the better moves in the poem— not only an escapist gesture on Bishop's part but also an exhilarating rush through space, an invitation to the reader to travel in imagination along with her. From this imagined height, she observes that "a wide shadow pulses" across the water. Is it the shadow of the airplane, some other unaccounted-for shadow, or perhaps the figurative shadow cast by the speaker's own supposedly aerial but somehow dejected disposition? The source of the trope remains indeterminate. Amidst almost hypnotic descriptive details ("long, leaning, submerged green grass"), these some-what coy emotional cues: what, we wonder, is the shadowy secret here, the psychological inducement for the words "poisoned" and "shadow"?

"Pulses," "burning-glass," "violently red bell-buoy," "neon-color," "vibrate," "glitters rhythmically," and "shocks of electricity": this dic-tion—all heat and physical sensation—suggests not only tropical bright-ness but also that the answer to that question of motivation may be located in frustrated sexual desire. If the receptive mind was likened to a still, walled-off swimming pool earlier, here the mind takes on the active, even destructive, intensity of a burning-glass: a convex lens for focusing the direct rays of the sun to produce heat or set fire to something. The poem that began with delicate, pastel hues and muted, avoided emo-tion has reached a crescendo of color (blue, green, red)—although the emotional import is still hinted at obliquely, with a light touch, through descriptive accuracies.

Suddenly, with the next line, the poem turns from description to more abstract declaration: "The sea is delight." Again, as with the earlier assertion that the water "goes its own way," this brief statement hovers between complementarity and contrast. Are we to understand that the voyager's mind is like the sea: vivid and luxuriant, a locus of delight? Or, given that the sexual sense of pleasure in "Pleasure Seas" has just been activated, is the speaker obliquely indicating that although her sur-roundings are delightful, sensual, and romantic, she herself (as an isolate plagued by loneliness, perhaps as a lover unrequited) is ironically at odds with the situation? If, as she goes on to announce emphatically, "The sea means *room*," should we then take this to mean that for the solitary

voyager the sea represents welcome opportunity for untrammeled imaginative play or rather that the watery expanse provides merely another
reminder of her own painful yearning for a romantic partner, as the rapid
transmogrification of sea to "*room*" to "ball-room" may suggest?[1] The
two readings, of course, are not mutually exclusive. Given free rein or
"*room,*" the mind (like a voyager) has a way of venturing out toward the
new, the exotic, only to return home, back to its wonted preoccupations.

Outward and backward, pleasure and grief, resolution and dissolution. With these paired oppositions, dreamily intermingled, the twenty-
eight-year-old Bishop drifts toward the end of her poem. And here the
romantic preoccupation is at last made explicit, or as explicit as the
reticent young poet can allow:

> And Love
> Sets out determinedly in a straight line,
> One of his burning ideas in mind,
> Keeping his eyes on
> The bright horizon,
> But shatters immediately, suffers refraction,
> And comes back in shoals of distraction.

The self-consciously artificial broaching of "Love" as a "he" or the
allegorical Cupid; the ironic adversion to Petrarchist cliché ("One of his
burning ideas in mind"); and the waggish silliness of the feminine rhyme,
"Eyes on" / "horizon": this passage is thickly overlaid with Bishop's
urbane defenses against bathos. ("*Suffers* refraction," by the way, the
most emotionally freighted phrase in the lines just quoted, replaces what
had been the more neutral "*goes through* refraction" in Bishop's earlier
draft (box 31, folder 472, VC): with such a leavening of wit, perhaps
she trusted that she could afford this single, more personally revealing
gesture.)

Just as she earlier switched her point of view to that of a distanced,
depersonalized airplane and then to the open ballroom of the sea, here in
the final lines Bishop redirects attention to both the human and inhuman
perspectives around her. In the swimming pool, in the airplane, and on
the yacht the people are said to be "Happy." Even the seawater is, as
the Elizabethans used to say, "in humor," as it throws itself against the
distant coral reef: "Lightly, lightly, whitening the air: / An acre of cold
white spray is there / Dancing happily by itself."

Everyone and everything except myself is "Happy," the speaker seems to say with mixed self-pity and self-exhortation. But then it is also impossible to read these last three especially lyrical lines without thinking that what is "Dancing happily by itself" is not merely external to the speaker, the water in the Florida keys, but also inside her, the solitary poet's psyche or (as Keats would have it) "working brain" that has endeavored to remain cheerfully dispassionate or "cold" like the sea spray, to find in solitary observation sufficient enjoyment ("Pleasure *Seas*" may punningly be read as "Pleasure *Sees*"), and to wear its not-quite-concealed unhappiness (that shadow over the poem that makes its title of course double-edged or ironic), "Lightly, lightly."

III

I have lingered so long on (or in) "Pleasure Seas," Bishop's exercise in extended image lists and couplets, because attention to a poet's slighter poems sometimes brings into relief what is essential to his or her project as a whole. One characteristic trait of this early poem is its engagement with what David Kalstone noted as "The Real Problem for Bishop: How to turn the descriptive poem into a narrative—while keeping it descriptive in nature."[2] The narrative here, as in so many of Bishop's poems and stories, records mental process—the mind's interaction with the world—even as it calls into question the easy distinction of those entities: "mind" and "world."

This descriptive/narrative method has its advantages as well as its dilemmas or limitations. The psychological "story" may be so buried under descriptive detail that it escapes our notice. We might feel that we are in the presence of an annoying coyness. In fact, Bishop seems gradually through her career to have taken stock of these problems, and without demoting description she would highlight first-person narrative in stronger, more mature poems such as "Crusoe in England" or "In the Waiting Room." In "The Bight," the Bishop poem that most resembles "Pleasure Seas" (because it also playfully and ruefully delineates a mental state while describing a body of water), we are provided with the epigraph, "On my birthday," that provides some emotional entree.

Some of the advantages of Bishop's descriptive/narrative method are obvious: the opportunity for inclusion of details that another poet might discount as too slight or as thematically irrelevant; the avoidance of what she would have considered sentimental or embarrassingly "confessional." [3] Other advantages are more rhetorically subtle. Her method immerses the reader not merely in scenery but also in mental process—an ongoing story, or a little history, of the interplay of internal and external forces that, although morally engaged, reaches no authoritative moral or philosophical conclusion. There is no solution proffered by this poem—unless it is the watery solution that, like the speaker's mind, is in restless, constant flux. What the mind observes is contingent on a certain environment; what is observed in that environment is contingent on a certain state of mind, and the very boundaries between these two dramatis personae of perception are blurred. The reader, in short, like the voyager, drifts on a sea of indeterminacy. And Bishop will offer no reassuring, transcendent vision—"vision" being for her, as she tells us in another poem, "too strong a word." [4]

But she is no dour indeterminist, and we wouldn't travel with Elizabeth Bishop unless she were good company. Bishop criticism has tended usefully to stress the recurrent psychological and philosophical dilemmas in her work, dilemmas becoming more apparent with the appearance of her final, most accessible and autobiographical book, *Geography III*. Here, I am emphasizing the playful rather than the troubled Bishop, because it provides a way to address the pleasure and quiet excitement of reading a poem by her (even a relatively slight poem) and because it helps to define what I think Bishop defined to herself throughout the approximately forty-year span of her writing career as poetic material. What material did Bishop consider suitable for poetic shaping; what were her standards for inclusion and exclusion? [5]

"Poemness"—if I may for a moment invent a clumsy term—poemness for Bishop consists in capturing "not a thought, but a mind thinking"; [6] not in drawing conclusions but in positing questions; and not in supplying eternal verities but rather, as I have just suggested, in offering (to herself as well as to her reader) the pleasure and freedom of shape-shifting, transmogrification, metamorphosis. Bishop above all loved the way, in poetry, things can change into other unexpected things.

Consider, for example, the well-known poem that resulted from Bishop's delight in the newspaper error that altered *mammoth* to *man moth* or her memorably ingenious metamorphosis of a writing desk into a battlefield in "12 O'Clock News." Then there is her lifelong obsession with changes of culture and scenery through travel as well as her fascination with dream transformations in poems such as "The Weed" or "Sleeping Standing Up." The radical shifts of perspective and of scale in her descriptions are too frequent and obvious to belabor (e.g., the sudden shift, noted earlier, to an aerial view in "Pleasure Seas"), as are her quirky changes of mind in the middle of a poem, as in "The Fish" ("and then I saw / that from his lower lip / —if you could call it a lip—") or in "Love Lies Sleeping" ("inverted and distorted. No. I mean / distorted and revealed"). And consider, finally, as a telling stylistic feature, Bishop's characteristic use of the simile, a device that delivers pleasure by almost magically turning one thing into another before our eyes: "the dead volcanoes / glistened like Easter lilies" ("Over 2,000 Illustrations and a Complete Concordance"); "the fireflies / begin to rise: / . . . exactly like the bubbles in champagne" ("A Cold Spring"); "Here and there / his brown skin hung in strips / like ancient wallpaper" ("The Fish"); "lupins like apostles" ("The Moose").

Of course, although Bishop's similes are unusually vivid, the simile is a common literary device, and given that poetry has roots in magic—the attempted manipulation of nature, time, and other people—lyric poems, even in their commitment to fixed perfection, are as a rule obsessed with transmutation or change. Still, as the list of thematic and stylistic choices above attests, changeability holds a uniquely preeminent place in Bishop's poetics.[7] When, in a poem written near the end of her own too-short life, Bishop wrote an elegy for her longtime friend and dearest rival, Robert Lowell (an obsessive reviser of his own poems), she singled out this as the hardest loss: "Sad friend, you cannot change" ("North Haven," *CP*, pp. 188–89).

The posthumously published "Sonnet" (*CP*, p. 192) rings its changes on the sonnet tradition and demonstrates what David Kalstone (1989, p. 134) noted as Bishop's predilection for "waywardness as a poetic strategy":

Caught—the bubble
in the spirit-level,
a creature divided;
and the compass needle
wobbling and wavering,
undecided.
Freed—the broken
thermometer's mercury
running away;
and the rainbow-bird

from the narrow bevel
of the empty mirror,
flying wherever
it feels like, gay!

While the traditional sonnet employs iambic pentameter, this pared-down, roughly dimeter sonnet does not. Whereas both Petrarchan and Shakespearean sonnets abide by restricted rhyme schemes, Bishop's unpredictable adaptation, anarchically, will not. If Shakespeare and other English sonneteers used the form to claim immutability, constancy, unchangingness even beyond this life, Bishop here uses her whimsical version of it to lay claim to (or maybe it is more appropriate to say to wish for) perpetual mobility, a kind of perdurable mutability.

In the drafts of this poem (Rare Books and Manuscripts, VC), we see how Bishop played with two pairs of images, the first pair having to do with constraint and the second with liberation. And we see how she tinkered to set those paired images into her very freely adapted rhyming form. This passage from entrapment to freedom and this restrained anarchy of form are the same general strategies noticed in the earlier "Pleasure Seas" (although there are no rhymes in the later "Sonnet" that seem as forced as "on the yacht" / "likely as not"). An early work sheet has Bishop trying out, "Oh, Brain, bubble," as her first line. Knowing this reinforces the sense that her brief poem (she could not have known that she would die suddenly of a brain aneurysm and that this would be her final poem) is concerned among other things with the final freeing of brain or spirit from the "leveling" body. At one point in the revision process, the brain/bubble was "slipping, shifting," which is not unlike the drifting mental action we noticed in "Pleasure Seas"—and in fact in that same early version of "Sonnet" the compass needle was even said to be "drifting." One work sheet shows Bishop trying out "rolling away" as the last line, but she stayed with her ordering of images and with the final word, "gay!" once she happened upon that richly connotative rhyme word.

And with this word, so much more freighted than the "pleasure" of her earlier poem, Bishop's gaiety and her gayness become indivisible. Although I do not see "Sonnet" as "a poem of explicit homosexuality," as does Robert Dale Parker (1988, p. 142) (because "gay" here means a number of things, including bright or varicolored, and the brief poem is in any case pretty cryptic for the adjective "explicit"), the available pun does tease us into further thought. If what I have called Bishop's poetics of change may be linked, as we have seen, to the pleasurable qualities or the gaiety of her poetry, how may it be seen as related to her sexuality, her lesbianism or gayness?

There cannot be a simple answer to such a question. For one thing, the issue of change is, as we know, bound up with other experiences in Bishop's life—her early loss of both parents and of her childhood home in Nova Scotia, most prominently. For another, the connections between creative practice and individual psychology remain mysterious, as Sigmund Freud acknowledged when he wrote of Leonardo da Vinci that "the nature of artistic achievement is inaccessible to us psychoanalytically" (Freud 1944, p. 119). And besides requisite intellectual humility, there remain questions about the point of focusing on Bishop's gayness, precisely because she did not publish poems of explicit homosexuality but chose instead to follow her own implied advice to the "confessional" poets and keep intimate matters to herself. (This of course at a time when identifying oneself as homosexual was less feasible, socially as well as legally, than today.)

Such considerations of tenability should not, it seems to me, be cavalierly dismissed in a cultural and academic environment that has grown all too accustomed to sensationalism and the purposeless exploitation of biographical materials. Nor, although I understand the motivations behind and the uses of specialized reading lists and anthologies, am I interested in relegating a poet who refused to appear in women's anthologies because she thought it was "a lot of nonsense, separating the sexes" (Starbuck 1983, p. 322) to the further-segregated category of "lesbian poet."[8]

I am interested in how these poems, which continue to appeal to a wide audience, work—and play. And Bishop's obsession with changeability now may be seen as entwined not only with her gaiety but also with other objectives of her work. These objectives include, as specified near the beginning of this essay, the questioning of gender boundaries and the exploration of the pleasures and anxieties of same-sex love. This complicated concatenation of concerns can be difficult to address at times because Bishop's work as a whole builds up a context in which the reader is expected at the same time to know and not to know about her sexual disposition.

These concerns of Bishop's, however, can be illustrated by looking at the way she delivers poetic pleasure—even as she both keeps and tells her "secret"—by means of two organizing figures or tropes that I will designate "inversion" and "thirdness." Although other important rhetorical figures recur in her work, these two tropes so inform her poetry from beginning to end that they are not merely useful literary devices deployed now and then but are actually ingrained habits of mind, powerful psychological gestalts producing many of Bishop's patterns of imagery and other poetic structures. I will return to Bishop's employment and final abandonment of these two tropes in "Sonnet," but first I want to trace, in a discussion intended as suggestive rather than exhaustive, their evolution in some of her earlier work.

IV

The most overt example of the inversion trope appears in *A Cold Spring*, Bishop's slim second book that contains what Alan Williamson (1983) has called her "seemingly little-read, little-discussed, love poems" (p. 96). "Insomnia" begins with an image of the moon reflected in a bedroom bureau mirror, and it concludes with these lines:

> So wrap up care in a cobweb
> and drop it down the well
>
> into that world inverted
> where left is always right,
> where the shadows are really the body,
> where we stay awake all night,
> where the heavens are shallow as the sea
> is now deep, and you love me.

(*CP*, p. 70)

This song-like poem, a sort of magical charm composed (with the single exception of the penultimate line) in the three-beat meter appropriate to magical incantation, raises a number of questions outside the purview of this essay. Where and how, for example, does the beloved, the "you," enter this poem? What can we make of Bishop's interest, here and elsewhere, in shadows? What is the relation of Bishop's "Sonnet" to Sir Philip Sidney's graceful sonnet-excursus in projection that begins, "With how sad steps, Oh Moon, thou climb'st the skies" (*Astrophel and Stella*, sonnet 31, in Sidney 1962)?

For the purposes of this discussion, my point is that the poignancy and wit of the quoted lines depend heavily on our understanding of what it means in this context to conceive of the "world inverted." In the first place, it means that reciprocal love, for the speaker, is only possible in a topsy-turvy or *Through the Looking Glass* world,[9] which is to say that re-quited love may be impossible, a mere fantasy. Secondly, it suggests that desire for this speaker belongs to the world of what Havelock Ellis in the late nineteenth century catalogued under the rubric of "sexual inversion" (Ellis 1936, pp. 261–62). (That implicitly negative term for homosexu-ality was still in common use in the 1950s, when the poem was written, as Lorrie Goldensohn [1988, p. 36] has noted.[10]) "By the Universe deserted" reverberates differently once we register this pun on inversion, as does the assertion "left is always right," which might then come to mean that what is "left" (meaning wrong or gauche or unwanted) in the everyday or heterosexual world would be both correct and desirable—"right"— in an inverted or gay world.

In Bishop's work this trope of inversion is multivalent, a pattern that imposes its energy onto the organization of many sensations and experi-ences that are in turn expressed via a multitude of motifs. It may express chagrin, estrangement, and a world-weary sense of impossibility, while at the same time conveying a sense of anarchic playfulness and a kind of covert self-assertion. Bishop manages to be both wistful and wayward not only in "Insomnia" but also in other poems that adopt inversion as a central organizing principle, such as "Sleeping on the Ceiling" or, more importantly, "The Man-Moth." In the latter poem the imaginary creature, standing in moonlight, "makes an inverted pin, the point mag-netized to the moon"; he lives underground and "always seats himself facing the wrong way" on the subway so that he "travels backwards."

Inversion, a radical change in position or perspective, manifests itself in a number of more subtle maneuvers. There is, for example, the inverted mirror image in "The Gentleman of Shallot" or the moment in "Ques-tions of Travel" when Bishop asks why "we are determined to rush / to see the sun the other way around?"—or the ominous moment in "Love Lies Sleeping" when the reader is invited to imagine how the world at morning looks in the eyes of a dead person,

> whose face is turned
> so that the image of

the city grows down into his open eyes
inverted and distorted.

(*CP*, p. 17)

In the two-sentence "Sonnet," we even see a small stylistic manifestation of this trope in the positioning of implied sestet before octave, a playful inversion of Petrarchan form.[11]

This recurrent pattern or gestalt, which I am suggesting is linked to Bishop's sense of herself as sexually atypical, is, not surprisingly, frequently played out as the inversion or upsetting of gender categories, as when Bishop adopts the masculine persona of the Prodigal or of Crusoe, for example, or when, in the uncollected poem "Exchanging Hats" she satirically depicts "Unfunny uncles who insist / in trying on a lady's hat" and "Anandrous aunts" who "keep putting on the yachtsmen's caps."

For a more subtle example of the blurring of gender boundaries, one might consider the conclusion of "At the Fishhouses," in which Bishop associates knowledge with seawater—a "bitter" draught that is life-sustaining:

> It is like what we imagine knowledge to be:
> dark, salt, clear, moving, utterly free,
> drawn from the cold hard mouth
> of the world, derived from the rocky breasts
> forever, flowing and drawn, and since
> our knowledge is historical, flowing and flown.
>
> (*CP*, p. 66)

The shift here from "mouth" to "breasts" is left confusing and evocative, but one way of reading this passage is as a compressed and hauntingly odd story of origin in which father and mother, male and female, are peculiarly conflated. Knowledge or human experience is linked to the sea, the origin of terrestrial life, and it issues from the world's "cold hard mouth," which may, without too much strain, remind us not only of fissures and faults in the earth's crust but also of the numerous creation myths in which some male god expectorates or speaks the world into being, including the account in Genesis of the creation of World from Word, the Logos of God, the ultimate father. But this origin story is baffling, because knowledge here becomes a nourishment and a need that we draw in like (or with) our mothers' milk from breasts "rocky" rather than soft and warm. Both implied parental figures, following this line of thinking, are associated with rock-like hardness or resistance, even as the image of seawater symbolically conflates more fluid male and female properties—seawater as semen, as amniotic fluid, or as mother's milk.

The questioning or blurring of gender boundaries implied in these last examples is effected to a certain extent as well by the organizing trope I have designated thirdness. By the use of this term, I do not mean to promote a homophobic version of gayness as oddity or unnaturalness but rather to condense into one word what seems to me Bishop's own sense, as communicated by her poetry, of vagary, indefiniteness, gender in-betweenness—together with her sense that in indefinition resides possibility, the chance for almost alchemical change into some other reality, some third thing or tertium quid.[12]

The most extended example of this trope may be found in Bishop's 1978 poem, "Santarém," in which she describes the confluence of two South American rivers:

> That golden evening I really wanted to go no farther;
> more than anything else I wanted to stay awhile
> in that conflux of two great rivers, Tapajós, Amazon,
> grandly, silently flowing, flowing east.
> Suddenly there'd been houses, people, and lots of mongrel
> riverboats skittering back and forth
> under a sky of gorgeous, under-lit clouds,
> with everything gilded, burnished along one side,
> and everything bright, cheerful, casual—or so it looked.
> I liked the place; I liked the idea of the place.
> Two rivers. Hadn't two rivers sprung
> from the Garden of Eden? No, that was four
> and they'd diverged. Here only two
> and coming together. Even if one were tempted
> to literary interpretations
> such as: life/death, right/wrong, male/female
> —such notions would have resolved, dissolved, straight off
> in that watery, dazzling dialectic.

(CP, p. 185)

This passage, witty in its built-in invitation to and dismissal of "literary interpretations," is unusually forthright for Bishop in some ways: the speaker, using the first-person pronoun, tells us repeatedly what she "wanted" and "liked"; the magical or alchemical transformation of ordinary reality evoked by "golden evening" and "everything gilded" is not seriously undermined by the force of the more unprepossessing "mongrel riverboats" or by the appended skepticism of the phrase "or so it looked." Conveying an almost religious sense of spiritual arrival, these lambent lines are reminiscent of the conclusion of "The Fish," with its "rainbow" in place of this poem's "golden" and its "little rented boat" in place of "mongrel riverboats."

The essential elements of a poetics are here. The captured moment resembles a Wordsworthian "spot of time"—although Bishop, who jokingly referred to herself as a "minor female Wordsworth" (Bishop to Robert Lowell, 11 July 1951, HL), modestly casts doubt on her own powers by beginning her poem, "Of course I may be remembering it all wrong." Paradoxically, and characteristically for this poet, the desire to recollect coexists with an equal passion for change; what she wants to hold on to is flux. The transfixed speaker wants "to stay *awhile*": her moment of spiritual arrival is also a moment of travel that takes place at the "con*flux*" of two rivers, which are themselves (and Bishop here repeats a favorite word) constantly "flowing." The location is watery, shifting (c.f., "Pleasure Seas," "The Bight," "The Fish," "At the Fishhouses"), and the time is evening, a time of change between night and day. (So many Bishop poems take place at the transitional times of dawn or evening—"Roosters," for instance, and "At the Fishhouses"—times linked to the liminal state between sleeping and waking that evidently enabled this poet's dreamy divagations and suited her sense of herself.) Here, in a place that is and is not like Eden, the homely ("mongrel riverboats") and the extraordinary ("everything gilded") merge, together with the Tapajós and Amazon rivers. Here, too, through the force of the concourse image, cardinal dualities are resolved by being dissolved[13]—as though immutable difference were merely a trivial matter of "literary interpretations."

Yet the evocative stanza, like passages in "Pleasure Seas" and elsewhere in Bishop's work, invites interpretation of the implied personal narrative beneath the description. In the view before her, the speaker sees herself, or rather her wish for herself. Out of paired oppositions, which include the dichotomy of "male/female," the notion of some third thing emerges, blurred and indistinct like the confluence of two distinct rivers. And for a moment that tertium quid meets with something like cosmic approval, as the scene is "gilded" by the evening sun. The traveler finds the watery setting "cheerful," rather than "awful but cheerful," as in "The Bight": in this late poem, Bishop is less qualified in her pleasure or gaiety, even as she is seemingly more at ease with her gayness.

We can see a much earlier and more troubled manifestation of third-ness in Bishop's Man-Moth, a composite creature or shadowy third thing that, like the watery "conflux," also emerges from the conjunction of two known things. One passage from the penultimate stanza of "The Man-Moth" is especially arresting in regard to this trope and disturb-ing in its implications about the young Bishop's experience of her sexual orientation:

He does not dare look out the window,
for the third rail, the unbroken draught of poison,
runs there beside him. He regards it as a disease
he has inherited the susceptibility to. He has to keep
his hands in his pockets, as others must wear mufflers.

(*CP*, p. 15)

A hyphenated monstrosity—a "mistake" created by a newspaper error—the Man-Moth suggests the witty young author's anxiety about her-self as somehow monstrous. (As in "Pleasure Seas," "Rainy Season; Sub-Tropics," "Some Dreams They Forgot," and other works, "poison" is here peculiarly associated with this poet's anxiety.) Like the young Bishop, the Man-Moth is fearful and yet persevering. A melancholic, with his slyly palmed tear, he is also by implication a sort of artist (his tear-production seen as an offering "from underground springs and pure enough to drink").

The same conjunction of elements found in this poem—strangeness or monstrosity, the evocation of darkness and dream life, fear and anxiety as prevalent emotions, the teardrop image, the suggestion of emergent artistry—Bishop readers can find also in "The Weed," another poem from the 1930s. "The Weed" offers a somewhat more subtle example of the trope of thirdness I have been discussing, because it recounts a dream in which, from the two halves of a severed heart, a third thing, the strange and transformative weed, emerges.

There are, of course, other obvious and subtle manifestations, but let me conclude this discussion of thirdness by touching on two related stylistic features. There is, first of all, Bishop's previously mentioned pre-dilection for trimeter, as in the metrical and incantatory "Insomnia" or in more loosely structured free-verse poems such as "First Death in Nova Scotia" or "In the Waiting Room." It is perhaps to be expected that a mind organized hoveringly above the prospect or promise of thirdness would find expression so often in a sculpted three-beat line. Second, in Bishop's penchant for verbal indecision—e.g., "commerce or contemplation" ("Large Bad Picture"), "enemy, or friend" ("Roosters"), "*Mont d'Espoir* or *Mount Despair*" ("Crusoe in England")—we see how a shadowy, if more apt, third term is implied by the oscillation between two opposing terms. In each of these cases (as well as in less clear-cut cases such as "Pleasure Seas," where we are poised between the opposing terms of "Grief" and "Pleasure," the "poisonous" and the "fabulous"), it is as if the poet positions her reader at the interstice, leaving the puzzle of an unsupplied term that would be part this and part that, a something else that exists only in imagination.

V

This brings the discussion back to Bishop's "rainbow-bird" in "Sonnet," yet another tertium quid—a creature part this and part that, hyphenated and hypothetical, like the Man-Moth. And it brings me to some final consideration of her final poem. "Sonnet" is a relatively minor production, but in it we can see condensed the poet's persistent interests, the three nouns in this essay's title. Colorful and cheerful, this is a poem of gaiety, like the early "Pleasure Seas," that moves toward freedom as it moves toward the final adjective, "gay." It contains, as has been indicated, the two recurrent tropes that I have linked to Bishop's sense of her lesbianism or gayness. Here, however, both tropes are evoked to be in some way discarded. That is, inversion—which shows up not only in the stylistic reversal, previously mentioned, of Petrarchan form but also in the conjured notion of a mirror image (familiar to us from "Insomnia" and "The Gentleman of Shallot")—is in a sense abandoned with the presentation of an "empty mirror" that cannot deliver a message of unsettling division or inversion. And the third thing here is not shadowy, fearful, or restricted to a single location. Instead, the bright, rather Ariel-like "rainbow-bird" flits off cheerfully, "wherever it feels like."

That is, of course, the happy ending. On the other hand, we must also acknowledge that another, less-cheerful narrative inhabits these few lines. To be at once free and gay in Bishop's poignant as well as playful short poem (and the words "free and gay" at one point in the re-vision process were the final words) is also in some way to have been "broken" like the thermometer or to be disembodied like the prismatic light that glances off the bevel of the ominously "empty mirror." Being free and gay may not, the poem suggests, be possible in this life. Like other Bishop poems, "Sonnet" possesses a double edge, what Octavio Paz (1983) called "the lightness of a game and the gravity of a decision" (p. 212).

Change, the third and final constant in Bishop's poetics, is here again apparent, and to conclude, I am interested in lingering for a moment on a particular embodiment of change—the "broken thermometer's mer-cury." This imagistic phrase suggests a mnemonic that can be associated with Bishop, containing as it does a single word encapsulating the poet's salient characteristics. Mercury, as the Roman god of the roads, was the patron of travelers. He was said to have invented the lyre (from which, *lyric*) by noon on the day he was born. From Mercury we get, of course, our elegant adjective for changeable. Devotees of mysticism and alchemy called him Hermes Trismegistus, associating him with magic, alchemical change, "hermetic" secrecy.[14] In a further association, the Greek Hermes conducted the souls of the dead to Hades and was the god of sleep and dreams. In both Greek and Roman views, Hermes/Mercury was the winged messenger of the gods. Under this rubric, Elizabeth Bishop is a lyric poet obsessed with change, a traveler of roads all over the globe, a bringer of new information from the silvery world of mirrors and dreams, a teller and keeper of secrets. Because Mercury was the god of gain and luck, he may also stand in this mnemonic for Bishop's gaiety, her insistence throughout her career on kaleidoscopic possibility—not ex-cluding, for all her presentation of the contrary condition, the possibility of pleasure.

Notes

1. The figure of sea as ballroom appears in Bishop's 1937 "Song" (*Uncol-lected Work*):

Summer is over upon the sea.
The pleasure yacht, the social being,
that danced on the endless polished floor,
stepped and side-stepped like Fred Astaire,
is gone, is gone, docked somewhere ashore.

2. This passage from David Kalstone's working notes is quoted by James Merrill in his afterword to Kalstone 1989, p. 252.

3. "You just wish," Bishop (1983) said of this new and indiscreet breed of American poets, "they'd keep some of these things to themselves" (p. 303).

4. See Bishop's "Poem," from *Geography III* (*CP*, pp. 176–77).

5. Bishop's choice of poetic material in relation to her adaptation of the projects of other Anglo-American poets (George Herbert, William Wordsworth, and Marianne Moore) is discussed in Merrin 1990.

6. In a college theme entitled "Gerard Manley Hopkins: Notes on Timing in His Poetry," Bishop quoted this phrase from Croll 1929 (Rare Books and Manuscripts, VC).

7. Carolyn Handa (1986) registers this fact and discusses change in somewhat different terms in "Vision and Change: The Poetry of Elizabeth Bishop," pp. 18–34.

8. Adrienne Rich (1983) discusses Bishop as a lesbian poet: "Moreover, it is only now, with a decade of feminist and lesbian poetry and criticism behind us and with the publication of these *Complete Poems,* that we can read her as part of a female and lesbian tradition rather than simply as one of the few and 'exceptional' women admitted to the male canon" (pp. 134–35). Rich also writes in this essay, and I concur, that "Bishop was critically and consciously trying to explore marginality, power and powerlessness, often in poetry of great beauty and sensuousness" (p. 135).

9. Elizabeth Taylor, in "Romance, Reality, and the Cryptic Nature of Elizabeth Bishop's 'Insomnia,'" a paper written for my spring 1991 graduate seminar in lyric poetry at Ohio State University, noted similarities between Lewis Carroll's and Elizabeth Bishop's worlds of inversion.

10. Adrienne Rich (1986) also acknowledges this sense of *invert,* referring to it as "the old jargon" (p. 129).

11. Charles Sanders (1982) makes this observation about the inverted form of Bishop's "Sonnet"; see pp. 63–64.

12. Some feminist critics have seen in lesbian subjectivity or identity (not necessarily linked by these critics to sexual preference and practice) a positive force for the destruction of sexual categories, classes, and contracts. For example, see Wittig 1981: "Lesbian is the only concept I know of which is beyond the categories of sex (woman and man), because the designated subject (lesbian) is not a woman, either economically, or politically, or ideologically" (p. 53); and Lauretis 1990.

13. Joanne Feit Diehl (1985) sees in this "alluvial dialectic" Bishop's "attempt to free herself from the Emersonian tradition" together with an eschewal on Bishop's part of "the hieratic distinctions of self-other which are its foundation" (p. 131).

14. Hermes/Mercury is also, of course, a trickster and the patron of thieves. I have let these associations go, although one might allude here to Bishop's rhetorical sleights of hand and to her adaptations of literary models such as George Herbert and Gerard Manley Hopkins. For critical discussions creatively linking the figure of Hermes/Mercury to signification, secrecy, and hermeneutics, see Derrida 1981 and Kermode 1979.

PART III

Bishop and Literary Tradition

JACQUELINE VAUGHT BROGAN

Elizabeth Bishop:
Perversity *as Voice*

THERE MAY BE no more traditional way of defining the "Poet" —and, by extension, the lyric itself—than that found in William Wordsworth's Preface to *Lyrical Ballads:* "What is a Poet? To whom does he address himself? And what language is expected from him?— He is a man *speaking* to men" (italics mine). In recent years, the philosophical assumptions underlying these three questions (specifically the nature of author, audience, and the Logos itself) have all been challenged by poststructuralist critics and theorists; the sexual bias that informs the presumption of a masculine identity for author (and audience) throughout most of our canonized literature and criticism certainly has been exposed by a number of recent feminist critiques.[1] Nevertheless, our tendency to associate the lyric as a genre with an authentic poetic voice has remained largely unchallenged.[2]

In the hands of Elizabeth Bishop, however, we see in praxis a deliberate subversion, even perversion (to adapt her own word), of what we might call the dominant (and dominating) poetics of the lyric, particularly as it is made manifest in the poetry of Wallace Stevens, that poet with whom, ironically, she is most often compared.[3] Although especially obvious in the contrast between her "Quai d'Orléans," written in 1938, and Stevens's "Idea of Order at Key West," written only four years before, Bishop's subversions of this particular genre extend from the "The Map" (*CP*, p. 3), which opens her first book of poetry, to her final "Sonnet" (*CP*, p. 192), published only a few weeks after her death. Far from being "one of the formulators" of "lyrically expositional verse," as she has been recently called (James William Johnson, 1986, p. 130), in any

175

traditional way, Bishop emerges as a poet who not only challenges our basic assumptions about the lyric, but one who does so in such a way that her poetic strategies have ramifications that extend well into the realm of feminist and political concerns. In this regard, that supposedly traditional, most reticent, even modest poet places herself ironically well on the side of social revolution.[4]

On the surface, Bishop hardly appears revolutionary, much less "perverse." Curiously, in a century marked by great poetic experimentation (Pound's well-known injunction to "MAKE IT NEW" also meant to "make it modern"),[5] Bishop repeatedly, perhaps perversely, turned to traditional lyric forms, such as ballads, sonnets, and sestinas, often using very traditional prosodic and rhetorical devices, such as tercets and anaphora, as well. In addition, her tone, one of almost inviolable civility, has seemed to most critics the model of poetic decorum: as Sherod Santos (1984) notes, Bishop's "sense of reserve, both in and out of her work, is famous by now" (p. 31). Furthermore, Bishop's work specifically calls attention to the genre within which she most characteristically works by appealing to that other traditional aspect of the lyric voice—its musicality. Lines such as "Shadows, or are they shallows, at its edges / showing the line of long sea-weeded ledges" or "Along the fine tan sandy shelf / is the land tugging at the sea from under" (*CP*, p. 3)—lines taken from the poem that opens both her first book of poetry and the *Collected Poems* as well—evoke, almost excessively, the musical charm that we associate with this genre.[6]

Yet it is precisely because her own lyrics seem so traditional and even reserved that Bishop challenges the lyric tradition—particularly the notion of the authentic lyric voice—as perhaps no other twentieth-century poet (or critic, for that matter) can. As Thomas A. Greene (1982) has noted in a somewhat different context, "The poetic word achieves its brilliance against the background of a past which it needs in order to signify but which its own emergence is tendentiously and riskily shaping" (p. 19)—a statement that could well apply to Bishop's verse. In fact, it may be fair to say that Bishop needs the tradition of a "man speaking to men" to reshape (perhaps tendentiously, but certainly with great risk) our culturally inherited conflation of the lyric with an authentic and authoritative voice. For all her apparent reticence, Bishop uses her own lyrics (and to some extent her prose and prose-poems, as well) to expose the lyric voice itself, with its implicit and traditional associations with authenticity, originality, and authority, as a manifestation of a traditionally dominant (and dominating) phallic poetics. That is, her lyrics

undermine the essentially logocentric and equally phallocentric belief in
that "constructive faculty" that "orders" chaos into meaning.[7]

This subversive, even perverse intent is nowhere more ironically
stated than in "Quai d'Orléans," first written and published in 1938:

Each barge on the river easily tows
    a mighty wake,
a giant oak-leaf of gray lights
    on duller gray;
and behind it real leaves are floating by,
    down to the sea.
Mercury-veins on the giant leaves,
    the ripples, make
for the sides of the quai, to extinguish themselves
    against the walls
as softly as falling-stars come to their ends
    at a point in the sky.
And throngs of small leaves, real leaves, trailing them,
    go drifting by
to disappear as modestly, down the sea's
    dissolving halls.
We stand still as stones to watch
    the leaves and ripples
while light and nervous water hold
    their interview.
"If what we see could forget us half as easily,"
    I want to tell you,
"as it does itself—but for life we'll not be rid
    of the leaves' fossils."

(*CP,* p. 28)

In the simplest and (I want to stress) most superficial of terms, "Quai
d'Orléans" is rather obviously concerned with linguistic representation
and its groundless relation to human consciousness. Ruthlessly, for all its
modest tone, this poem exposes the apparently unavoidable projection of
human consciousness onto nature as an imprisoning act, while simultaneously disclosing nature's utter indifference to and lack of responsibility
in this scripting.

The "wake" that trails "Each barge" appears, but only to the human mind, analogous to a "giant oak-leaf of gray lights / on duller gray." The imaged "giant leaves" rapidly take on more anthropomorphic terms, the "Mercury-veins" of the ripples evoking a rather gruesome analogy to the human hand. The projection of human consciousness extends from the ripples, leaves, and veins to the heavens where (again, implicitly) the brevity of a falling star evokes a sense of the brevity and consequent preciousness of human life. Yet it is much to the point that these human analogies are never directly stated but instead are something that we, as readers, provide. This scripting continues until the human is finally and ironically described in terms of nature ("We stand still as stones"), thus inverting the direction of the reading—which is, precisely, reflection. The irony here is that the presumed liberation of human consciousness becomes literally a conscription, an escalating act of the mind that finds itself increasingly caught in its own reflections. In contrast, "what we see" forgets itself, while the human, the victim of consciousness, cannot get "rid / of the leaves' fossils." The final image at once represents the ironic awareness of mortality and the inescapable temporality of consciousness itself that records or engraves this mortality. We have, then, an almost perfectly Paul-de-Manian poem but with no authorial (or authoritative) delusion that some logocentric resolution for this catastrophe will be achieved through the metaphors of the poem.

Yet, as I suggested, such a reading is superficial and finally reductive. Although this text is disturbing enough, what is even more chilling is the subtext, which is figured imagistically (and perhaps phonically) by the quai itself and signalled by the single word *modestly,* that so femininely laden word.[8] Both gesture toward the poem's white writing, which can be heard only as and in con-text.

Although the total context of this poem is quite complicated (including, as I think it does, women's gaining of political voice only one decade before, as well as the rather consistent denigration of women poets when Bishop first began practicing her craft),[9] the most critical con-text of this poem is the genre within which it is written—specifically, the prevailing assumption that the lyric is defined by a spoken, authentic voice, an assumption that extends from before Wordsworth well into the twentieth century. As different as we may consider modernist and postmodernist poetry to be from that written before, we have largely retained some notion of authenticity in the lyric voice as an unchallenged assumption that has continued to be disseminated until the most recent of critical discussions. For instance, even in 1957 (and through the various reprintings of *Anatomy of Criticism* over the next decade), Northrop Frye (1965) defined the lyric in that most influential of his works as being "preeminently the utterance that is overheard" (p. 249). Even though (in contrast to Wordsworth) the audience has disappeared from Frye's definition, the idea that an authentic voice is somehow present in the text—and ultimately identical to the lyric genre itself—is one that remains intact. Only recently has this assumption been challenged. As Jonathan Culler (1985) notes, "Critics are beginning to consider the fact that voice in lyric is a *figure* and to explore the role of this figure of voicing" (p. 50), as does Paul de Man (1985), for example, when he questions whether the "principle of intelligibility" in the lyric really "depends on the phenomenalization of the poetic voice" (p. 55).

Nevertheless, such critical speculations were clearly not part of the context when Bishop began writing her own verse. But other contemporary lyrics were. As a part of that particular context, Wallace Stevens's "Idea of Order at Key West" (first published in 1934 and reprinted as the title poem of *Ideas of Order* in 1935 and again in 1936) may be said to epitomize the assumptions inherent in the traditional lyric context, even con-text, against which "Quai d'Orléans" achieves, quite literally, its resonance. Stevens's poem may even be the specific pro-vocation for Bishop's poem (providing a con-text that is signalled by the homophonic pun of *quai* and *key*), and in this regard it is interesting to note that Bishop corresponded with Marianne Moore specifically about Stevens's verse (although, perhaps surprisingly, they did not correspond much about the work of other contemporary poets) and that she intended two years after writing "Quai d'Orléans" to produce what a friend described as a " 'tript-itch' of Key West poems" (Bishop to Marianne Moore, 26 February 1940 [in reference to "Cootchie," *CP*, p. 46], in MacMahon 1980, p. 146). And even though mere biographical and geographical accident might explain the latter intention, nonetheless, "Sunday at Key West," a poem Bishop enclosed in a letter (dated 14 February 1938) to Marianne Moore (MacMahon, p. 209), points rather obviously toward Stevens:

> The rocking-chairs
>   In rapid motion
> Approach the object
>   Of devotion.
> Rock on the porches
>   of the tabernacle:

With a palm-leaf fan
> Cry Hail, all Hail!

(*CP*, p. 206)

While this lyric (like many of Stevens's) challenges traditional religious structure and orders, the revisionist focus of this small poem appears to mock both the alternate "devotion to the sun" posited in Stevens's "Sunday Morning" (Stevens 1954, p. 70) and the "Blessed rage for order" praised in "The Idea of Order at Key West" (p. 130).[10] In addition, although Bishop says that "Sunday at Key West" is really "about" her landlady (*CP*, p. 206), there is notably no woman in Bishop's poem (either "complacent," as in "Sunday Morning" or "singing," as in "The Idea of Order") but rather a figurative absence or negation between the "rocking" and the "Rock" that yields, if it does, ironically and with great resistance to the discourse of authority. The effect of this resistance is to contradict the very presumptions of "originality"—those words "of ourselves and of our origins" (Stevens 1954, p. 130)—so authoritatively voiced in Stevens's poems, specifically in "The Idea of Order at Key West."

Although it would be a serious mistake to reduce Stevens's entire corpus to espousing one particular stance,[11] Stevens's "The Idea of Order at Key West" (reprinted in part below) is a "supreme" expression of that belief in poetic/phallic dominance:

> She sang beyond the genius of the sea.
> The water never formed to mind or voice,
> Like a body wholly body, fluttering
> Its empty sleeves; and yet its mimic motion
> Made constant cry, caused constantly a cry,
> That was not ours though we understood,
> Inhuman, of the veritable ocean.
>
> . . . .
> It was her voice that made
> The sky acutest at its vanishing.
> She measured to the hour its solitude.
> She was the single artificer of the world
> In which she sang. And when she sang, the sea,
> Whatever self it had, became the self

That was her song, for she was the maker. Then we,
As we beheld her striding there alone,
Knew that there never was a world for her
Except the one she sang and, singing, made.

Ramon Fernandez, tell me, if you know,
Why, when the singing ended we turned
Toward the town, tell why the glassy lights,
The lights in the fishing boats at anchor there,
As the night descended, tilting in the air,
Mastered the night and portioned out the sea,
Fixing emblazoned zones and firey poles,
Arranging, deepening, enchanting night.

Oh! Blessed rage for order, pale Ramon,
The maker's rage to order words of the sea,
Words of the fragrant portals, dimly-starred,
And of ourselves and of our origins,
In ghostlier demarcations, keener sounds.

Contrary to most criticism on this poem, it is not the supposedly elo-
quent and elegantly figured muse nor the assertion that "when she sang,
the sea / Whatever self it had, became the self / That was her song, for
she was the maker" (Stevens 1954, p. 129) that is ultimately the most
striking about this poem, but rather the utterly self-conscious way in
which "she" is exposed or appropriated within the fiction of the poem
as a figure for Stevens himself and his "rage to order." This particular
circumscription may well be the most revealing mark of the nature of
the "idea of order" Stevens has in mind: at the specific moment that
he breaks into the text, abruptly addressing Ramon Fernandez with the
question about the "Mastering" of the night and the "portioning of the
sea" (thus implicitly questioning the very idea of order that he is positing), Stevens places himself in a textual and hierarchical order above
nature, above friend, and above the muse as artificer, inscribing himself as the author/authority of the world in which he sings. Here logo-
and phallocentric assumptions of order coincide, forming a textual crux
that glosses over the apparent exposure of the fictionality of the poetic
word. It is not without significance that the muse is always referred to
in the past tense: she literally is not present in the text. Thus, although

the conclusion of the poem may imply that words are much like Derrida's "trace" (only "ghostly demarcations," even de-marcations), the tone of this poem is one of unwavering faith in poetic/phallic dominance. There is none of that uncertainty, reticence, or prolonged and painful questioning so characteristic of Bishop's verse.

Seen in this context, Bishop's "Quai d'Orléans" becomes a highly subversive text that is engaged in re-marking, if not violating, the terms and intent of this male canon. Notably, in both poems, the two figures (the presence of whom is withheld until the end) standing or walking by water contemplate the relation between the human and the natural world. In both, this problematic relation is dramatized by the speaker's unexpected intrusion into the voice of the poem. And in both poems the final words point to the ironic contradiction between the human's conscious linguistic constructs and the unconscious (and therefore potentially unstructured) phenomenological world. At this point any similarity between the poems ends, however, and Bishop inverts the constraints necessitated by this possible contextual allusion—but certainly by the expectations of an authentic lyric voice—into a subversion of feminine constraint (and restraint) itself. As Alicia Ostriker (1982) points out, "Whenever a poet employs a figure or story previously accepted and defined by a culture, the poet is using myth, and the potential is always present that the use will be revisionist; that is, the figure or tale will be appropriated for altered ends . . . ultimately making cultural change possible" (p. 69). From this perspective, Bishop's poem might be called "Ideas of (Dis)Order." From her vantage point, Bishop sees a space in which is configured not instances of creative domination but rather instances of modest disappearing, even extinction. Furthermore, in Bishop's poem there is no muse—no figure to be appropriated as confirmation of poetic authority. But even more provocative is the fact that, in contrast to Stevens's very authorial voice, the supposed speaker of the poem does not speak but only "want[s]" to say.

This intensely ironic inversion, in which the quoted words remain unspoken within the fiction of the text, reveal the speaker to be a writer, thus essentially deferred from the presumed authenticity of the lyric. That is to say, this poem cannot be understood without engaging in the fiction that it does not exist precisely because it is not spoken. And yet, there it is, "word for word" (Stevens 1954, p. 512), as Stevens "says" in one of his later poems. The almost shimmering tension between the text's presence and its ironic representation of itself as an absence hollows the space (however ironically we may describe it) where Bishop is most acutely heard. In contrast to the expected lyric voice, we are offered here only silence—that empty cipher of feminine erasure—which is inscribed quite deliberately into the text as a sign of what the writer wants to say and cannot do (that is, re-mark). The subject of this subtext, then, is perversely a nonperformative, the very performance of which ironically instantiates its conditions and undermines its terms.

As such, this poem seems to me a tour de force of feminine repression and of feminist expression. Yet what may ultimately be even more perverse, even more disturbing, about this poem is its implicit degendering of its readers—a radical subversion achieved through the conversation between its surface text and subtext. This poem at least implies that the prison of consciousness is metonymic for the cultural position of women or that the cultural conscription of women is metonymic for the conscription of all human consciousness. At this point gender distinctions break down: we are all *women*, victimized by the very consciousness that tries to impose order, even if that order is meaning. This is a highly disturbing, even perverse, suggestion, but one that ultimately and successfully escapes the binary oppositions that, I think, Bishop is trying to escape in the very subversion of the expected "lyric voice" itself.

We find similar strategies in Bishop's "In Prison," a story of sorts written the same year as "Quai d'Orléans" that could, if pursued, present its own challenge to genre expectations.[12] Yet what is important here is that this work not only uses similar subversive techniques as those found in "Quai d'Orléans" but that it clarifies the purpose of such subversions. Whereas the title leads us to expect a dramatic situation in which a character is already in prison, the presumed speaker of the story begins with this rather odd statement: "I can scarcely wait for the day of my imprisonment" (*CProse,* p. 181). As surprising as this may be, this desire is made even more peculiar by the following aside, which follows immediately in the text: "The reader, or my friends, particularly those who happen to be familiar with my way of life, may protest that for me any actual imprisonment is unnecessary, since I already live, in relationship to society, very much as if I were in a prison" (*CProse,* p. 181). Addressed to the reader, this aside encourages us to think not of the expected speaker but of a writer. I find it almost impossible not to think of the writer—that is, Bishop herself—and of her relationship to society as a woman.[13]

The most critical passage in this work occurs toward the end, however, when the writer explains the hope to be given in prison "one very dull book to read . . . perhaps the second volume, if the first would familiarize me too well with the terms and purpose of the work. Then I shall be able to experience with a free conscience the pleasure, *perverse,* I suppose, of interpreting it not all according to its intent" (*CProse*, pp. 187–88; italics mine). The specific conjunction of the word *perverse* (etymologically "per-verse," "through the turn") with books, their "terms," and their "intent" underscores the narrative and textual desire of this piece to escape both intellectual and linguistic dominance. This motif continues throughout the story, most obviously in the one paragraph that is (unexpectedly) *labeled* "Writing on the Wall." Here, this dramatic monologue, now more clearly a monograph, becomes specifically textual and con-textual: "I have formulated very definite ideas on this important aspect of prison life. . . . The voice of a new inmate will be noticeable, but there will be no contradictions or criticism of what has already been laid down, rather a 'commentary' " (*CProse*, p. 188).

Although this intention may not appear, at least initially, very subversive, the critical and even specific textual irony is that Bishop, once again, is inverting the notion of voice itself. There is no voice, neither of a "new inmate" nor of the author, for in both cases the supposed speaker is a writer and, like language itself, already silent, erased, even conscripted. As the writer finally explains, however, there is subversive purpose to this conscription: the intention is to be, within the severe constraints of prison, "unconventional, rebellious perhaps, but in shades and shadows" (*CProse*, p. 189) and further, by means of a "carefully subdued, reserved manner" to become "an *influence*" (italics Bishop's) and an "authority" (*CProse*, p. 190)—which also means author. This intention, I think, could well describe the intention of the writer—that is, of Bishop herself—in many of her works, most notably in her supposedly reticent and modest lyric poems.

As an ironically concealed manifesto, "In Prison" provides additional insight not only into the intent of "Quai d'Orléans" but also into many other of her lyrics as well. In "Insomnia," for example, we "drop . . . down the well / into that world inverted" (*CP*, p. 70); and in "Sleeping Standing Up," the "world turns half away / through ninety dark degrees" (*CP*, p. 30), both poems (also written in 1938) turning upon visual rather than vocal inversions. Such techniques are in fact so consistently thematized throughout her work that our recognition of them seems nearly inexhaustible once we attend them. The mountains in "Questions of Travel" look "like the hulls of capsized ships" (*CP*, p. 93), another example of her many visual inversions. Even in "The Monument," that superficially most structured of poems, it is precisely the carefully constructed "view's perspective" (*CP*, p. 23) that becomes disordered within the poem itself, leaving us as disoriented as the disembodied "voice" that unpredictably appears:

> "Why does that strange sea make no sound?
> Is it because we're far away?
> Where are we? Are we in Asia Minor,
> or in Mongolia?"

> (*CP*, p. 23)

Though perhaps not in any obvious way aligned with feminist expression, Bishop's continued attempts to disorder visual perspective are, quite specifically, the revisionary counterpart to her attempt to dismantle the largely phallocentric perspective that dominates not only our dominant poetics but our culture as well. As such, it is almost inevitable that Bishop's subversion of the lyric would frequently challenge reigning political structures as well.

This aspect of Bishop's work has, so far, been almost completely ignored, a fact that, in itself, points to the consequences of those very political structures. As already suggested, it has become almost a critical commonplace to remark on this female poet's "decorum," her "modesty," and her "reticence." Not surprisingly perhaps, there is a "history" to this critical attitude as well: as Lloyd Schwartz and Sybil Estess note in their introduction to *Elizabeth Bishop and Her Art* (1983), in 1946 Oscar Williams set the "tone" for "years of critical misconception, effusion, or condescension" by "praising her 'exquisite detail' and 'charming little stained-glass bits' " (p. xvii) (phrases notably reminiscent of those used to describe—and to criticize—other female poets such as Emily Dickinson and Amy Lowell).[14] Nonetheless, with only a few notable exceptions, this misconception continues to inform current critical appraisals of Bishop's work.[15] For example, Nathan A. Scott (1984) notes that "hers was, of course, a sensibility too chaste for her ever to have moaned about falling on the thorns of life," before concluding that "she appears as one of the most remarkable poets to have graced the American scene, no doubt not a major figure—not in the range of a Frost or a Stevens or a Carlos Williams—but one whose legacy will long be a bench mark against which false sentiment and specious eloquence will be severely judged" (p. 275). Scott makes overt what I find to be an implicit qualification, if not denigration, of Bishop's literary merits that can be found in much criticism of her poetry. At least in this instance, the implication is that Bishop's real talent lies in acting like a twentieth-century, even if somewhat anachronistic, Anne Elliot.

This is not to say that Bishop's work has not been genuinely appreciated. Her own contemporaries regarded her work quite highly, and many notable critics, such as Helen Vendler, John Hollander, Marjorie Perloff, and Robert Pinksy (to name only a few), assume her recognized place in the canon of major literature. Harold Bloom (1983) even suggests that she may be superior to other poets of her own generation (including Theodore Roethke, Robert Lowell, John Berryman, Randall Jarrell, and Charles Olson) and places her "securely in a tradition of American poetry that began with Emerson, Very, and Dickinson, and culminated in aspects of Frost as well as of Stevens and Moore," a tradition he further describes as being "marked by firm rhetorical control, overt moral authority, and sometimes by a fairly strict economy of means" (p. ix). It is not without significance, however, that Bishop's assumption here into a primarily male canon is made through presumptions of essentially masculine notions of poetic "control" and "authority." These are clearly words of domination and finally do not describe Bishop's poetry any more accurately than do words of reticence or modesty.

It is important to recognize that in almost all of her lyrics Bishop consistently undermines domination, whether poetically, phallically, or politically conceived. Just as she dismantles our expectations about the authority of lyric voice, she inverts a seemingly reticent language (the received legitimate linguistic domain of women) into a white writing that is designed to be, quite ironically, intensely revolutionary rather than merely reactionary.

Occasionally, as in "To Be Written on the Mirror in Whitewash," Bishop's white writing is not all that reticently inscribed:

> I live only here, between your eyes and you,
> But I live in your world. What do I do?
> —Collect no interest—otherwise what I can;
> Above all I am not that staring man.

(*CP*, p. 205)

Although the "staring man" points most directly to the ironic condemnation of phallocentric descriptions of women, even here there is a white (or silent) text that makes an even more ironic, if not perverse commentary.

Even as it is literally described, what is not inscribed is the effacement of women not by men but by women themselves as they adopt the dominant phallic perspective and learn to see themselves precisely as objects of reflection. Such commentary thoroughly belies the apparent humor of its whitewash. In addition, the pun on "interest" encourages a political (even Marxist) interpretation of the intersection of gender relations in this culture with the dominant economic structure of this culture.

In fact, well in advance of *Questions of Travel* (1965), a book that self-consciously questions the legitimacy of a Western European/American perspective, Bishop rather consistently uses her "subversive" lyrics to raise what I see as highly subversive, political questions. For example, in her first book of poems, *North & South* (the title of which recalls the social and political divisions of this supposedly unified country), the whole (il)logic of the opening poem "The Map" depends on a literal and figurative questioning of our normal modes of ordering the world:

> Or does the land lean down to lift the sea from under,
> drawing it unperturbed around itself?
> Along the fine tan sandy shelf
> is the land tugging at the sea from under?
>
> (*CP*, p. 3)

Within this particular visual inversion, it is quite in keeping with the poems previously discussed that Bishop reenvisions the peninsulas, a rather obviously phallic image, as women feeling the texture of cloth. What is more important here, however, is that in the poem's concluding lines Bishop questions not only the dominant phallic perspective of our culture but its corollary political categories, hierarchies, and prejudices as well:

> Are they assigned, or can the countries pick their colors?
> —What suits the character or the native waters best.
> Topography displays no favorites; North's as near as West.
> More delicate than the historians' are the map-makers' colors.

From a topographical perspective, this poem dismisses the legitimacy of such phrases as the *Far East* (with the concurrent privileging of the West) or the *northern hemisphere* (with the concurrent denigration of the southern). Yet, as the poem rather unnervingly suggests when the "names of cities" on the map "cross the neighboring mountains," even the relatively neutral mapmaker (like the poet) fixes a text—that is, fixes some perspective, however tolerant or liberal that perspective may be. Textuality, then, is as inescapable as it is conscripting. It is all the more critical, Bishop implies, that the perspective governing any text (whether political or poetic—if, indeed, they can be separated) be questioned.

Questions of perspective, phallocentric dominance, and the possible political consequence converge in many of Bishop's lyrics. In "The Roosters," for example, written during World War II, Bishop juxtaposes "the many wives / who lead hens' lives / of being courted and despised" (*CP*, p. 35) with the roosters

> making sallies
> from all the muddy alleys,
> marking out maps like Rand McNally's:
>
> glass-headed pins,
> oil-golds and copper greens,
> anthracite blues, alizarins,
>
> each one an active
> displacement in perspective.
>
> (*CP*, p. 36)

As she clarifies in a letter written to Marianne Moore, the "pins" refer to "the pins that point out war-projects on a map"; furthermore, the roosters have their source in the "violent roosters Picasso did in connection with his GUERNICA picture" (Bishop to Marianne Moore, 17 October 1940, in MacMahon 1980, p. 149). The total con-text, then, criticizes not only gender relations and roles in this culture but also the political and military structures that were realized as and in the two world wars.

We see a similar critique in "12 O'Clock News" (*CP*, pp. 174–75), a prose-poem written immediately after the official end of the Vietnam War, that appropriately dismantles even the categories that give rise to genre classifications. Although the prose text imitates the kind of voice and script heard on the nightly news, the marginalia (provided by Bishop as part of the text) glosses the "news" as the objects with which the news itself is written (*"typewriter," "typed sheet," "ink-bottle,"* etc.).[16] In the last two paragraphs, the Western "superior vantage point" is exposed not only as a text (that is, the supposedly neutral voice describing events is once again written) but also as a "deceptive illumination" that is biased,

oppressive, and ultimately aggressive. Yet, the identification of the supposed subject as the objects with which the news is written—and with
which the prose-poem is itself written—also implicitly reminds us that
such textuality (although unavoidable) is ultimately arbitrary, socially
bound, and finally groundless, even as it also reminds us that we are in-
capable of having a perspective, even the rather subversive one that the
prose-poem gives us, without a text.

Of all her poems, however, "In the Waiting Room" (the title of
which notably bears a certain affinity to "In Prison") most successfully
combines Bishop's ongoing concerns with the assumptions that underlie
poetic voice and phallic and political dominance. The superficial plot of
this late poem is that a child (revealed by the name inscribed within the
poem to be the poet as child, aged seven, and trapped, as it were, in
the waiting room) comes to a point of identification of herself and with
others at a critical textual intersection. While waiting for her Aunt Consuelo, the child reads the *National Geographic,* where she sees, among
other things,

> Babies with pointed heads
> wound round and round with string;
> black, naked women with necks
> wound round and round with wire
> like the necks of light bulbs.

(*CP,* p. 159)

The response of this well-bred, New England girl, is to continue reading:

> I was too shy to stop.
> And then I looked at the cover:
> the yellow margins, the date.
> Suddenly, from inside,
> came an *oh!* of pain
> —Aunt Consuelo's voice—
> not very loud or long.

(*CP,* pp. 159–60)

With a deft and intensely ironic repetition of cultural prejudices, Bishop
has the self-as-child then admit,

I wasn't at all surprised;
even then I knew she was
a foolish, timid woman.
I might have been embarrassed, but wasn't.

Then the child goes on to "say" something that is completely surprising:

What took me
completely by surprise
was that it was *me:*
my voice, in my mouth.
Without thinking at all
I was my foolish aunt,
I—we—were falling, falling

into the *National Geographic,* into the cultural text—and into the poem itself (*CP*, p. 160).

As Lee Edelman (1985) has already shown, critics have assumed that the child's identification is with the rest of humanity (largely a male concept in our existing linguistic constructs), whereas the specific provocation of this identification is, textually, with the others being victimized and objectified—that is, with the women and babies in the text (see in particular pp. 182–83, 191–92). In fact, the degree of Bishop's perversity in this poem may be most evident in the way she almost completely erases the child's identification with the women by having her say outright, "you are an *I*, / you are an *Elizabeth,* / you are one of *them*" (*CP*, p. 160). It is much to the point that it is almost impossible to hear her and that we as readers are tempted to see this painful moment of identification as a constructive act, in its Freudian, Oedipal, and essentially phallic sense.

Yet, as in several of the works discussed above, there is an even more important and subversive content to this particular poem, one aspect of which is found in the conjunction between the two culturally inscribed deformations; on the one hand, the binding of the women and children, reforming them as objects; and on the other, the unconsciously held but equally dehumanizing assumption that the aunt is dismissive as a "foolish" and "timid woman." The superficial contrast between the two cultures and their more significant similarity in their dominant and dominating perspectives is not readily cognizant to the child. But it is available to the adult poet, who writes in such a way that the vocalized pain comes literally from inside, at once from inside the child, from the aunt heard beyond the waiting room, and from the closed magazine or text itself. Yet in (utter) opposition to our expectations, *inside* in Bishop's poem fails to evoke immediacy, originality, much less our normal expectation of voice. Instead, from all its various sources, voice is experienced here as a "zero," a "void," a "figure in some predetermined social text" (Edelman 1985, p. 196). Yet it is critical to note that this text is extended by the date 1918 (inscribed both on the cover on the *National Geographic* and as the last word of the poem), which moves the poem into a specifically political context. Although clearly a feminist poem, the date of the poem encourages us to transfer the child's experience to the violent disorder and senseless victimization of those caught in the world at war. Much as she does in "Quai d'Orléans," Bishop manages to imply that the feminine experience may be equally metonymic and synecdochic for the whole violated human condition. The unspoken, white writing of this poem thus points toward the very cultural (and phallocentric) presuppositions about voice, author, and authority that encourage dominance, therefore suppression, and finally aggression in what may be called the genre of political war.

In this regard, "Manners" (subtitled "For a Child of 1918") proves especially intriguing. It is, as are many of Bishop's poems, ostensibly humorous in a wry and nostalgic sort of way. A grandchild, schooled by a grandfather in "good manners," learns the lesson well. Even in the face of dust thrown up by passing automobiles (the only overt sign in the poem of the changing times), the child riding in a wagon still shouts, "Good day! Good day!"—just as "good manners required" (*CP*, pp. 121–22). But with what we have seen of Bishop's other lyrics, we should be careful to attend to that which is not voiced. What is not spoken at the narrative level of the poem is precisely the issue of the "lost generation," an unspoken term implicitly evoked by the dedication that manages in this poem to include both sexes. Where in this time of war, which would so radically reconstruct the very constructs being prescribed by the grandfather, is the mother? And where is the father? "All our knowledge is historical" (*CP*, p. 66), as Bishop says in another poem; and it is ironically only with our most recent, even revisionary, historical knowledge that we can trace the empty ciphers of this poem with awareness of both the destructive and also liberating consequences of this time.[17] Ultimately, it is precisely a historical consciousness that will allow us to experience much that is not overtly articulated in Bishop's texts: the pain of subservience in "Cootchie" (*CP*, p. 46); the racial, sexual, and economic anguish in such seemingly humorous poems as "Songs for a Colored Singer" (*CP*, pp. 47–57) and "A Norther—Key West" (*CP*, p. 202); or the humiliation Bishop must have felt when she was forced to assume a male pseudonym on her first job as a teacher at place named (ironically and appropriately enough) the "U.S.A. School of Writing" (*CProse*, p. 48).

Yet despite such anguish, there is always about Bishop a certain humor, a certain health, that is ultimately essential to her voice, however subversive, even perverse, it may be; and it is a humor she exploits even in her last subversion of the lyric. Published in the *New Yorker* of 29 October 1979 only three weeks after she died from an aneurysm on 6 October, "Sonnet" perhaps ironically anticipates her unexpected death. In doing so, however, it also explores (and exploits) the final freedom from conscripting "literary interpretations" ("such as: life/death, right/wrong, male/female," as she writes in another very late poem, "Santarém" [*CP*, p. 185]). Although technically a sonnet in some ways because it has fourteen lines, an octet and sestet, Bishop's last lyric subverts the most famous lyric form by inverting the position of octet and sestet and by reducing the expected iambic pentameters to half-lines. Yet as this poem amply demonstrates, there is freedom, gaiety, and even (perversely) a kind of authority to be gained through such subversions. As she says in the (strictly speaking) fragment of the concluding octet to "Sonnet,"

> Freed—the broken
> thermometer's mercury
> running away;
> and the rainbow-bird
> from the narrow bevel
> of the empty mirror,
> flying wherever
> it feels like, gay!
>
> (*CP*, p. 192)

Finally, Bishop is neither reticent nor reactive but specifically active, both in terms of gender and in terms of political concerns, in ways that our critical enquiries have only recently begun to appreciate. In fact, she achieves as a poet what Frank Lentricchia (1983) has recently described as the "value" of Emerson's "active soul"—an intellectual "activity which does not passively 'see' " but which "constructs a point of view in its *engagement with textual events,* and in so contructing produces an image of history as social struggle, . . . an image that is not 'there' in a simple sense but is the discovery of the active intellectual soul" (p. 11, emphasis added). What remains to be discovered about her poetry will depend upon our ability to reevaluate her position and purpose in our canon. But, as Bishop optimistically concludes in another highly "perverse" poem ("Cirque d'Hiver"), "Well, we have come this far" (*CP,* p. 31).

Notes

1. I am assuming here a basic familiarity with both feminist writings and deconstruction, particularly the exposure of the traditional privileging of the spoken over the written and the corollary privileging of male over female, although the various works of such critics as Hélène Cixous, Sandra Gilbert, Susan Gubar, Luce Irigaray, Julia Kristeva, Alicia Ostriker, and Monique Wittig (as well as that of Jacques Derrida) would be helpful here.

2. Although the idea that voice is somehow more original (or logocentric) than the written sign has been thoroughly challenged by poststructuralist theorists, and although the cultural bias that encourages us to interpret voice as male has been exposed by feminist theorists, the application of those insights to our presumption of the authentic (and phallic) lyric voice in the lyric genre itself has been largely ignored. Two feminist critics do address the lyric as genre in *Lyric Poetry: After the New Criticism,* but they do so without exploring that aspect of lyric voice with which I am concerned here: see Barbara Johnson 1985 and Mary Nyquist 1985.

3. The word *perverse* is critical to "In Prison" (*CProse,* pp. 181–91). It is worth noting that although Harold Bloom acknowledges Wallace Stevens's influence on Bishop by noting that her late poem "The End of March" is, in part, an "affectionate ripose" of Stevens's *lion* (a figure for "the poet's will-to-power over reality"), Bloom emphasizes Bishop's relatively lighthearted "play of trope" rather than suggesting the more subversive strategy and intention I am describing here. See Bloom 1983, p. xi; and Stevens 1954.

4. In this way, Bishop satisfies Julia Kristeva's injunction, albeit in a way entirely different from what I think Kristeva intends, for women to adopt "a *negative* function: reject everything finite, definite, structure, loaded with meaning in the existing state of society." Such an "attitude," Kristeva adds, "puts women on the side of the explosion of social codes: with revolutionary movements." See Gauthier 1980, p. 166.

5. Although the self-conscious desire to be modern informed artistic developments throughout the early twentieth century, it was a desire expressed most eloquently perhaps, given our purposes here, in Wallace Stevens's 1940 lyric "Of Modern Poetry" (Stevens 1954, pp. 239–40).

6. As Barbara Johnson notes, "the musical element is intrinsic to the work [i.e., the lyric] intellectually as well as aesthetically" (Preminger 1986, p. 122).

7. The phrase is taken from Albert Gelpi's (1985) recent discussion of Wallace Stevens's and William Carlos Williams's shared belief in the poet's creative ability, which "pieces together connections from fragments . . . and thereby composes in a lifetime of poetry his relation to the world, his place in it, his passage through it" (see p. 7). In fact, the presumption of dominance in literary composition (and woman's displacement in that presumption) has had widespread currency.

8. In this regard, consider the fact that when the author is a woman, the adjectives that critics most consistently use to describe the work are not *great, forceful,* or *true* but (as Alicia Ostriker [1986] points out), "the diminutives: *graceful, subtle, elegant, delicate, cryptic,* and above all *modest*" (p. 3). Given the kind of reviews of contemporary woman poets that were published when Bishop was a young teenager (see below), she may have had this specific critical context in mind not only as she wrote the line cited above but also as she acted out the script of the modest female poet throughout her career.

9. Even Marianne Moore, for example, who was in many ways a mentor for Bishop, is negatively reviewed by Rolphe Humphries (1925) for her "clipped restraint" or her lack of "passion" (p. 16). It is much to the point that Humphries refers, in a derogatory fashion, to Moore and Emily Dickinson as "these girls" (p. 16). A similar, unconscious sexist assumption that authors should be male is ironically revealed in Eda Lou Walton's (1925) review of Martha Ostenso and Hildegarde Flanner: the cover of the magazine announces, "Two Girl Poets Reviewed" (see *Measure* 51).

10. David Kalstone (1983b) notes that "Bishop seems uninterested in Moore's modernist connections," aside "from some detailed exchanges about Wallace Stevens" (p. 118). In addition to Stevens's poems mentioned in the text, note the similarity between the concluding lines of "Sunday at Key West" and Stevens's "Hymn from a Watermelon Pavilion" (Stevens 1954, pp. 88–89), first published in 1922: "You dweller in the dark cabin, / Rise, since rising will not waken, / And hail, cry hail, cry hail."

11. I have made the point (Brogan 1986) (as have others) that Stevens is not reducible to one interpretation even though he evolved his own poetically and politically subversive lyrics in response to the objectivism of William Carlos Williams and the outbreak of the Second World War. See also Brogan 1987. I have also discussed the phallocentric implications of "The Idea of Order at Key West" at greater length in Brogan 1988.

12. It is curious that although critics tend to refer to "In Prison" as a short story, Bishop described it in a letter to Marianne Moore (31 January 1938) as "another one of these horrible 'fable' ideas" that seemed to "obsess" her (MacMahon 1980, p. 146). I think it likely that here, too, Bishop was subverting expectations of genre, especially the idea that a fable makes a moral point. Indeed, this 'fable' does make a moral point, but it is in total opposition to the written desire of the main character.

13. David Lehman (1983) asserts that "Miss Bishop takes pains to distinguish the speaker's gender from her own" because the supposedly masculine character "has thought of enlisting in the armed services—and of playing on the baseball team" (p. 69). Besides the fact that the speaker is specifically a writer, it seems to me that Bishop deliberately makes the gender of the character indeterminate precisely to

disorder our phallocentric expectations of authorship and authority. In addition, see Bishop's description of Marianne Moore in "Efforts of Affection," where Bishop praises the other female writer in terms largely reminiscent of "In Prison": "Now that everything can be said, and done, have we anyone who can compare with Marianne Moore, who was at her best when she made up her own rules and when they were strictest—the reverse of 'freedom'?" (*CProse,* p. 145).

14. For instance, Williams's attention to Bishop's "charming little stained-glass bits" sounds much like Maxwell Anderson's negative review of Amy Lowell in *Measure* 49 (1921), p. 18, in which Lowell is derided as a "cutter of gems." It is ironic that Dickinson is (condescendingly) praised by Humphries for occasionally, in contrast to Marianne Moore, letting a "passion for life" outrank her usual "passion for observation," *Measure* 53 (1925) p. 16.

15. Two notable exceptions to the generalization I am drawing here are Lynn Keller and Christanne Miller (see Keller and Miller 1984), and Lee Edelman (see Edelman 1985), reprinted in this volume, above.

16. In an otherwise excellent discussion, Mutlu Konuk Blasing (1987) regards the objects identified in the marginalia *not* as the objects on a news reporter's desk but strictly as the "artifacts on the poet's desk" (p. 348). Although recognizing that the poem is, itself, a written text is certainly part of the intention of the piece, the most immediate subversion of this prose-poem is the disruption of our assumption that our supposedly factual news is, in any way, objective.

17. Sandra Gilbert (1983) convincingly argues that as men left for war, women were liberated from the home.

BARBARA PAGE

Off-Beat Claves, Oblique Realities:
The Key West Notebooks
of Elizabeth Bishop

DURING HER RESIDENCE in Brazil, Elizabeth Bishop gave a number of manuscript items to a friend, Linda Nemer, including several
notebooks, two of which date mostly from the period when for the first
time since college she settled down in one place. Following her travels
in Europe and a brief residence in France, Bishop returned to the United
States, uncertain about her vocation, her residence, or her possibilities
for enduring relationships. Around New Year's 1937, she made a visit
to Florida and in the following year bought a home in Key West, which
is among the "loved houses" mentioned in "One Art." Her residence in
Florida was interrupted often by stays in the North, a sojourn of nearly
a year in Mexico, and other travels, and after the war, Key West, as she
said, "wasn't the same" (Brown 1983, p. 299). But for more than a decade she continued to circle back to the place that had been for a time
the center of her emotional and "observatory" (KWN 1, p. 34) life.[1] In
this period, as the notebooks reveal, Bishop's uncertainties and unease
play off against a gradual clarification of her artistic principles, as she
ponders not only her relation to other poets and artists but also the resources of art unexpectedly found in her very condition of disconnection
and marginality.

In this essay I shall read the Key West/Nemer notebooks through the
double lens of my interest, on the one hand, in poetic process and, on
the other, in the woman artist as a gendered subject. First, I shall discuss
Bishop's transition into Key West, taking note of her continuing preoccu-

pation with dreams and her interest in and criticism of surrealism. In the notebooks—and also in letters from this period—Bishop articulates her own aims as a poet and measures herself against her poetic forebears, sometimes diffidently but also with striking independence and resistance to authority. In this regard, I shall draw on Harold Bloom's theory of the anxiety of poetic influence, as it has been adapted and challenged by feminists who are concerned with difference, particularly the problematic relation of the woman artist to tradition.[2] Then I shall take Barbara Johnson's (1987) critique of Erich Auerbach's effort to resubsume the woman artist under masculinist universals as a point of departure in addressing Bishop's struggle to find in her experience of discontinuities and marginality a valuable principle of composition. I shall argue that in the desuetude of Key West, at the geographical periphery of the country, Bishop found a place corresponding to her own disposition for the margins. Here she exercised her spirit of adventure and her powers of observation, while practicing the "vagrancy" and evasions that gave room to her ambition as a woman poet.

II

Bishop's notebooks are, by and large, working papers, not intimate diaries. They are highly fragmentary, filled with observed details, ideas for poems and stories, and drafts toward poems, many of them stillborn. Only very occasionally does one find mention of deeply felt matters that she did not allow entry into her published work. The most poignant example in these notebooks alludes to a serious automobile accident she was in while motoring in France with two college friends, in which the arm of one friend was severed. Afterward, Bishop composed a dialogue spoken by the arm at the moment it discovers its inexorable separation from the body. In the margin, in tiny handwriting, she added the comment: "This is what it means to be really 'alone in the world' " (KWN 1, p. 51). Although the dialogue of the severed arm probably owes its formal inspiration to Bishop's reading in the extravagant conceits of the metaphysical poets, its mood is informed by her own experience of being cut off from family and society as a result of her orphaning and perhaps also of her sexuality. And the comment from the margin of her own text, a graphic whisper, gives evidence of a heartbreaking effort to come to terms with a sense of immeasurable loss.

Of particular interest in the Key West/Nemer notebooks are Bishop's accounts of her dreams, which often provide in their oblique way an adumbration of her mental territory and preoccupations. At least from the beginning of college, Bishop had thought it worthwhile to record her dreams, a disposition further authorized by the surrealist artists whose ideas both attracted and alarmed her in their attack on the rule of reason and their exploration of the unconscious. But even while she continued to examine her own dream world, she drew a line that limited her mental travels at the point where memory led her back to experiences too painful to be renewed. In her notebook she wrote, then cancelled, these lines: "I could never bear to go back there, / Even in the armored cars of dreams / That let us do so many dangerous things" (KWN 1, p. 10).[3]

During her first visit to Florida, Bishop had a dream that in many ways anticipated her transition into a new element through an immersion that might have proved dangerous but in fact opened the way to a source of material that would feed her poems for decades to come. This dream concerns an encounter with a fish—not surprising in that Bishop went to Florida to fish and in fact went fishing often while she lived there. In her dream, the fish is "about 3 ft. long, large scaled, metallic like a gold fish only a beautiful rose color." By comparison, she remarks, "I myself seemed slightly smaller than life-size." The dreamer follows the kindly fish, who glances around "every now and then with his big eyes" to see if she is following. In his mouth, he carries a new galvanized bucket of air that he is taking to the other fish. Dreamer and fish had met at the margin of land and sea where he was gathering this sampling of air "to be used . . . for some sort of celebration" (KWN 1, p. 15).

Here, as in certain of her later poems, the poet allows herself to be guided by an unorthodox natural spirit into an alien but enticing region. To steady herself and sanction her vagrancy, she makes a meticulous record of what she sees, like a good Darwinian naturalist. In this dream, the guide is male, as is the great creature she catches and describes so closely in her poem "The Fish," which culminates in a transfigurative moment of ecstatic vision and (literal) release: "Rainbow, rainbow, rainbow! / And I let the fish go." These encounters of the ordinary with the marvelous, at the boundaries of the elements of air and water, anticipate Bishop's poems of the Sublime, in the Romantic tradition but in her distinctively contemporary manner. These are "The Riverman," from Brazil, and, from a remembered experience in Canada, her visionary "The Moose," a poem begun in 1946 but not completed until the 1970s. In "The Riverman" (*CP*, pp. 105–9) the speaker is male and the guide, the water spirit Luandinha, is female. In "The Moose" (*CP*, pp. 169–73), as the bus driver exclaims, "Look! It's a she!" But at this earlier moment in her career, as Bishop ventures with cautious courage into the offbeat, outdoors life of Florida, her guide is male. It is hard to say with confidence what these shifts in sexual distribution signify in Bishop's poems of the Sublime. In her discussion of Bishop and the American Sublime, Joanne Feit Diehl (1985) argues, with reference to "The Map," that "Bishop's eye . . . evades as it questions the distinctions of both geography and gender, envisioning in their stead a world that invites a freer conception of sexual identity and a highly particular sense of place— the dissolution of all externally imposed hieratic distinctions" (pp. 134– 35). Ultimately, Diehl believes, Bishop's poems aim at freedom from the dualistic tradition of the Sublime and indeed of Western literature.[4] This is a strong statement of what in Bishop's work unfolds with characteristic indirection, although in one late poem, "In the Waiting Room," she presents herself with autobiographical insistence as a female subject. In her poems of the Sublime, we can say at the least that there is a good deal of shifting around of gender assignment, suggesting that Bishop did want to evade any fixed assignment of sex to seeker, guide, and inspiration.

In Bishop's poems, as in her travels, acts of attention work to forestall vertigo and fear even when the mood shifts from celebration to menace in the alien element. In this regard, an unfinished poem in her notebook, entitled "Current Dreams," bears comparison to her dream of the fish. In it the air turns to salt water as "we" descend some stairs, drawn by marimba music:

> But when we get there it is silent.
> Around us the impettalled fish
> swim seriously;
> it is not a cabaret at all.
> It is an endless wax-works, dimly lit,
> where rows of lonely figures sit
> whose fresher tears naturally cannot fall.
> (KWN 2, p. 33)

These lines contain a peculiar confluence of Baudelairean marimba music and Tennysonian tears, but they also announce themes arising from childhood experience that Bishop would write about later, especially her bafflement before the fact of death. The grotesque incongruity of lively cabaret music and deadly waxworks calls to mind, for example, the weird humor in "First Death in Nova Scotia," when the child is brought in to view her dead cousin Arthur laid out in his coffin, a "little frosted cake," eyed by a stuffed loon, that "Since Uncle Arthur fired / a bullet into him, / . . . hadn't said a word" (*CP*, p. 125).

In the Key West/Nemer notebooks, Bishop's ongoing interest in dreams is connected with notations concerning Freud, understandably, whom she called "the prophet of touch only" (KWN 1, p. 6), but also with the surrealists and other modernist artists who challenged norms of representation. Like the surrealists, Bishop refused to make a sharp distinction between the conscious and the unconscious, and sought glimpses into truths that cannot be seen "full-face" (letter to Anne Stevenson, Stevenson 1966, p. 66), although she did not share their enthusiasm for irrationalism in art.[5] In this regard Bishop might be aligned with another American poet, Robert Frost: both valued the glimpse as a means of reaching beyond systematic observation, yet both balanced skepticism against outbreaks of the marvelous and insisted that poetry should be regulated by formal order. But in pursuing the possibilities of spontaneous, unauthorized observation, Bishop worked toward a principle of artistic expression outside of those regimes of authority and claims to universal perception that feminist critics have rightly identified with masculinist art. We can see in the notebooks a sifting of the heritage of art for alternatives to the grand style in an oblique, understated, deceptively casual address to experience. Of the cubist painter Juan Gris, for example, Bishop remarked, "Things are caught looking the way they look when we aren't quite looking at them (KWN 2, p. 189). Crucial to the success of such observation is that it not be premeditated self-consciously. The naive stare and the fugitive glance of the vagrant traveler become signatures of Bishop's art, as she determinedly locates herself away from centers, hierarchies, and authorities.

But no matter how often Bishop denied having ambition in life, she was ambitious as a poet and in the notebooks can be seen eyeing—sometimes anxiously—the "strong poets," to borrow from Harold Bloom's theory of poetic influence, who preceded her. For a woman artist, the burden of the past is doubly heavy. Not only is there the anxiety of influence by "master" poets, but there is also masculinist contempt and denial of the human or artistic worth of women. And for Bishop, there was as well the minatory presence of the accomplished and publicly recognized Marianne Moore, who also embodied, in David Kalstone's (1989) words, a "wise, eccentric aunt" who attempted at times to inscribe "proper" feminine manners in her spiritual niece (p. 109). Bishop's strategies for evading this burden and repression while marking out fresh territory are of great interest and are in full evidence in her comments on other poets in notebooks and letters. Despite her admiration for Moore, who, she said, stood, with Gerard Manley Hopkins, at the top of "observatory" poets, Bishop refused Moore's efforts to correct her "Roosters," insisting on her own "violence of tone" and a diction attuned to the "sordidities" of everyday life (KWN 1, p. 34). Despite her deep regard for Moore as mentor and her diffidence as a young woman before an elder, Bishop resisted Moore's tutelage in terms that suggest a daughter's refusal of a mother's effort to pass on the "refinements" of gender inhibition. In Bishop we hardly encounter a Whitmanian barbaric "rough," yet she saw her difference from Moore exactly in terms of a greater freedom— like that accorded to boys—to engage in the rough and tumble of an outdoors world.

Even more surprisingly, we find Bishop objecting on similar grounds to a finicky retentiveness in those male poets who, in Bloomian terms, comprise, if not poetic fathers, at least elder brothers. Against the poets of the Auden circle, she objects in her notebook: "They . . . still seem to be holding onto their poetry. It's still in their own grasp. . . . It's that deliberately unfinished—can't let-go—monkey with his hand in a bottle—feeling that I don't like. They the poems aren't 'on their own' " (KWN 1, p. 74). By now, Bishop was beginning to turn her experience of being cut off—like the severed arm—from continuity and preestablished order into a principle of new composition that would inform her own practice as a poet of discontinuities, cultural incongruities, and dilapidated things. In this regard, Wallace Stevens was perhaps more daunting to Bishop than the poets of the Auden circle in that he had preceded her not only into publication in the journals to which she was sending poems but also into the Floridian landscapes about which she was beginning to write. Against his method she placed her own surrealist-inspired blurring of the line between waking and dream, attacking Stevens's over-controlled polish: "What I tire of quickly in Wallace Stevens is the self-consciousness—poetry so aware lacks depth. Poetry should have more of the unconscious spots left in" (KWN 1, p. 89). Self-consciousness for a woman artist, it should be remarked, is laden with debilitating prohibitions against physical freedom and aspirations to art. In Stevens's ideas of order at Key West or anywhere else, a woman may sing, but it is the male artist who will write a poem about her. Bishop needed a

Key West of her own—in dreams and in the geographical peripheries of real places—in which she might unravel the order that excluded her and her kind.

In her poem "The Monument" Bishop articulated both what attracted her to the surrealist artists and what she found it necessary to resist in the practice of Wallace Stevens, and the process through which she passed is graphically visible in her notebook jottings and sketches. Although "The Monument" was not published until 1946, she had formed a clear notion of its central image as early as 1937, while she was still actively pondering the surrealist art that had preoccupied her in France, specifically Max Ernst's technique of frottage—forming a suggestive image by rubbing a pencil over paper placed on a grainy floorboard. Midway in the notebook that opens with commentary on Stevens's *Owl's Clover* (published in 1936), she produced a pen-and-ink sketch of the figure she would describe in "The Monument," in its setting at the shore, preceded by a lined-off text reading, "Take a frottage of this sea."[6] In her sketch, the fleur-de-lis that surmounts the wooden boxes is detached, half toppled, adding to the desuetude of the monument's ornamentation. In form and tone, Bishop's "The Monument" answers Stevens's "Old Woman and the Statue" and "Mr. Burnshaw and the Statue," in *Owl's Clover,* poems almost crushed by the burden of the past, in which mannered minds fend off the death of things in the impending night of cultural collapse. By contrast, Bishop visually and verbally builds a figure of undetermined possibilities by insisting not on the preestablished meaning of the thing but on the activity of making it, like a child at the shore unconcerned with the source of the flotsam incorporated in her sand castle. Deceptively casual words at the bottom of the sketch announce the germination of the poem:

> this is the beginning of a painting
> a piece of statuary, or a poem,
> or the beginning of a monument.
> Suddenly it will become something.
> Suddenly it will become everything.
> (KWN 1, p. 100)

This sudden beginning of significance that makes the most dilapidated artifact worth commemorating is the act of investing desire, wanting "to cherish something." What "gives it away as having life" is the act of attention itself: "Watch it closely."[7]

In her rendering of "The Monument," the apparent modesty of ambition, merely to begin "something" by compiling a fragile and tottering assemblage imprinted with preexisting forms, yields suddenly to a much larger result, becoming "everything." Composed of weathered materials bearing the impress of the sea, Bishop's assemblage stands on the shore, incorporating "something" from inheritance (the fleur-de-lis), which holds—even takes—place because it is watched. Taking a frottage of the sea would be impossible except by what the eye can catch and hold in a glimpse. In this poem, the speaker seems little concerned with the belatedness that wearies Bloom's male poets, and, instead, by a casual act of bricolage—using the means at hand—constructs from broken down materials marked by church and state a new-old, idiosyncratic monument. It is a composition both heroic and homely.

III

In an essay on Zora Neale Hurston, Barbara Johnson (1987) argues that avoidance of a godlike stance and the universalizing language of metaphor is characteristic of certain women writers' narrative voice, a view that has cogency for Bishop's poetic practice as well. Johnson takes on Erich Auerbach, from *Mimesis,* in his discussion of Virginia Woolf's *To the Lighthouse.* Auerbach, reflecting on the preoccupation of modernist writers with "the minor, the trivial, and the marginal," as Johnson puts it, argues that "the complicated process of dissolution which led to fragmentation of the exterior action, to reflection of consciousness, and to stratification of time" in fact tends toward an "approaching unification and simplification." Johnson conjectures that Auerbach's wish to see unity through what he calls "minor, unimpressive, random events" arises because the primary text he is addressing was written by a woman. In Johnson's view, "Auerbach's urge to unify and simplify is an urge to resubsume female difference under the category of the universal, which has always been unavowedly male" (see p. 165). The tendency toward the representation of dailiness that Auerbach identifies is undoubtedly found among modernist writers, male and female, from Flaubert on, and my point is not to claim it for women artists but rather to point out that Bishop—who felt her own marginality keenly, because of orphaning, because of her sex, and because of her sexuality—in her search for literary forebears seized upon this tendency, which she discovered in writers earlier than those of the modern movement. In her notebooks from Key

West, we can see her turning over the problems of experiencing life in terms of disconnections and views from the sidelines, and then working slowly toward an aesthetic clarification of that experience and of the disposition of her art.

Bishop's mind was occupied by artifacts picked up in her travels, and she is a justly celebrated artist of "found objects." But the syntax connecting them troubled her. In a moment of discouragement over having produced only a handful of phrases she could reread without embarrassment, she confessed in a letter to Marianne Moore: "I have that continuous uncomfortable feeling of 'things' in the head, like icebergs or rocks or awkwardly-shaped pieces of furniture—it's as if all the nouns were there but the verbs were lacking—if you know what I mean. And I can't help having the theory that if they are joggled around hard enough and long enough some kind of electricity will occur, just by friction, that will arrange everything—But you remember how Mallarme said that poetry was made of words, not ideas—and sometimes I am terribly afraid I am approaching, or trying to approach it all from the wrong track" (11 September 1940, V 05:02, RM).

It is not at all surprising that Bishop's mind embraced both icebergs and furniture, the nomenclature of her refusal to choose, as Helen Vendler (1983) has shown, between the domestic and the strange. For Bishop, though, the difficulty was with predication, with how to put things together. Turning again to Barbara Johnson, I want to sketch out the points of her argument that help explain what underlies Bishop's struggle with poetic syntax and her success. Johnson argues that the imposition of binary poles on discourse (the ones Johnson is considering are black/white and man/woman), even when complicated into tetrapolar grids, unifies experience into systems of exclusion and subordination and prevents the recognition of self-difference—or the play of mind—that allows one to escape from oppressive roles and from totalizing systems of knowledge. Drawing on the linguist Roman Jakobson, Johnson distinguishes between the metaphoric urge to universalize or totalize knowledge and the metonymic urge to name and rename things in succession. Bishop's often noted refusal to choose between binaries achieves its final expression in her late poem "Santarém," about her arrival at a confluence of two great rivers in Brazil, with the lines:

> Even if one were tempted
> to literary interpretations

such as: life/death, right/wrong, male/female
—such notions would have resolved, dissolved, straight off
in that watery, dazzling dialectic.
(*CP*, p. 185)

Bishop's poems rarely allow even grandly monumental metaphors to remain central, because they are observed by a speaker who is herself either
marginal or self-divided and who establishes a vantage point outside of
metaphorical control. This was true in early poems as well as late; her
"The Imaginary Iceberg," for example, contains in its last line a crucial
corrective (which I have italicized) against absorption in the image:

Icebergs behoove the soul
(both being self-made from elements least visible)
to see them so: fleshed, fair, erected indivisible.
(*CP*, p. 4)

Although Bishop is a poet of many inventive similes, she distrusted
facile assimilations. On the other hand, as she remarked in her notebook,
"*Rhyme* is *mystical*—asserting, or pretending to assert, powerful connections between" things (KWN 1, p. 140). In her Key West notebooks
we find distillations of a long meditation, focused on the unlikely pairing
of Pascal and Poe, through whom she argued out the conflict between
the irreducible separateness of things and the mystical power of art to
make connections. Her method, in Barbara Johnson's terms, remains
steadfastly metonymic.

Pascal had figured as an exemplary writer of baroque prose in an
essay by Morris Croll that Bishop read at Vassar and continued to refer
to in her notebooks. In the passage from Croll (1929) often cited as a
key to Bishop's method—"Their purpose was to portray, not a thought,
but a mind thinking"—Croll's essay continues, "or in Pascal's words, *la
peinture de la pensée*" (p. 430). According to a letter to Moore, Bishop
began to read Pascal's *Pensées* at about the time she made her first visit to
Florida, finding them "full of magnet-sentences that accumulate strayed
objects around them," and "a happy correspondance [*sic*] of the book to
the scenery—the French *clarity* and the mathematics fit in so well with
the few, repeated natural objects and the wonderful transparent sea!"
(5 January 1937, V 04:31, RM). In her notebook entries, Bishop pon-
dered Pascal's notion of nonconnection in nature in relation to a theory
of art. One notation reads, "Inconsequence of maps," then quotes from

the *Pensées*: "Nature has made all her truths independent of one another. Our art makes one dependent on the other. But this is not natural. Each keeps its own place" (KWN 1, p. 13). Some pages later Bishop asks enigmatically: "Does the pt., the 'secret success,' of the poem come in at the pt. the real is lacking—(the factor that the imagination cannot supply) . . . . . . Poe's 'each law of nature depends at all points on all the other laws'—Versus Pascal's 'Nature has made all her truths independent of one another—' " (KWN 1, p. 34).

Bishop's long-standing interest in Poe's theories was nourished by her reading of Baudelaire and the French symbolists, and in Key West she worked on a poem, never finished, entitled "Edgar Allan Poe & the Juke-Box." In "The Poetic Principle," Poe had written that poetry moves us to tears, not of pleasure but of sorrow at our inability to grasp the joys of which we attain a brief glimpse through the poem (Poe 1984, p. 77). Bishop's draft includes this comparison: "Poe said that poetry was *exact.* / But pleasures are mechanical / and know beforehand what they want." Jukebox pleasures, unlike poetry, obtain a "single effect" that "can be calculated like alcohol / or like the response to the nickle" (KWN 1, p. 239). The pleasures of the senses, here represented dangerously by alcohol as well as jukebox music, hint at all sorts of disappointments in the making with desires that are calculated and happiness that does not last. Against these stands poetry that is exact and makes connections, through the mysticism of rhyme, between discrete, isolated effects.

Against Bishop's somewhat murky meditation on Poe's claim that we attain through poetry only a glimpse of the interconnections in nature stand her reflections on Pascal, which hearken back to Croll's "Baroque Style in Prose." In one passage Croll describes a method of juxtaposing statements without connection or merely "by *and, or,* or *nor,*" conjunctions having "no logical *plus* force whatever." These conjunctions merely connect "two efforts of the imagination to realize the same idea; two as-it-were synchronous statements of it." Citing Bacon's distinction between the " 'Magistral' method of writing books of learning and the method of 'Probation' appropriate to 'induced knowledge,' " Croll again takes note of conjunctions that disjoin the members they join and "allow the mind to move straight on from the point it has reached," avoiding commitment "to a pre-determined form" (see Croll 1929, pp. 437, 441, 443).

An isolated notebook jotting distills Bishop's reflections on these matters into the gnomic line that would become the fulcrum of her poem "Over 2000 Illustrations and a Complete Concordance," the words " 'and' and 'and.' " In this poem, she begins, "Thus should have been our travels: / serious, engravable," like the images of domestic warmth associated with the engravings in the family Bible, as David Kalstone has shown. Instead, loss of parents, narrative loss, and loss of faith in unified truth in nature—or at least the possibility of our knowledge of it—conjoin in her poem (Kalstone 1989, p. 130). Disparate travels, loosely linked ("And at St. Peter's," "And at Volubilis," "And at Dingle,") lead to the line—note the lack of a verb—"Everything only connected by 'and' and 'and.' " Here, Pascal's independent truths remain unconnected; Bishop's art, instead, confers unexpected "plus force" on a conjunction that marks the gap between what should have been and what was. In this poem, Bishop's refusal to choose and her rejection of overfinished, totalizing rhetoric become principles of syntax, a substitution of the metonymic sequence of the tourist for the metaphoric domination of the linguistic imperialist.

In "Over 2000 Illustrations" the engraver's burin and in "The Monument" the overall frottage of wood emblemize the power of formal art, "magically interlocking ideas making associations," as she writes in one notebook fragment, which like rhyme, asserts or pretends to assert powerful connections between things (KWN 1, p. 140). Although Bishop's method arises from the necessary resistance of the woman artist to the imperial tradition in masculinist art, she retains the fundamental ambition of the artist to make resonant and revealing connections. Her struggle has a psychological origin, as well. She did not want the effect of nonconnection in her poems, and in a notebook she remarked that the effect in "semi-surrealist poetry" of "the mind being 'broken down' " terrified her (KWN 1, p. 193). In a jotting near the sketch of her monument, she wrote: "posing an *imaginary* question—form of art— artificiality we *lay over* the world as [we?] prepare to grasp it—taking a cloth to unscrew a bottle-cap (partly but poorly expressed in 'S. & its Shore')" (KWN 1, p. 95). The world—her world—did not readily hang together or offer security of station, and it is probably not incidental that Bishop was drawn to poets like Baudelaire and Poe, who suffered from social ostracism and marginalization, even though she did not follow them in representing extreme conditions and emotions in poems. Like these poets, Bishop embraced form, the "artificiality we *lay over* the world," as a means of overcoming the refusal of "things" to connect.

Although the postwar period can be seen in hindsight as the artistic culmination of Bishop's early maturity (she was now in her mid-thirties and *North & South* had finally been published to discerning critical praise), the letters reveal that she suffered a crisis of confidence and uncertainty about what to do with herself, provoked in part by the unraveling of the life she had built in Key West. Before she left Florida for good, however, she turned the frowsy disorder that had drawn her there in the first place into a paradoxical statement of her stance as an artist. In 1948 she wrote to her new friend Robert Lowell about the "beautiful view over the harbor" of her new apartment, but then warned him, "when somebody says 'beautiful' about Key West you should really take it with a grain of salt until you've seen it for yourself—in general it is really *awful* & the 'beauty' is just the light or something equally preverse [*sic*]." Then, in her letter, comes the descriptive germ of her poem "The Bight": the water that looks like "blue gas" and the harbor a mess of junky little boats, some "splintered up from the most recent hurricane," which, she says, "reminds me a little of my desk" (12 January 1948, HL).

In "The Bight," as in "Over 2000 Illustrations and a Complete Concordance," Bishop stresses the making of connections, offering simile after simile, from the idiosyncratically "perverse" eye of the poet: pelicans like pickaxes, man-of-war birds with tails like scissors or like wishbones, shark tails like plowshares, and finally the little white boats piled up, "not yet salvaged, if they ever will be, from the last bad storm, / like torn-open, unanswered letters." In the subterranean life of the poet, visible only in the subtitle, "On my birthday," a connection has been felt between the storm-damaged boats and unanswered letters, which will not be "explained" autobiographically but by a leap of wit, when Bishop writes: "The bight is littered with old correspondences," invoking Baudelaire's poetic principle of *correspondance*. Toward the beginning of the poem Bishop had alluded to Baudelaire's method of making connections not by logic but through synesthesia. At low tide in the bight, the water doesn't wet anything; it is the color of gas: "One can smell it turning to gas; if one were Baudelaire / one could probably hear it turning to marimba music." This mention of Baudelaire is one outgrowth of her close reading of the poet, recorded in extensive jottings in her notebook, which also contains the remark that "B[audelaire] is supposed to have removed the hands from his clock & written on the face 'it is later than you think!'" (KWN 2, p. 176). The untended or broken off affairs represented by the unanswered letters on her desk give evidence of Bishop's worry about the connections in life that she found difficult to make and sustain. An old interplay of hope and disappointment takes shape in her notebook in an unfinished lyric for music, drawn from an anxious dream of a postman:

The postman's uniform is blue.
The letter is of course from you
& I'd be able to read, I hope,
my own name on the envelope
but he has trouble with this letter
which constantly grows bigger & better
& over & over in despair
he vanishes in blue blue air.
(KWN 1, p. 99)

Rigorous acts of description in "The Bight" (*CP*, pp. 60–61) displace and control the possibilities of correspondence—as art, as the medium of love and friendship, as the mysterious nonconnection of things in nature. The drafts of "The Bight" show that while Bishop had Baudelaire and his marimba music in mind from the start, only in the third draft did she substitute "correspondences" for the disorderly desk mentioned in her letter to Lowell. In between—in a rather more nihilistic mood—she has the gaseous air igniting the deskful of letters: "Maybe it will burn everything up sooner or later, this afternoon, / a conflagration / awful but cheerful." In the final version, though, it is against old correspondences that the heard music of present activity plays. Bishop measures her distance from Baudelaire's exotic marimba music, preferring what comes to her own ear, "the dry perfectly off-beat claves" of the little ocher dredge. Refusing to rest within the poles of its comparisons, the poem resists the formal closure of beauty in favor of ongoing present life: "All the untidy activity continues, awful but cheerful."

In "The Bight," against her own expectations, perhaps, the poet becomes a situated, if not a centered, self, one who has a birthday and therefore parentage, one whose eye, ear, and mind confer the affectionate distinction of oddity on the minor, the trivial, and the marginal. And for her readers, her acts of attention produce a dramatic revaluation upward into lasting memory of the "ordinary" life represented in the poem, even as she seems to reject classical finality. In her disposition toward disorderly detail, she belongs in the line of women artists, practitioners, as Barbara Johnson puts it, of "de-universalization," from Penelope the unweaver to Mrs. Ramsay, whose brown stocking is never finished, and Hurston, whose capacity for redirection allows her to avoid men's fixated horizons. That this had become a philosophical as well as a poetic principle for Bishop becomes evident in the memorial to Robert Lowell, "North Haven" (*CP*, pp. 188–89), composed near the end of her own life. The sorrow of Lowell's death is that: "You can't derange, or rearrange, / your poems again. (But sparrows can their song.) / The words won't change again. Sad friend, you cannot change."

Against the finality of closure, Bishop asserted her preference for unofficial and unstable positionings—like that at Key West—for which she found justification in the work of Marianne Moore. In a notebook jotting of 1948, Bishop describes a method of Moore's applied to what she called an "interstitial situation": "oblique realities that give one pause that glance off a larger reality. . . . I see the man hammer, over at Toppino's (or saw him chopping wood at Lockeport) then hear the sound, see him, then hear him, etc. The eye and ear compete, trying to draw them together, to a 'photo finish' so to speak. . . . Nothing comes out quite right" (KWN 2, p. 189). Bishop's experience of the recalcitrance of "things" and of nonconnections had a good deal to do with her own early displacement from family, just as her vagrancy and instinct for the margins had to with her sex and sexuality. The remarkable fact, though, is that these conditions, of severance and loss, became the premises of her art, achieved—as she said—by the "mysticism" of rhyme, but also by her willingness to enter into a new element, like an observant naturalist, and to pick up the cadences of off-beat claves. By the time she moved on from Key West, she had herself become a poet of "interstitial situations," truant from the rules governing the lives of women, in but not altogether of the club of male poets, the artist of oblique realities.

Notes

1. For Bishop's recollection of the dates of her residence in Florida, see Brown 1983, p. 299. Bishop gave 1939 as the date she took up residence in Key West, but her letters to Marianne Moore show that she spent the first half of 1938 there.
2. The origin of this theory will be found in Bloom (1973). Among the many feminist appropriations and critiques of Bloom's theory, Sandra Gilbert and Susan Gubar (1979) offered one of the earliest concerted interrogations of the masculinist bias in Bloom's Freudian notion of literary inheritance; see especially chapter 2.
3. In "Sleeping Standing Up," Bishop writes of the "armored cars of dreams, contrived to let us do / so many a dangerous thing," chugging at the edge of thoughts that appear as "a forest of thick-set trees" (*CP*, p. 30).

4. Bishop's alignment with poets of the Sublime is not exclusively American. In a letter to Robert Lowell she remarked that she saw herself as a "minor female Wordsworth" (11 July 1951, HL). Her willingness to identify herself as female raises further questions about the degree to which, in Diehl's thesis, she wished to transcend gender. The remark was rueful, however, in both its adjectives.

5. Richard Mullen (1982) argues that "within Bishop's poetry, despite the specific surrealist parallels . . . , there is never the attack on the Word itself which underlies all surrealist verse" (p. 70).

6. Bishop wrote to Marianne Moore about "Montrachet-le-Jardin": "I didn't like the Wallace Stevens poem much—he and his old mother-of-pearl inlaid guitar—but phrases & verses are self-consciously beautiful" (24 January 1942, V 05:03, RM).

7. For discussions of Bishop's use of frottage in "The Monument," see Stevenson 1966 and Mullen 1982, pp. 66–67.

Epilogue

VICTORIA HARRISON

Recording a Life: Elizabeth Bishop's Letters to Ilse and Kit Barker

> Then I started the introduction [to *The Diary of "Helena Morley"*] and fussed and fussed over it, trying to get everything just right. Burton went to Diamantina in 1861, and as usual he is endlessly talkative, and absolutely accurate about everything . . . he is amazing, and I bet his passion for exactitude and information drove his Brazilian friends mad! Then just as I got it done and would probably have written you a long letter I did something you may have seen in the paper—got the Pulitzer Prize—to my astonishment. [. . .] Well, it's been very nice and lots of fun.
> (5 June 1956, folder 5, PU).

ELIZABETH BISHOP had a casual, chatty style, filled with the intonations of speech. It seems, often, that the voice in her stories, memoirs, poems, and letters is in the room, talking to you. Elizabeth Bishop liked Dona Alice, pseudonymously named "Helena Morley," and in late 1954 took on the translation of her adolescent diary, because she was fresh, pensive, and witty and knew how to tell a good story. As Bishop notes in the introduction to her translation of the diary, she has "a sense of the right quotation, or detail, the gag-line, and where to stop" (p. xxviii). With the same instincts at play, Bishop took to letter writing, which became perhaps her most prolific genre, especially when she was living in Brazil (from 1952 until 1971, off and on in the later years), when most of her friendships became, of necessity, correspondences.

In her letters she found a place for honesty and for a good, embellished story; she could write about the clouds outside her window in the mountains above Rio or trips to the dentist or her proud purchase of a new MG with the money from the sale of a story; she wrote about other writers, about her own writing, about writing in general; she recorded her losses—the deaths, mental illnesses, estrangements of those she cared for. There is nothing remarkable in all of this—she wrote letters.[1] What is vitally important, however, about Elizabeth Bishop's letters is that in the absence of a published biography, they tell her life; in the virtual silence from her in terms of criticism or essays about writing, they are a locus for her opinions and philosophies. And despite her lifelong dissociation from the notion of the "woman writer," letters were her private forum for testing her opinions of and affinities with other women writers. Especially when her correspondent was another woman writer less accomplished than she, Bishop played the role of mentor, guiding her friend with praise and patient nudging, as she explored her own writing process.

In her letters to Ilse and Kit Barker, German-born writer and translator and British painter, respectively, Bishop explored all these aspects of her life. Although Bishop saved only eight of the Barkers' letters, leaving her readers unfortunately without a dialogue, the Barkers preserved some 225 of Bishop's letters over twenty-seven years—one of her most sustained correspondences, both in number of letters and in the honesty and generosity of detail. The letters are mostly two to four typed pages each, with penned additions, corrections, and an occasional sketch.

Although Bishop wrote to the two of them together, opening her letters with such endearments as "Dearest Barkerzinhos," the letters often become a conversation of two, be they about books ("I've almost finished the first 2 volumes of Edel, Ilse—" [2 May 1963, folder 12, PU]) or babies ("Lota and I followed your daring independent decision about feedings, Ilse,—breathless!—"[15 May 1963, folder 12, PU]).[2] In this paper, thus, I explore a writing relationship that spanned much of a lifetime and allowed Bishop to be not only a friend and confidante of an artist couple who loved and respected her but also a mentor of a fellow woman writer and, indeed, when she let down her guard, a woman writer herself.

Bishop met the Barkers at Yaddo in 1950, during one of the more difficult periods of her life. She had come to that writers' colony after a physically and emotionally straining year as poetry consultant at the Library of Congress, where she had often been ill and had felt surrounded

by poets constantly more productive than she, a fear that kept her pan-
icked and depressed. At Yaddo, although she continued to have the bouts
of drinking, asthma, and depression that had plagued her in Washington,
she did become poetically productive. She wrote "The Prodigal" there,
reporting in letters to Dr. Anny Baumann, her personal physician and
confidante, that she was generally working well. And she developed some
lasting friendships, including that with the Barkers. The Barkers were
in residence for four months during the winter of 1950–51, one of three
stays there during the years they spent in the United States between 1949
and 1953. Bishop saw them off at midnight on a Greyhound trip to San
Francisco; by the time they returned to New York she had left for Brazil.
They saw each other on several other occasions over the years: Bishop
visited them at their home in Sussex, England, alone in July 1964 and
with her Brazilian friend Lota de Macedo Soares in 1966; the Barkers
saw Bishop in Boston in 1973 and stayed with her and Alice Methfessel at
North Haven, Maine, in 1978; and Bishop and Methfessel visited them in
England in 1979, a few months before Bishop died. Between the last two
visits they exchanged several letters regarding a pen-and-ink drawing of
North Haven that Kit Barker was doing for publication as a broadside
along with Bishop's memorial poem to Robert Lowell, "North Haven,"
a poem she wrote during the Barkers' Maine visit.[3]

Bishop began writing to the Barkers shortly after she settled, unexpectedly but happily, in Brazil. Her planned vacation to Brazil and to
other parts of Latin America in early 1952 had become instead a fairly
permanent residence there as a result of a debilitating allergic reaction
to the fruit of the cashew and the care and love of Macedo Soares, whom
she had met in New York in 1942. Macedo Soares asked her to live
with her at "Samambaia," the home she was having built in the mountains above Petrópolis, two hours from Rio de Janeiro. Both Bishop and
Macedo Soares were interested in every aspect of art and architecture;
they oversaw and took part in the designing and building of their home,
making decisions about terraces, interiors, and Bishop's studio, which
was a short walk from the house and overlooked a cliff and waterfall.
Macedo Soares was descended from old aristocratic Brazilian families on
both sides and so knew many of the major Brazilian architects, painters,
writers, and political leaders. Bishop was immediately surrounded, as
much as she chose to be, by interesting people; she often elaborated on
their visits with great amusement in her letters to the Barkers.

She did, of course, tell her stories on many occasions to several friends, often borrowing from her own descriptions. Her two most important literary correspondences were those with Robert Lowell and Marianne Moore. For various personal reasons, however, she limited her range of subjects and moods with them more than she did with the Barkers. She and Lowell were writers together. Yet she was self-defensive about her newly domestic happiness, as if she had to justify not being among her fellows in New York to him and perhaps to herself:

> I am extremely happy, for the first time in my life. I live in a spectacu-
> larly beautiful place; we have beteen [sic] us about 3,000 books now; I
> know, through Lota, most of the Brazilian "intellectuals" already and I
> find the people frank,—startlingly so, until you get used to Portuguese
> vocabularies—extremely affectionate—an atmosphere that I just lap
> up—no I guess I mean loll in—after that dismal year in Washington and
> that dismaler winter at Yaddo when I thought my days were numbered
> and there was nothing to be done about it.—I arrived to visit Lota just
> at the point where she really wanted someone to stay with her in the
> new house she was building. [. . .] She wanted me to stay; she offered
> to build me a studio—picture enclosed—I certainly didn't really want
> to wander around the world in a drunken daze for the rest of my life—
> so it's all fine & dandy. (28 July 1953, HL)

Her defensiveness was well placed; Lowell's response was humorous but chastising: "I think about you continually—you and your studio and your Brazilian world. I'm sure you are as happy as you sound. But I don't approve at all. Like a rheumatic old aunt, I would gladly spoil all your fun just to have you back. I think I'll try and have payments on your trust fund stopped" (29 November 1953, VC). The emotional and professional intimacy of the early years of their friendship became strained when Bishop moved to Brazil.[4] They wrote less frequently, in part because the physical distance made them lose track of each others's lives, in part because during these years Lowell suffered repeated psychotic breakdowns. Bishop seemed often to hold back her own stories in order to say the right thing during or after a breakdown. Their respect for each other as people and as poets remained mutual and unconditional, nonetheless, and the discussions in their letters of poets and poetry, as well as of the Brazilian political situation, are some of Bishop's most interesting.

Marianne Moore, Bishop's dear friend, mentor, mother figure, and longest-term correspondent, was receptive, Bishop knew from the beginning of their friendship, only to certain kinds of news and conversation.[5] Love—and her joys or difficulties with her lovers—was a taboo subject. They disagreed about most political issues, so they avoided politics. They did commiserate over each other's health quite regularly. But their relationship thrived on their pride in and discussion of each other's work, as well as their wide reading in philosophy, psychology, and literature. They had a mutual love of the eccentric and the exotic: Moore brought out in Bishop the side of her that was awestruck at the world and some of her most stunning descriptions: "I don't mean to complain about the mails—they are part of the really lofty vagueness of Brazil, where no one seems to know quite what season it is, or what day of the week, or anyone's real name,—& where a cloud is coming in my bedroom window right this minute" (3 March 1952, V 05:04, RM).

Theirs was always a generational relationship—Moore was the mother/mentor, Bishop the daughter/protégée—even when Moore became self-deprecating in her later years, and her pleasure in Bishop's poems sometimes verged on sadness that her own moment had passed. Eight years after the first publication of Bishop's playful poem "Invitation to Miss Marianne Moore," Moore was still thanking her: "Never could I deserve so lovely a thing. I shall always be trying to justify it. Furthermore, it gives me some standing. Several times this summer I have been ardently received as having been the occasion for it" (29 August 1956, VC). Overcome by emotion, Moore then quickly moved on in the letter to a subject still very much her own, the Dodgers and Roy Campanella. Bishop's letters to Moore have the love and respect owed to an admired old friend, but they do not have the freedom of an intimate.

Bishop's letters to the Barkers range wide, and their tone of love and generosity suggests that theirs was a friendship deeper and more sustaining than the topics they discussed. Consequently, some of Bishop's freshest insights about herself and her writing, her feminism, and her position as exile emerge in these letters, which often served as testing ground for her half-formulated ideas. At the same time, when she was troubled and in need of unconditional support, she turned to the Barkers with her fear, regrets, and pain. Ilse Barker characterized their friendship with Bishop as a "complete" one (letter to the author, 4 March 1987). They loved her and she them, unconditionally and unproblematically.

One of her first letters to them records her newly found happiness in Brazil: "The social life up here where I am is very limited—a few friends make it up the mountain over the week-ends, [. . .] but the rest of the time we go to bed to read at 9:30, surrounded by oil-lamps, dogs, moths, mice, blood-sucking bats, etc. I like it so much that I keep thinking I have died and gone to heaven, completely undeservedly. My New England blood tells me that no, it isn't true—Escape does not work; if you really are happy you should just naturally go to pieces and never write a line—but apparently that—and most psychological theories on the subject, too—is all wrong. And that in itself is a great help" (12 October 1952, folder 1, PU). Pleased to have found a stopgap for pain far easier than the psychiatric treatment she had undergone in New York beginning in 1944,[6] Bishop delighted in an "escape" that offered both newness and home. In the early years of her correspondence with the Barkers, Bishop's constant fascination with the scenery, her household of servants, and Brazilian culture in general predominated. She reported regularly on the progress of the building of their house, which won first prize in a Brazilian exhibit: "Lota is busting with pride because . . . all the good ideas were hers and not the architect's [Sergio Bernardes, whose work was featured in the 1950s in international architecture magazines] at all" (5 February 1954, folder 3, PU). Bishop regaled the Barkers with details of the house. Aside from her studio, she seemed most pleased with the bathroom: "Well—the new bathroom has three walls of white tiles—the only kind you can get here—and we thought we'd paint the third, back, wall, all pink to liven it up. Then L had an inspiration—it is now going to be diamonds, harlequin style about 18″ high—the wall is about 9′ × 12′ I guess—maybe longer—We're preparing it for frescoe now. [. . .] We're all going to paint diamonds until the wall looks the legs of Picasso's clowns, only better" (13 July 1953, folder 2, PU). She went on to tell them about the gray floor, also with diamonds. In honor of the bathroom's completion, Kit Barker painted a watercolor of a harlequin for Bishop.

The house was filled for years with construction workers and children, the constantly multiplying family of an adopted, married son of Lota as well as the servants' children. (Later, in the early 1960s, their friend and neighbor Mary Morse began adopting children, who often stayed at their home.) Bishop was able to work, nevertheless, better than she ever had. Not yet comfortable enough to write the nuances of Brazil, she began for the first time in her career to publish writing about her childhood. After her father's death in her first year of life and her mother's hospitalization in a mental institution, she lived for several years with her grandparents and two of her mother's sisters in Nova Scotia. As she wrote to the Barkers, "It is funny to come to Brazil to experience total recall about Nova Scotia—geography must be more mysterious than we realize, even" (12 October 1952, folder 1, PU). The connections between her Brazilian life and her Nova Scotia memories have been drawn by Howard Moss and others: countryside, family, animals abounding, the elements that made Nova Scotia "home" for the first seven years of her life seemed importantly re-created here in Brazil. Her newfound contentedness and stability allowed her to put her childhood into verbal perspective: her most acclaimed story, "In the Village," gives voice to the articulated scream of her mother, home very impermanently between hospitalizations, and to her own inarticulable scream—her helplessness as a young child in the face of this inexplicable pain. Bishop's distance of time and place in writing also allows her child to discover sustenance, even pleasure, in the world beyond the scream, which almost—but not quite completely—blocks it out and protects her from it. When she writes about "In the Village" to the Barkers, this distance is clearly felt. She is now the artist crafting a story, manipulating her autobiography, enjoying the result:

> I'm really writing this [description of the bathroom] I must say, ungraciously, because I'm so sick of re-typing my best story. [. . .] I've re-done a little, but will concede not another comma for clarity's sake. [. . .] But one tires of typing even a masterpiece I find. (13 July 1953, folder 2, PU)

> I am really getting interested in what I now think is the Art of story-writing. I just wrote off some prose-poetry from time to time before—I'm afraid "In the Village" is pretty much that, too—but now I am taking it more seriously and thinking about *people,* balancing this with that, time, etc.—and I'm hoping whatever I write will be a little less precious and "sensitive" etc, in the future . . . Which mostly means that I appreciate what you are trying to do more. (29 August 1953, folder 2, PU)

> I know I'm not a story writer, really—this is just poetic prose. And completely autobiographical. [. . .] I've just stuck a few years together. Fortunately the aunt most involved in it all [. . .] likes it very much—and even corrected some names, and reminded me of this and that—we have equally literal imaginations. [. . .] Cal Lowell said it reminded him of a "ruminating Dutch landscape." (25 February 1954, folder 3, PU)

> One nice thing—I've had three or four letters from old Nova Scotians, two of them actually spotted the exact Village—even though

I've changed things around some—and one said he'd *left* in 1890-something—"I think you must be the daughter of Grace B——" he said, naming my favorite aunt—then they all make little corrections—it was McKim, not McClean; the barn was on the other side of the road, etc etc. (22 May 1954, folder 3, PU)

The pain of the story is off the page of her present text, her letters here, from Brazil. She playfully matches a little self-deference with a little praise for Ilse Barker: her own ease during these years is reflected in the sensitivity with which her letters address their audience. Concerned about Barker's frustration that her own stories were not being accepted for publication, Bishop mentions her fan mail here but neglects to cite the high praise of her friends, fellow poets, and critics.[7]

As a letter writer she was sensitive to her audience, except when she was most in pain. As a critic she was ruthless. Barker sent Bishop her own writing throughout their correspondence, and Bishop scrutinized it word by word, as she did for manuscripts she received from all her friends.[8] She did the same with Lowell's writing, but when Bishop and Lowell read each other, they both knew they were reading highly accomplished writers. Their professional relationship was always first a personal friendship, and never, finally, hierarchical. Marianne Moore's work was the important exception to Bishop's critical method: Bishop praised it unequivocally in letters to her, even as she was criticizing especially Moore's later work to others.

But Bishop was definitely the mentor in the Bishop-Barker relationship, and the position was an important one for her. She knew that Barker took her comments very much to heart and made consequent changes and improvements in her writing. At times she would let her concern range into brutal honesty. Responding to a story of Barker's, "The Lion of Heyst,"[9] Bishop began by trying to be nice, thanking her for sending it. She then pointed to a "mistake in sentence 3" and followed her correction with, "It is a most mysterious little tale, all right." She wanted Barker to cut through the mystery with more direct and realistic detail, "I know you don't want to make it *un*-mysterious, but somehow I felt a bit put-upon by my ignorance as to what the 'lion' *really* was," and ended by suggesting extensive reshaping, "sometimes in your stories the preliminary part is too long for the dramatic part" (28 July 1968, folder 17, PU).

She was just as careful and aggressive, though, with her praise. She did like Barker's novel *Return,* devoting most of a four-page letter

(22 March 1959, folder 8, PU) to discussion of it. Several paragraphs about Barker's handling of the international theme of this novel praise her realistic use of detail and setting: "Certain English mannerisms that frighten us, the English habit of 'attack' in conversation, of casualness that can strike us as coldness or rudeness—are all there and properly understood—as well as the American 'kindness' that Santayana made so much of, and our national concern with doing the right thing." Citing individual sentences and their effect on her of homesickness and anger, she has read it, observant exile herself, immersed in every detail. With the pride of a mentor, Bishop compared this novel with William Dean Howells's *Indian Summer* to praise Barker's natural ease with the international novel genre. At the same time, Bishop was the teacher, who included a page-long exposition on punctuation, especially on Barker's use of the comma.

Bishop was the senior writer, with experiences and advice to share. At the end of a long and chatty letter, for instance, she gave detailed consideration to Barker's publishing frustrations:

> I do hope you've been able to get to work again—I have been in a dreadful slump for over a month now and I know how awful it is—I keep starting poems and working like mad for one day and then the next I think my god! how could I have ever thought of anything so *corny*—or else it still is a good idea but there just isn't any form for it. I've decided that possibly it gets harder rather than easier as one gets older—discouraging thought—because when you first start off you don't stop to think so much—you're delighted to have the idea at all—when you're older you realize the possibilities too much—the different treatments, the different tones, the different levels, etc. Don't you think so?
>
> [. . .] I do sympathize with you with all my heart. It *is* necessary to push more—pushing rarely does pay off, thank goodness, in writing—to "sell" and it must be very hard if one isn't naturally made that way. [. . .] I liked you and Kit right off because you didn't show any signs of it [go-getting]. It is one reason why I am content to leave New York for good. I think—everybody is so intent on using everybody else that there is no room or time for friendship any more.
>
> As you say—work's the thing. When I'm busy I don't give a damn what anyone thinks except the very few people I really care for. (8 October 1953, folder 2, PU)

Bishop knew Barker's worries; she herself published only two or three poems a year through most of her life. But her personal frustration here gives way to professional encouragement when she analyzes that frustration for her friend.

At the same time these letters, as well as those to Lowell, served as Bishop's own informal notebooks, where she tested literary judgments and generalizations. As Ilse Barker wrote about her, "she had an opinion about everything" (letter to the author, 4 March 1987). But because she never thought of her own critiques as literary criticism, a form for which she often said she had no aptitude, she rarely formalized or even completed the articulations she dropped casually into her letters. Discussing Howells's *Indian Summer,* for instance, she began what might have led to an interesting discussion of influence: "I feel sure that James got the idea for THE AMBASSADORS from it, and even stole quite a bit from it—it's ten years or so earlier" (22 March 1959, folder 8, PU). She stopped short of analysis, although she was equipped to do it given her reading—most of Howells, and, as she wrote to the Barkers in 1956, all of Henry James, Alice James's journal, William James's essays, and Matthieson's *The James Family* (23 March 1956, folder 5, PU). Likewise, rather than write a review or a memorial note on Dylan Thomas, by whose death she was deeply affected, she tucked a single sentence into a letter to the Barkers, "T's poetry is so narrow—just a straight conduit between birth & death, I suppose—with not much space for living along the way" (23 November 1953, folder 2, PU). In letters to other writers Bishop frequently followed her comments about writing with an apology that she was not a better critic, but with the Barkers she did not feel she needed to posture. She could muse and let insights come as they did, free of the "go-getting" New York literary rigor she had escaped.

Thus, when it came to discovering her literary influences, Bishop shared her amazement with the Barkers over an affinity with Sarah Orne Jewett that she mentioned nowhere else that I have seen.[10] When asked in interviews, she always gave the place of influence to George Herbert, Gerard Manley Hopkins, and, of course, Marianne Moore.[11] Bishop had a complex relationship with poetry of Emily Dickinson, which she admired but by which she was troubled, as she was by Dickinson's letters. She struggled similarly with Virginia Woolf, with whose work she renewed her confrontation periodically throughout her life.[12] Bishop began to read Jewett perhaps in response to a passing reference by Lowell, who wrote her after seeing her Nova Scotia stories "Gwendolyn" and "In the Village" that she should do a "growing-up novel," "what K. A. Porter's childhood stories aim towrds [*sic*], or a super Miss Jewett" (1 January 1954, VC). In Jewett's prose, in her tough, sturdy characters, in her contemplation of the landscape and its connection to personal history, Bishop saw her own. Specifically recommending Jewett's lyrical Maine novel, *The Country of the Pointed Firs,* to the Barkers, she wrote that the stories that make it up are

> dated now, but still sometimes marvellous stuff and worth reading. I had only read one and I was appalled when I recently read a whole book—I'm sure anyone who read my story ["In the Village"] would think I was imitating her shamelessly—whole phrases, even—it is very strange; I had really never laid eyes on the ones that are like mine. (21 July 1954, folder 3, PU)

> And it's all so completely true, you know—I wish I could read her without weeping. [. . .] And even some of the more frankly sentimental ones, if they were "translated from the Russian" or something, I'm sure would be world–famous—[. . .] But it was a shock to me to find how closely I'd paralleled things she'd said in spots—I've even had to change some things in two unfinished Nova Scotian stories. (19 January 1955, folder 4, PU)

Twenty-four years later, she seemed to forget her early enthusiasm. After spending the summer of 1979 reading all of Jewett's work, she wrote to Howard Moss that she thought she would turn down a request that she make selections and do an introduction for a new edition (14 August 1979, NYP). (She was negotiating with William Goodman of David R. Godine, Inc., but had signed no contract by the time of her death on 6 October 1979.) Still, when her own Nova Scotia writing coincided with her reading of Jewett, she not only saw the similarities but also responded to Jewett's world with tears, as if through it she were revisiting her own.

Identifying with women's writing was rare for Bishop. Perhaps she so limited her acknowledgment of Jewett as a literary mother because she sensed in it the potential contradiction: her refusal to identify herself as a woman writer in a period when American women writers were discovering their common voice, seemed to conflict with her unavoidable identification with Jewett. So as not to be misunderstood, she tried in her next letter to the Barkers to formulate her stance with regard to women's writing. Distinguishing between what she called Jewett's sentimentality and others', here particularly that of Elizabeth Bowen, Virginia Woolf, Rebecca West, and Rosamund Lehman, she asserted that it's a fault one almost never finds in men's writing, or if one does in a different form. It is that they are really boasting all the time. There's a sort of intonation of the "She-has-such-a-*lovely-home* . . ." sort about it. They are secretly pointing out, for you to admire, their beautifully-polished old silver [in the margin she wrote, "Well—maybe Waugh shares it with the ladies—"], their taste in clothes, their intellectual and, frequently, social standing, their husbands, etc.—and ultimately their sexual irresistability . . . (men writers do this last of course, but not in such sly ways) It's the "How nice to be nice!" atmosphere that gets me, and I think women writers must get quite away from it before they ever amount to a hill of beans. I see I've mentioned English ladies— well, there are plenty of American ones, too—Mary McCarthy does it, Jean Stafford less, maybe, but sometimes, Eudora Welty less but also sometimes—

[. . .] I suppose it is at bottom a flaw in reality that irritates me so—not so much of being protected,—you can't blame them for that— but of wanting to show that they are even if they aren't. (28 February 1955, folder 4, PU)

Becoming increasingly aware of issues of class during these years in Bra-zil, Bishop accuses these women writers of more than simply a defensive and unself-conscious retreat into their class privilege; it is their "female" means of doing so that most bothers her. Not only does the superficiality of such female manners make for bad writing, but also the manners lie. These women writers' cowardly adherence to privilege, Bishop asserts, evades the reality of whatever, beneath the defense, they might love or fear. Yet the vehemence of Bishop's tone cannot be attributed alone to her righteousness about these pretensions. Rather, she senses that her own writing position is threatened by these other women writers' trans-gressions. She must attend to the foibles of women's writing that keep it from being simply writing: details of reality must be served; reality lies elsewhere than in the silver.

To ask women writers to pay attention not to the drawing room or kitchen but to the world's activity, as she did more specifically in 1970 in some unfinished book reviews, is to ask them not to legitimize dif-ferent male and female worlds. Bishop's form of feminism, a word she chose for herself in several 1960s and 1970s interviews (see Starbuck 1983, p. 322, Spires 1981, p. 80, and Hale and Byatt 1978, p. 61), be-lieved in dissolving distinctions between men and women, rather than understanding or accepting gender difference. She told George Starbuck (1983), for instance, that "I never made any distinction; I never make any distinction. However, one thing I should make clear. When I was in college and started publishing, even then, and in the following few years, there were women's anthologies, and all-women issues of magazines, but I always refused to be in them. I didn't think about it very seriously, but I felt it was a lot of nonsense, separating the sexes. I suppose this feeling came from feminist principles, perhaps stronger than I was aware of" (p. 322).

It is a rare moment in Bishop's letters, one I have seen repeated nowhere else, when she reverses her gender terms and finds minute attention to detail to be a special interest of women. In a 6 February 1965 letter addressed to Ilse (and not to both Barkers, as her letters usually were) she picked up the thread of a former letter that described a visit to Ouro Prêto with a male friend:

> I can take a little [literary gossip and discussion of literary theories], but when it comes to a choice between a baroque chapel and say, Allen Tate—give me the chapel . . . while it's under our nose, I mean. But it is my chief complaint against the opposite sex, anyway—with the exception of the poets and painters—they don't *see* things. They're always having ideas & theories, and not noticing the detail at hand . . . I have a small theory of my own about this—that women have been *confined*, mostly—and in confinement details count.—They *have* to see the baby's ear; sewing *makes* you look closely.—They've had to do so much appeasing they do feel moods quickly, etc. There may be nothing in it, and as I said,—it doesn't apply to artists, or not to good ones. (folder 14, PU)

Domestic life, grandmothering, and a steady exchange of details with Ilse Barker about "the baby's ear" and everything else have allowed Bishop to generalize outward to other women, from her own attention to detail to theirs: she acknowledges that her seeing is her artist's as well as her female vision. Although she became notorious in feminist poets' circles for her mainstream poetry (see, for example, Cooper 1974, pp. 43–44, Fraser 1977, p. 157, and Rich 1979, p. 36) and her refusal to be part of women writers' anthologies, when the pressure to identify with the philosophies of a group was off, as it clearly was with the Barkers, she felt free to make just such identifications.

Observing detail was an activity built in to Bishop's self-exile in Brazil—her voluntary move from "home" to an unknown place—just as it was a means toward making a home in Brazil, or placing herself. Especially when she was translating the *Diary*, looking over "Helena

Morley's" shoulder at the daily episodes of her life, Bishop recognized her own rural childhood. The wholly different character of this world overlapped with those memories, as she showed especially in nostalgic letters to her aunt, Grace Bowers, in Nova Scotia. Her letters to the Barkers during the translation project are filled with anecdotes from the book and from her own experiences in connection with it. Similarly, her poetry about Brazil re-creates the position of the observer who also has a part. Narrative voice in many of these poems belongs to observers and explorers, often, as the title of her poem "Under the Window: Ouro Prêto" signifies, acknowledging their own point of reference as they record what they see. She and Barker did not discuss their mutual exile as an issue; rather, they went about inspecting cultures not their own by writing the details of their lives—lives that were doubly infused with the present cultures and their absent native ones.

When she began to sense the conflict between these, Bishop first applied the term *exile* to her state, which she was realizing by 1963 could no longer offer her her doubled vision: "I want to get away badly these days—I feel like those moments I've jus [*sic*] been watching on the beach when two waves going at angles to each other meet and an immense confusion of helpless ripples and foam and upheavings result . . . Lota wonders how we keep corresponding, Ilse, and I think—besides the fact we both like to write & get letters—perhaps it is partly because we are both exiles in a way, even if voluntary and cheerful ones—" (2 May 1963, folder 12, PU). Rather than living at the juncture of cultures Bishop found herself at the swell of conflict. By the mid 1960s, Brazil's government and economy were becoming less and less stable, and the country was turning less than paradisiacal for Bishop and Macedo Soares. In 1960, when Carlos Lacerda was elected governor of the new state of Guanabara, Macedo Soares's friendship with him led to her appointment as coordinator of architects and landscape designers in the planning and building of a six-kilometer park in Rio de Janiero. Though Macedo Soares was honored and excited by the responsibility, their life changed drastically when she accepted the position. The work was much more than full time; so that she could be near the park, they moved to an apartment in Rio, returning to their quiet Samambaia life only one or two weekends a month. Macedo Soares's close ties with Lacerda brought her into the middle of his turbulent anti-Goulart politics. She found, to her increasing exhaustion and frustration, that his state government, no less than the government of the president he opposed, was inefficient and sexist and, toward the end of his tenure in 1965, corrupt, even dangerous.

The upheavals became more and more literal, and although Bishop continued in the mid-1960s to write long and cheerful letters to the Barkers—she averaged a letter every three weeks from 1963 to 1965—she began to voice her frustration. In the middle of five pages about Lota's typhoid fever, her own ten-day hospitalization in a "rest home," an attempted assassination of Lacerda by Goulart men, tension about whether President Goulart would declare a state of seige in Rio, as well as chatty stories about one of Mary Morse's daughters, about Mary McCarthy's *The Group,* and about Dos Passos's visit to Brazil, Bishop articulated her own position: "Oh God—poor Brazil—my feelings are so mixed. I read in an Eng. review of Fellini's '8½' that it was about someone—artist— who 'was stuck because he was feeling too many things at once'—and realized that describes my state of the last two years exactly. The necessary elimination, sequestration, concentration, etc. have been harder & harder" (14 October 1963, folder 12, PU). A writer who thrived on escape, as she put it in her 12 October 1952 letter to the Barkers, Bishop had become immersed in a world whose personal and political chaos demanded her full attention. Her solution was, once again, to get away: she and Macedo Soares went to Europe in 1964 and 1966. She took several trips, for work and rest, to Ouro Prêto, an area by which she was mesmerized—"18th century pure and simple" (17 January 1965, folder 14, PU). In August 1965 she bought an eighteenth-century house there as a renovation project and spent two and a half months living next door at a friend's, writing and overseeing the work. Needing money and needing to get even farther away, she accepted her first teaching job, a semester at the University of Washington in Seattle in 1966. But her escapes served, finally, as added aggravation. Macedo Soares became very ill, physically and emotionally. In September 1967 she flew to New York to visit Bishop, who was working there on a never-finished book of prose pieces about Brazil; in New York Macedo Soares took an overdose of valium and died.

Bishop wrote to the Barkers less frequently but with deep honesty during this period. She confided to them her grinding frustration over what seemed irresolvable difficulties for Macedo Soares and herself. In short letters, trusting in an audience who would intuit all that was not there, she recorded her shock and grief over Macedo Soares's death. She wrote them about her problematic move to San Francisco with a friend whom she had met in Seattle and about the flood of corruption she faced when the two of them returned to Ouro Prêto in 1969, both from lawyers handling Macedo Soares's still unsettled will and from the contractors and workmen she had hired for her house. She filled these letters with her bitterness toward Brazil and her worry over her companion's mental health through all of this. Until the end of the decade, Bishop's necessarily great effort to hold her life together is subject and tenor of her letters to the Barkers, who were, aside from Dr. Baumann, her most constant correspondents during these years.

As her life gradually reached emotional calm in the early 1970s, she became more active professionally than she ever had been. She began teaching at Harvard in the fall of 1970, temporarily replacing Lowell, who was on a leave of absence. From then until her death in 1979, she taught at least one semester a year, often two, at Harvard, the University of Washington, New York University, and the Massachusetts Institute of Technology and gave several readings a year all over the country.

Her letters to the Barkers in the 1970s became, consequently, less chatty, less introspective, and less frequent. The "activity and *clarity*" (30 August 1979, folder 28, PU) of life in Boston intervened, and letters became only rarely the sanctuary where Bishop recollected herself, as they had been for so many years in Brazil. She wrote about the trips she took with Alice Methfessel, her friend whom she had met her first year at Harvard, when living at Kirkland House, where Methfessel worked. Most intrigued by their first vacation to the Galápagos Islands, she also wrote about their travels in the United States and abroad and their several summers in North Haven, Maine. Bishop wrote about the Lewis Wharf apartment she bought in 1973, "I've already had the walls all arranged to suit me and ordered a Franklin stove, etc. so I guess I'm settled for the rest of my life now . . ." (30 July 1973, folder 22, PU). She wrote about her illnesses, her classes, her poetry readings. On the rare occasions when she had the time during these years simply to sit and write, however, her voice did pick up its old tone, its curiosity and playfulness. Thanking the Barkers for a present of a kaleidoscope (11 November 1974, folder 23, PU), Bishop defies the smog and oil tankers she complains of in this letter, as well as a depressing visit to her old aunt in a nursing home and classes that were only "fair"; she became lost in the details of her new toy:

> At first it didn't seem to move at all, then I had the bright idea of warming it up a bit—and that makes it work—hold near a light bulb—I also discovered the obvious—it is much better through my reading glasses! [. . .] I do have 2 others—one I've had since I was 15—a beauty, an old one set on a stand like a microscope and filled with pieces

of Venetian glass,—I found it in an antique shop for $5.00 and have carried it about the world with me—but I don't think you've ever seen it. Then I have one of the newer U S, I think, models, in which nothing really moves—you point it at *outside* things [. . .] So you see I am a sort of amateur of kaleidoscopes [. . .] and I am very fond of them. Sometimes your [*sic*] looks like 5 yellow butterflies, or 5 buttercups—

Although Bishop usually corrected her typing errors, she missed a typo near the end of her last letter to them (30 September 1979, folder 28, PU) that seems to characterize the defiant escape of her kaleidoscope fascination and of so much of her life. Writing about a close friend of Methfessel who was planning to visit on the way to the airport, Bishop says, "The fog is so thick I don't see how anything's going to fly—but perhaps iy will lift." Perhaps, indeed, she did. The pun of her typo is uncanny in its echo of the close of her poem "Sonnet," published in the *New Yorker* after her death. Like the mercury that breaks out of the thermometer, "flying wherever / it feels like, gay!" Bishop unwittingly intimates to the Barkers her own escape into death six days later. Yet her letter meant to suggest no such closure. Having recorded the details of both inside and "*outside* things" over the duration of a long friendship, Bishop ended her correspondence with Ilse and Kit Barker in the midst of its process: "I think now that I'll have to write you another chapter of this—and re-read your last 3 letters again."

Notes

All letters not otherwise marked are quoted from the Elizabeth Bishop Collection, Letters to Kit and Ilse Barker (C0270), at the Princeton University Library, excerpts copyright © 1988 by Alice Methfessel. Princeton purchased the collection from the Barkers in October 1985. It is available for reading with unrestricted access. My thanks to Ilse and Kit Barker for reading this manuscript and generously giving their time, suggestions, and corrections. I thank the literary executors of the estates of Elizabeth Bishop, Robert Lowell, and Marianne Moore—Alice Methfessel, Frank Bidart, and Marianne Craig Moore, respectively—and the Princeton University Library (PU), the Vassar College Library (VC), the Houghton Library, Harvard University (HL), and the Rosenbach Museum and Library, Philadelphia (RM), for their permission to examine and quote from manuscript material. Brackets distinguish my ellipses from Bishop's use of the ellipsis as punctuation.

1. Robert Giroux's edition of Bishop's letters is forthcoming with Farrar, Straus & Giroux.

2. Although I do not discuss this aspect of the correspondence here, when she did write more directly to Kit Barker it was to address art in Brazil and abroad, especially his art, many pieces of which he sent her over the years. She always had

plans to bring the Barkers to Brazil, and she often made hypothetical arrangements of Brazilian exhibits of Kit's work or offered suggestions of positions at museums or universities. For various reasons, none of these plans materialized. Art, nonetheless, was always important to her—she painted over three dozen watercolors herself—and a topic of lively discussion.

3. Barker's drawing is of the view from the house at which they stayed together in North Haven, looking toward Penobscot Bay and Mount Megunticuk. The broadside was published in 1979 by the Lord John Press, Northridge, California, in 150 signed copies. See MacMahon 1980, pp. 118–19, for further reference.

4. David Kalstone (1985 and 1989) gives an account of the early period of Lowell's and Bishop's relationship.

5. For discussion of the Bishop-Moore relationship, see Kalstone 1983b, Keller 1983, and Costello 1984.

6. See letters from Marjorie Stevens to Bishop (26 November 1944, VC) and from Bishop to Anny Baumann (5 August 1948, VC).

7. In their letters to Bishop, Marianne Moore (20 December 1953, VC), Robert Lowell (1 January 1954, VC), V. L. O. Chittick (2 January 1954, VC), May Swenson (25 January and 16 March 1954, WU), and Marjorie Stevens (22 February 1954, VC), among others, tell her how impressed they are with the story's language, the style, and the accurateness of detail.

8. See also Gioia 1986 and Wehr 1981 for humorous portraits of Bishop's classroom teaching method: she expected the same attention to detail of her surprised and unprepared classes as she expected of her fellow poets and herself.

9. Both this story and the novel *Return* were published under the pseudonym that Barker used for her writing, Kathrine Talbot.

10. There is a gap in Bishop's letters to Lowell from 5 December 1953 to 20 November 1954. If there is a missing letter during this year, it would be the logical place for her to have mentioned Jewett's influence on her, were there to be such a mention at all. Bishop refers on 20 May 1955 to a long missing letter, but it is unclear whether she means a letter during that 1954 gap or another one entirely. She suggested to May Swenson during this period that she read Jewett but claimed no personal affinity.

11. See especially "Elizabeth Bishop: Influences," a version of a talk Bishop gave on 13 December 1977 in a series of "conversations" sponsored by the Academy of American Poets. Bishop reiterated these influences in slightly varied form in the interview conducted by Brown 1983, p. 292, and in Hale and Byatt 1978, p. 61.

12. Bishop published two book reviews about Dickinson in the early 1950s (see "Love from Emily," review of *Emily Dickinson's Letters to Doctor and Mrs. Josiah Gilbert Holland,* by Theodora Van Wagenen Ward, *New Republic* 125 [August 1951]: 20–21; and "Unseemly Deductions," review of *The Riddle of Emily Dickinson,* by Rebecca Patterson, *New Republic* 127 [August 1952]: 20). Bishop attempted a poem about Dickinson and Hopkins in 1955 and again in the mid-seventies and addressed her difficulties with Dickinson in mid-fifties letters to Lowell. She discussed her reading of Woolf in Starbuck 1983, p. 322, and in letters to Lowell (27 July 1960, HL) and to the Barkers (28 February 1955), where she generalized about women writers.

BRETT CANDLISH MILLIER

Elusive Mastery: The Drafts of Elizabeth Bishop's "One Art"

IN THE ELEVEN YEARS that passed between the publication of her volumes *Questions of Travel* (1965) and *Geography III* (1976), Elizabeth Bishop suffered such losses that it must have seemed to her that her life was ending very much as it had begun—in fear, uncertainty, and solitude. As a child, she had lost her father before she knew him, when he died of Bright's disease eight months after she was born. Her mother was deeply disoriented by her husband's death and spent the next five years in and out of mental institutions until, in 1916, she was diagnosed as permanently insane. Her five-year-old daughter would never see her again. Little Elizabeth had managed, with the uncanny adaptability of a child, to construct herself a secure world in the home of her maternal grandparents in Great Village, Nova Scotia. But her father's wealthy Boston family, worried that their only grandchild would grow up backward there among the ignorant, uprooted her a year later, and she began what would become a lifetime of living as a guest in other people's homes. In 1967, the most secure of these guest homes, in Petrópolis, Brazil, was violently disrupted when her hostess, friend, and lover of fifteen years suffered a breakdown and committed suicide, and Bishop was once again cast out. She landed awkwardly at Harvard University in September 1970. In the fall of 1975, the young woman who was the saving grace of Bishop's years in Cambridge sought to break their ties, and Bishop was again devastated. As if to address this renewed sense of loss, the poems of *Geography III,* written for the most part in Cambridge in the years following Lota de Macedo Soares's death, are "carefully revealed" elegies. The combination of age (Bishop turned sixty in 1971), poor health, alcoholism, the radical displacement forced upon her by the circumstances of

Lota's suicide, and her own financial condition begin to account for the weighty melancholy of these final poems. For a while, perhaps, Bishop thought she would write no more poetry. Throughout the manuscripts, correspondence, and galley proofs of her 1969 *Complete Poems,* the title of the volume alternated between *complete* and *collected,* as if the poet were weighing the likelihood that she would continue to write.

Later, in the long, slow process of gathering poems for her next book, *Geography III,* Bishop promised her publisher a long piece with the working title "Elegy." When she did not finish the poem in time, she decided it would be book-length itself and indicated on a 1977 Guggenheim Foundation application that this and a new volume called *Grandmother's Glass Eye,* would be her project. Only the barest outline of "Elegy" is left among Bishop's papers. It indicates that she planned to write the poem "in sections, some anecdotal, some lyrical different lengths—never more than two short pages." The poem was to be an elegy for Lota, for her "reticence and pride," her "heroism brave and young"; her "beautiful colored skin"; "the gestures (which you said you didn't have)." And also for specific memories: "the door slamming, plaster-falling—the cook and I laughing helplessly"; for her "courage to the last, or almost the last—"; "regret and guilt, the nighttime horrors, the WASTE." Bishop never finished "Elegy," although among her papers there is a very rough draft of a short poem called "Aubade and Elegy" (box 30, folder 456, VC), apparently written in 1969 or 1970. It mourns Lota in terms of two great facts of Brazilian life: "No coffee can wake you no coffee can wake you / no coffee / No revolution can catch your attention." The poem recalls the lichens of Bishop's first poem for Lota, "The Shampoo" written in 1955, (*CP,* p. 84): "No your life slowed then to that of the lichens circles, then of the rocks." It ends with a sad inventory of Lota's "things": "Oh God, the yellow hat."

Despite the fact that among these rough notes are several important words and ideas that turned up later in "One Art"—notably "gestures" and jokes and the pain of losing "things"—the villanelle does not replace that lost book-length elegy but rather incorporates it. There is no doubt that the crisis behind this poem was the apparent loss to Bishop of Alice Methfessel, the companion, caretaker, secretary, and great love of the last eight years of her life. Although its method is the description of the accumulation of losses in the poet's life, its occasion is the loss of Alice.

"One Art" is an exercise in the art of losing, a rehearsal of the things we tell ourselves in order to keep going, a speech in a brave voice that cracks once in the final version and cracked even more in the early drafts. The finished poem may be the best modern example of a villanelle and shares with its nearest competitor, Theodore Roethke's justly famous "The Waking"—"I wake to sleep and take my waking slow"—the feeling that in the course of writing or saying the poem the poet is giving herself a lesson, in waking, in losing. Bishop's lines share her ironic tips for learning to lose and to live with loss.

> The art of losing isn't hard to master;
> so many things seem filled with the intent
> to be lost that their loss is no disaster.
>
> Lose something every day. Accept the fluster
> of lost door keys, the hour badly spent.
> The art of losing isn't hard to master.
>
> Then practice losing farther, losing faster:
> places, and names, and where it was you meant
> to travel. None of these will bring disaster.
>
> I lost my mother's watch. And look! my last, or
> next-to-last, of three loved houses went.
> The art of losing isn't hard to master.
>
> I lost two cities, lovely ones. And, vaster,
> some realms I owned, two rivers, a continent.
> I miss them, but it wasn't a disaster.
>
> —Even losing you (the joking voice, a gesture
> I love) I shan't have lied. It's evident
> the art of losing's not too hard to master
> though it may look like (*Write* it!) like disaster.

(CP, p. 178)

More than once in the drafts of Bishop's published poems, one finds that she came to express in the final draft nearly the opposite of what she started out to say. As Barbara Page (1981–82) has pointed out, for example, in the seven available drafts of her poem "Questions of Travel," Bishop develops the key line of the final stanza from an early "The choice perhaps is not great . . . but fairly free" (box 31, folder 436, VC) to its final "The choice is never wide and never free," as the poet comes to realize restrictions that bind the traveler by articulating them in the poem (*CP*, pp. 55–57). The very late poem "Santarém," which describes from an eighteen-year distance a stop on Bishop's 1960 trip down the Amazon River, offers a similar development. In the final version of that poem, Bishop describes the confluence of "two great rivers," the Tapajós and the Amazon, and remembers that she was enchanted by this coming together. The last lines of the central stanza read in the final draft:

> Even if one were tempted
> to literary interpretations
> such as: life/death, right/wrong, male/female
> —such notions would have resolved, dissolved, straight off
> in that watery, dazzling dialectic.

(*CP*, p. 185)

The earliest drafts of this poem (box 31, folder 470, VC) show that Bishop was at first concerned, in trying to articulate the emotion she felt in seeing the conflux of two great rivers, with choosing between them, between the literary interpretations she dismisses in the final version. The poem originally evaluated, as "Questions of Travel" had, the traveler's possibilty for "choice"; the resolution the conflux first offered was the chance to decide: "Choice—a choice! That evening one might choose," she wrote in the first draft. In the final draft, even the idea of choice has disappeared and the place offers only resolution, as the poet lets go of her need to choose.

Something similar occurs within the seventeen available drafts of "One Art" (box 30, folder 456, VC). Bishop conceived the poem as a villanelle from the start, and the play of "twos" within it—two rivers, two cities, the lost lover means not being "two" any more—suggests that the two-rhyme villanelle is a form appropriate to the content. Bishop told an interviewer that after years of trying to write in that form, the poem just came to her. "I couldn't believe it—it was like writing a letter" (Spires 1981, p. 64). A letter with seventeen drafts, perhaps. The poem does seem to have been written over a period of about two weeks— ending on 4 November 1975—much shorter than her usual period of composition.

The first extant draft is a series of partly worked-up notes, appar- ently a basis for developing the rhymes and refrains of the final version. Its overall thematic shape is familiar in the final poem, with the evidence of the speaker's experience at losing followed by a somewhat strained application of that experience. In its unedited catalog of losses, it is heartbreaking to read.

The draft is tentatively titled "HOW TO LOSE THINGS," then "THE GIFT OF LOSING THINGS" and finally, "THE ART OF LOSING THINGS." (The title "One Art" appears to have been arrived at very late in the process.) This draft begins with the suggestion that the way to acquire this art is to "begin by mislaying" several items that remain in the final draft—keys, pens, glasses. Then she says,

> —This is by way of introduction. I really
> want to introduce myself—I am such a
> fantastic lly good at losing things
> I think everyone shd. profit from my experiences.

She then lists her qualifications: "You may find it hard to believe, but I have actually lost / I mean lost, and forever, two whole houses." Among her other losses: "A third house, . . . / I think, 'mislaid' . . . / . . . I won't know for sure for some time,"

> one peninsula and one island. . . .
> a small-sized town . . . and many smaller bits of geography or scenery
> a splendid beach, and a good-sized bay. . . .
>
> a good piece of one continent
> and another continent—the whole damned thing!

In the end, she writes:

> One might think this would have prepared me
> for losing one average-sized- not ~~especially~~ exceptionally
> beautiful or dazzlingly intelligent person
> (except for blue eyes) (only the eyes <u>were</u> exceptionally
> beautiful and the hands <u>looked</u>
> intelligent) the fine hands
> But it doesn't seem to have, at all. . .

The draft trails off with "He who loseth his life, etc.—but he who / loses his love—neever, no never never never again—."

In Elizabeth's handwriting in the margins of this typed draft are notations about possible rhymes for the villanelle, including "ever/never/

forever," "geography/scenery," and a version of her final choice, involving "intelligent" "continent," "sent," "spent," and "lent." This catalog served to set the terms for working into the form. By the second draft, the poem is an incomplete villanelle with "The art of losing isn't hard to master" as the first line, and the "no disaster" play in the third line. The final stanza is crossed out, although legible under the scoring is "But your loss spelt disaster." The marginalia, handwritten like the draft, consist of more work on rhyme and suggest other directions in which Bishop might have taken the poem. One set—"gesture," "protestor," "attestor," "foster," "boaster"—suggests a possible angry, almost litigious response to loss, and the words *evident* and *false* are set to one side of the scribbled-over final stanza, ready to be worked in.

The following drafts work mostly on the first four stanzas, whittling the catalog of losses into a discreet and resonant form and setting the rhyme scheme firmly. It is not until the fifth draft, which consists otherwise of a simple list of end-rhymes, that Bishop once again breaks her controlled tone in the final stanza. Here the original refrain is dutifully repeated, but the poetic frame, for a moment, won't bear the emotional weight:

> The art of losing's not so hard to master
> ~~But won't help in~~ think of that disaster
> No—I am lying—

This transformation of the "false"/"evident" play into "lying" is Bishop's first major change aimed at solving to her logical, emotional, and aesthetic satisfaction the problem of how the experience of losing car keys, houses, and continents could apply in handling this truly, as she perceived it now, disastrous loss. In the sixth draft, the final stanza reads: "The art of losing's not so hard to master / until that point & then it / fails & is disaster—." The poem bogs down here; the seventh draft stops short of the final stanza, and the eighth is sketchy, with such lines as "losses nobody can master" and "the art of losing's not impossible to master / It won't work . . ."—most of which are crossed out.

It appears that some time passed between the eighth and ninth drafts, for all of the later attempts are typed and contain completed versions of all six stanzas. In the ninth draft Bishop develops in the last stanza a more complete version of the "lying" theme:

> All that I write is false, it's evident
> The art of losing isn't hard to master.

oh no.
anythng at all anything but one's love. (Say it: disaster.)

The formalized spontaneity of "(Say it: disaster.)" enables the poem to accommodate the overflow of emotion that had, to this point, disarrayed the final stanza and made the villanelle's ritual repetitions inadequate to manage the emotional content. Bishop was fond of this technique of self-interruption or self-revision in a poem. She learned it from Gerard Manley Hopkins and from Baroque sermon writers and spoke of it as "portraying the mind in action" ("The Baroque Style in Prose," box 27, folder 395, VC).

The next version of the final stanza begins with the first real exploration of possible code words that might stand for "you," a phrase or aspect that would bring the lover wholly into the poem. The line is: "But, losing you (eyes of the Azure Aster)"—recalling the "remarkable" blue eyes of the first draft. This awkward and self-consciously poetic phrase would hang in through several drafts, until both its awkwardness and Bishop's need to generalize caused her to discard it for the more discreet and more melodious "gesture," which had been haunting the edges of the final stanza in the previous few drafts. Here, in the tenth, the idea is still that "I've written lies above" (which she has crossed out in pencil, with "above's all lies" written in) and "the art of losing isn't hard to master / with one exception. (Say it.) That's disaster." In draft eleven, the final stanza is reworked five times and the last line becomes, as Bishop had written and crossed out in the previous draft, "with one exception. (*Write it.*) Write 'disaster.' " Here both words in the phrase *write it* are italicized, as they would be until the poem was collected in *Geography III*—a slight but significant alteration of tone. The change in her means of affirmation or validation from "say it" to "write it" is the crux that, once solved, let the poem speak its curiously independent truth.

For midway through the twelfth draft, quite abruptly, "above's all lies" becomes "above's not lies" and then "I haven't lied above." And yet, still, "The art of losing wasn't hard to master / with this exception (*Write it!*) this disaster." This draft reworks the last stanza four tortured times and clearly wavers on whether or not "above's all lies," and on whether this loss is an example or an exception. Versions of both feelings are tried and crossed out and even the parenthetical outburst, "write it," alternates with "oh isn't it?" a disaster. What remains is the idea that whatever the brave speech or the possibilities for mastery, this loss still looks like disaster.

The thirteenth draft is the last that thoroughly reworks the final stanza, and it is at this point that the "gesture" becomes a "special voice," then a "funny voice," and finally the "joking voice." There are two tentative versions of the ending. First:

And losing you ~~now (a special voice, a gesture)~~
doesn't mean I've lied. It's evident
the loss of love is possible to master,
even if this looks like (Write it!) like disaster.

And, mostly crossed out,

In losing you I haven't lied above. It's evident
. . .
The loss ~~of love is something one must master~~
even if it looks like (Write it!) like disaster.

Firmly in place is the idea that this apparent disaster does not mean that losing cannot after all be mastered, even though when Bishop sat down to write the poem the first time, it must have seemed that it did. In the fourteenth draft, the words "not too hard to master" indicate Bishop's approach to the final version—the colloquial tone is a trademark of her polished style. The fifteenth draft makes few changes in the poem—notably in line two "so many things seem really to be meant" to be lost becomes "so many things seem filled with the intent to be lost." The draft is typed and has an almost-finished version of the final stanza—though handwritten notes show Bishop still struggling with how to express the "above's not lies" idea—"these were not lies" is the typed version; the handwritten notes offer "I ~~still do~~ can't lie" and "I still won't lie." The draft that Frank Bidart has seems to be a cleanly typed carbon version of draft fifteen with changes dictated to Bidart over the telephone by Bishop. The two major changes are the "filled with the intent to be lost" change, and, as is not in the version labeled draft fifteen at Vassar, in the second line of the final stanza, "these were not lies" becomes the now seemingly inevitable "I shan't have lied." What is odd about this late change is that "I shan't have lied" is technically in the future perfect tense. The phrase retains the past-tense sense of "I haven't lied above"—referring to the list of mastered losses in the rest of the poem—yet also poses a possible resolution in the future: "after I come to terms with this loss, then I won't have lied, but right now I don't know." The most significant ramification of the change to "I shan't have lied" is that it

reminds us forcefully that this poem is a crisis lyric in the truest sense—
"Even losing you" comes to mean "Even if I lose you"—and we know
that this is not emotion recollected in tranquillity, but a live, as it were,
moment of awful fear, with relief only a hoped-for possibilty.

One way to read Bishop's modulation from "the loss of you is impossible to master" to something like "I may yet master this loss even
though it looks like disaster" is that in the writing of such a disciplined,
demanding poem [*"(Write* it!)"] lies a piece of the mastery of the loss.
Working through each of her losses—from the bold, painful catalog of
the first draft to the finely honed and privately meaningful final version—
is a way to overcome them or, if not to overcome them, then to see the
way in which one might possibly master oneself in the face of loss. It is
all, perhaps, "one art"—elegy-writing, mastering loss, mastering grief,
self-mastery. The losses in the poem are real: time, in the form of the
"hour badly spent" and, more tellingly for the orphaned Elizabeth, "my
mother's watch"; the lost houses, in Key West, Petrópolis and, the one
still in doubt, Ouro Prêto, Brazil. The city of Rio de Janeiro and the whole
South American continent were lost to her with Lota's suicide. And currently, in the fall of 1975, she thought she had lost her dearest friend and
lover, she of the blue eyes and fine hands. Yet each version of the poem
distanced the pain a little more, depersonalized it, moved it away from
the tawdry self-pity and confession that Bishop disliked in many of her
contemporaries. The effect of reading all these drafts together one often
feels in reading the raw material of her poems and then the poems themselves: the tremendous selectivity of her method and her gift for forcing
richness from minimal words. An example is how, in the first draft of
"One Art," the lines "I am such a / fantastic lly good at losing things /
I think everyone shd. profit from my experiences" introduce her list of
qualifications. In the final version the two words "And look!" serve the
same purpose.

Elizabeth's letters to her doctor, a brilliant woman then in her seven-
ties, describe the despair of the fall of 1975. Elizabeth was sure that she
had lost the last person on earth who loved her. The letters agonize over
her prospect of a lonely old age, crowded with fans and students and
hangers-on but empty of love. Out of this despair, apparently, came the
villanelle "One Art." But my reading of the poem still wants to make
it Bishop's elegy for her whole life, despite its obvious origins. Elizabeth apologized to her friends for the poem, saying "I'm afraid it's a
sort of tear-jerker" (December 1975, PU)—she was clearly somewhat

uncomfortable with even this careful approach to the confessional. It is well known that her friends remained for a long time protective of her personal reputation and unwilling to have her grouped among lesbian poets or even among the other great poets of her generation—Robert Lowell, Roethke, and John Berryman—as they self-destructed before their readers' eyes. Elizabeth herself taught them this reticence by keeping her private life very private indeed and by investing what confession there was in her poems deeply in objects and places, thus deflecting biographical inquiry. In the development of this poem, discretion is a poetic method and a part of a process of self-understanding, the seeing of a pattern in one's own life.

The poem arose from an immediate crisis, but Bishop's papers and correspondence reveal that its elements had been with her for a long time. Her letters to Frani Blough Muser reveal that the two teenaged, then college-aged, girls had a kind of running joke about losing things— a letter of 5 September 1929 (VC) includes the following lines, apparently written by the eighteen-year-old Bishop, parodying Longfellow:

Lives of great men will remind us
We can mold life as we choose,
And departing leave behind us
Towels, safety pins and shoes.

A couple of years later, as Elizabeth contemplated a walking tour of Newfoundland, she had hopes of visiting the remote village of St. Anthony, "for after all, isn't St. Anthony the patron of lost articles?" (letter to Muser, 8 July 1932, VC). As it turned out, they couldn't get there; the village was "practically inaccessible." To Ilse and Kit Barker, Bishop wrote, referring to letters missing in the Brazilian mails, "I have a feeling some things have been lost in both directions—but now probably we'll never get it straightened out until all things are straightened out in eternity— at least that might be one way of filling up eternity, finding lost and mislaid articles" (6 October 1960, PU). More humorously, after the poem was published, Elizabeth temporarily lost her writing case in a Boston taxicab. To the Barkers she wrote, "Oh why did I ever write that cursed villanelle?" (28 August 1976, PU).

The joking voice, which people who knew both women tell me evokes its owner as surely as blue eyes would have done, is as well something that recurs in Elizabeth's life, that she loved in nearly all her friends and lovers, all the people whose loss had schooled her in the art of losing, and whose losses are implied in the catalog of "things" in the poem. A letter written to Anne Stevenson predicts the poem: "I have been very lucky in having had, most of my life, some witty friends,—and I mean real wit, quickness, wild fancies, remarks that make one cry with laughing. . . . The aunt I liked best was a very funny woman: most of my close friends have been funny people; Lota de Macedo Soares is funny. Pauline Hemingway (the 2nd Mrs. H.) a good friend until her death in 1951 was the wittiest person, man or woman, I've ever known. Marianne [Moore] was very funny—[e.e.] Cummings, too, of course. Perhaps I need such people to cheer me up" (8 January 1964, WU).

The "joking voice," the gesture Elizabeth loved (and, in fact, employed), she loved in Alice, she had loved in Lota, she loved in these other friends dead and gone—the phrase brings them all into the poem. In Bishop's distillation of immediate crisis into enduring art, the lesson in losing becomes even more a lesson one learns over and over, throughout one's life. The tentative resolution offered in the poem was not, alas, a real one; Elizabeth struggled terribly with this loss for months afterward. Only the lost one's return solved it. The poem is a wish for resolution or a resolution in the sense of a determination to survive—"I will master this loss; I will."[1] It is also a means of assessing the true magnitude of the present disaster in the middle of the crisis, a kind of "How bad is it?" question. And it explores the means of having one's loss and mastering it, too, which is the privilege of the elegist.

Notes

With exceptions as noted, all Elizabeth Bishop manuscripts quoted in this essay are among her papers at the Vassar College Library and are reproduced exactly as she left them. The collection holds seventeen drafts of "One Art," which Vassar has numbered.

1. The Oxford English Dictionary devotes several closely printed pages to the distinction between *will* and *shall* and reports, significantly, that "In the first person, *shall* has, from the early ME period, been the normal auxiliary for expressing mere futurity, without any adventitious notion a) of events conceived as independent of the speaker's volition. b) of voluntary action or its intended result. Further, I *shall* often expresses a determination in spite of opposition, and I shall not (colloq. I *shan't*) a peremptory refusal" (p. 152).

Select Bibliography

Contributors

Index

Select Bibliography

Select Primary Published Sources

Bishop, Elizabeth. 1930. "The Thumb." *The Blue Pencil* 13 (April): 6–9. (Reprinted in the *Gettysburg Review* 5 [Winter 1992]: 28–31.)

———. 1967. "Second Chance." *Time*, 2 June, p. 69.

———, ed. and trans. 1977. *The Diary of "Helena Morley,"* by Alice (Dayrell) Brant. Reprint. New York: Ecco Press.

———. 1983. "On 'Confessional Poetry.'" In Schwartz and Estess 1983, p. 303. (Excerpted from "Poets," *Time*, 2 June 1967, pp. 35–42.)

———. 1984. *Elizabeth Bishop: The Collected Prose*, ed. Robert Giroux. New York: Farrar, Straus, and Giroux.

———. 1985. "Elizabeth Bishop: Influences," ed. Henri Cole. *American Poetry Review*, January–February, pp. 11–16.

———. 1991. *Elizabeth Bishop: The Complete Poems, 1927–1979*. New York: Farrar, Straus, and Giroux.

Interviews

Bishop, Elizabeth. 1978. "Elizabeth Bishop Speaks about Her Poetry." *New Paper* (Bennington College) 4 (June).

Brown, Ashley. 1983. "An Interview with Elizabeth Bishop." In Schwartz and Estess 1983, pp. 289–302. (First published in *Shenandoah* 17 [Winter 1966]: 3–19.)

Johnson, Alexandra. 1978. "Poet Elizabeth Bishop: Geography of the Imagination." *Christian Science Monitor*, 23 March 1978, pp. 24–25.

Merrill, James. 1988 Interview from "Elizabeth Bishop, One Art," in the PBS *Voices and Visions* series. New York: Center for Visual History Productions.

Spires, Elizabeth. 1981. "The Art of Poetry, XXVII: Elizabeth Bishop." *Paris Review* 23 (Summer): 56–83.

Starbuck, George. 1983. "'The Work!': A Conversation with Elizabeth Bishop." In Schwartz and Estess 1983, pp. 312–30. (First published in *Ploughshares* 3 [1977]: 11–29.)

Archival Material

Bishop-Lowell Correspondence, Houghton Library, Harvard University, Cambridge, Mass.

Bishop-Moore Correspondence, Rosenbach Museum and Library, Philadelphia, Pa.

Select Bibliography

Bishop-Stevenson Correspondence, Elizabeth Bishop Papers, Olin Library, Special Collections, Washington University, St. Louis, Mo.
Elizabeth Bishop Collection, Special Collections, Vassar College, Poughkeepsie, N.Y.
Elizabeth Bishop Letters to Ilse and Kit Barker, Barker C0270, Rare Books and Special Collections, Princeton University, Princeton, N.J.

Secondary Material

Ashbery, John. 1977. "Second Presentation of Elizabeth Bishop." *World Literature Today* 51 (Winter): 9–11.
———. 1983. "The Complete Poems." In Schwartz and Estess 1983, pp. 201–5. (First published in the *New York Times Book Review*, 1 June 1969, pp. 8, 25.)
Bidart, Frank. 1983. "On Elizabeth Bishop." In Schwartz and Estess 1983, pp. 214–15.
Blasing, Mutlu Konuk. 1987. "'*Mont d'Espoir* or *Mount Despair*': The Reverses of Elizabeth Bishop." Chap. 6 in Blasing's *American Poetry: The Rhetoric of Its Forms*. New Haven: Yale Univ. Press. (First published in *Contemporary Literature* 25 (1984): 341–53.)
Bloom, Harold. 1973. *The Anxiety of Influence: A Theory of Poetry*. New York: Oxford Univ. Press.
———. 1983. Foreword to Schwartz and Estess 1983, pp. ix–xi.
———, ed. 1985. *Elizabeth Bishop: Modern Critical Views*. New York: Chelsea House Publishers.
Brogan, Jacqueline Vaught. 1986. *Stevens and Simile: A Theory of Language*. Princeton: Princeton Univ. Press.
———. 1987. "Wallace Stevens: Poems against His Climate." *Wallace Stevens Journal* 11 (Fall): 75–93.
———. 1988. "Sister of the Minotaur." *Wallace Stevens Journal* 12 (Fall): 102–18.
Bromwich, David. 1985. "Elizabeth Bishop's Dream-Houses." In Bloom 1985, pp. 159–74. (First published in *Raritan* 4 [Summer 1984]: 77–94.)
Ciardi, John, ed. 1950. *Mid-Century American Poets*. New York: Twayne.
Cixous, Hélène. 1981. "The Laugh of the Medusa." In *New French Feminisms: An Anthology*, ed. Elaine Marks and Isabelle de Courtivron, trans. Keith Cohen and Paula Cohen, pp. 245–64. New York: Schocken Books.
Cooper, Jane. 1974. "Nothing Has Been Used in the Manufacture of This Poetry That Could Have Been Used in the Manufacture of Bread." In her *Maps and Windows*, pp. 29–58. New York: Macmillan.
Corn, Alfred. 1977. Review of *Geography III*. *Georgia Review* 31 (Summer): 533–41.
Costello, Bonnie. 1983. "The Impersonal and the Interrogative in the Poetry of Elizabeth Bishop." In Schwartz and Estess 1983, pp. 109–32.
———. 1984. "Marianne Moore and Elizabeth Bishop: Friendship and Influence." *Twentieth Century Literature* 30 (Summer–Fall): 130–49.

————. 1988. "Writing Like a Woman: A Review of Alicia Ostriker's *Stealing the Language.*" *Contemporary Literature* 29 (Summer): 305–10.

Croll, Morris W. 1929. "The Baroque Style in Prose." In *Studies in English Philology,* ed. Kemp Malone and Martin B. Ruud, pp. 437–43. Minneapolis: Univ. of Minnesota Press.

Culler, Jonathan. 1985. "Changes in the Study of Lyric." In Hošek and Parker 1985, pp. 38–54.

De Man, Paul. 1985. "Lyrical Voice in Contemporary Theory: Riffaterre and Jauss." In Hošek and Parker 1985, pp. 55–72.

Derrida, Jacques. 1981. "Plato's Pharmacy." Sections 3 and 4 of his *Dissemination,* trans. Barbara Johnson. Chicago: Univ. of Chicago Press.

Diehl, Joanne Feit. 1985. "At Home with Loss: Elizabeth Bishop and the American Sublime." In *Coming to Light: American Women Poets in the Twentieth Century,* ed. Diane Wood Middlebrook and Marilyn Yalom, pp. 123–37. Ann Arbor: Univ. of Michigan Press.

————. 1990. *Women Poets and the American Sublime.* Bloomington: Indiana Univ. Press.

Easton, Elizabeth Wynne. 1989. *The Intimate Interiors of Edouard Vuillard.* Washington, D.C.: Smithsonian Institution Press.

Edelman, Lee. 1985. "The Geography of Gender: Elizabeth Bishop's 'In the Waiting Room.'" *Contemporary Literature,* 26 (Summer): pp. 179–96.

Elliott, Charles. 1969. "Minor Poet with a Major Fund of Love." *Life,* 4 July 1969, p. 13.

Ellis, Havelock. 1936. "Sexual Inversion among Women." In his *Sexual Inversion,* pp. 261–62; vol. 2 in *Studies in the Psychology of Sex.* 1897; rpt. New York: Random House.

Estess, Sybil. 1977. "History as Geography." *Southern Review* 13 (Autumn): 705–27.

————. 1983. "Description and Imagination in Elizabeth Bishop's 'The Map.'" In Schwartz and Estess 1983, pp. 219–22.

Fraser, Kathleen. 1977. "On Being a West Coast Woman Poet." *Women's Studies* 5, no. 2: 153–60.

Freud, Sigmund. 1944. *Leonardo da Vinci: A Study in Psychosexuality.* New York: Vintage Books.

Frye, Northrop. 1965. *Anatomy of Criticism.* Princeton: Princeton Univ. Press, 1957. Reprint: New York: Atheneum.

Gallop, Jane. 1988. *Thinking through the Body.* New York: Columbia Univ. Press.

Gauthier, Xavière. 1980. "Oscillation between Power and Denial." Interview with Julia Kristeva. In *New French Feminisms,* ed. Elaine Marks and Isabelle de Courtivron, trans. Marilyn A. August, pp. 165–66. Amherst: Univ. of Massachusetts Press.

Gelpi, Albert. 1985. "Stevens and Williams: The Epistemology of Modernism." In *Wallace Stevens: The Poetics of Modernism,* ed. Albert Gelpi, pp. 3–23. Cambridge Univ. Press.

Gilbert, Sandra. 1983. "Soldier's Heart: Literary Men, Literary Women, and the Great War." *Signs* 8 (Spring): 422–50.

Gilbert, Sandra, and Susan Gubar. 1979. *The Madwoman in the Attic.* New Haven: Yale Univ. Press.

Gioia, Dana. 1986. "Studying with Miss Bishop." *New Yorker,* 15 September 1986, pp. 90–101.

Goldensohn, Lorrie. 1988. "Elizabeth Bishop: An Unpublished, Untitled Poem." *American Poetry Review* 17 (January–February): 35–46.

————. 1991. *Elizabeth Bishop: The Biography of a Poetry.* New York: Columbia Univ. Press.

Greene, Thomas M. 1982. *The Light in Troy: Imitation and Discovery in Renaissance Poetry.* New Haven: Yale Univ. Press.

Hale, Sheila, and A. S. Byatt. 1978. "Women Writers in America." *Harpers & Queens,* July, pp. 58–71.

Hall, Donald. 1970. *Marianne Moore: The Cage and the Animal.* New York: Pegasus.

Handa, Carolyn. 1986. "Vision and Change: The Poetry of Elizabeth Bishop." *American Poetry* 3 (Winter): 18–34.

Hollander, John. 1977. "Questions of Geography." *Parnassus* 5 (Spring–Summer): 360–66.

————. 1983. "Elizabeth Bishop's Mappings of Life." In Schwartz and Estess 1983, pp. 244–51.

Hošek, Chaviva, and Patricia Parker, eds. 1985. *Lyric Poetry: Beyond New Criticism.* Ithaca: Cornell Univ. Press.

Hulme, T. E. 1958. *Speculations, Essays on Humanism and the Philosophy of Art,* ed. Herbert Read. London: Routledge & Kegan Paul.

Humphries, Rolphe. 1925. "Precieuse, Model 1924." *Measure* 53: pp. 15–17.

Johnson, Barbara. 1980. "The Frame of Reference: Poe, Lacan, Derrida." Chap. 7 of her *The Critical Difference: Essays in the Contemporary Rhetoric of Reading.* Baltimore: Johns Hopkins Univ. Press.

————. 1985. *"Les Fleurs du mal arme:* Some Reflections on Intertextuality." In Hošek and Parker 1985, pp. 264–80.

————. 1987. "Metaphor, Metonymy, and Voice in *Their Eyes Were Watching God.*" Chap. 14 of her *A World of Difference.* Baltimore and London: Johns Hopkins Univ. Press.

Johnson, James William. 1986. "Lyric." In *The Princeton Handbook of Poetic Terms.* Ed. Alex Preminger. Princeton: Princeton Univ. Press.

Johnson, Osa. 1940. *I Married an Adventure.* New York: J. B. Lippincott.

David Kalstone. 1983a. "Elizabeth Bishop: Questions of Memory, Questions of Travel." In Schwartz and Estess 1983, pp. 3–31. (First published in his *Five Temperaments: Elizabeth Bishop, Robert Lowell, James Merrill, Adrienne Rich, John Ashbery,* pp. 12–41 [New York: Oxford Univ. Press, 1977].)

————. 1983b. "Trial Balances: Elizabeth Bishop and Marianne Moore." *Grand Street* 3 (Autumn): 115–35.

————. 1985. "Prodigal Years: Elizabeth Bishop and Robert Lowell 1947–49." *Grand Street* 4 (Summer): 170–93.

————. 1989. *Becoming a Poet: Elizabeth Bishop with Marianne Moore and Robert Lowell.* New York: Farrar, Straus, and Giroux.

Keller, Lynn. 1983. "Words Worth a Thousand Postcards: The Bishop/Moore Correspondence." *American Literature* 55 (October): 405–29.

Keller, Lynn, and Christanne Miller. 1984. "Emily Dickinson, Elizabeth Bishop, and the Rewards of Indirection." *New England Quarterly* 57 (December): 533–53.

Kermode, Frank. 1979. "Carnal and Spiritual Senses." Chap. 1 of his *The Genesis of Secrecy: On the Interpretation of Narrative.* Cambridge: Harvard Univ. Press.

Lauretis, Teresa de. 1990. "Eccentric Subjects: Feminist Theory and Historical Consciousness." *Feminist Studies* 16 (Spring): 115–49.

Lehman, David. 1983. " 'In Prison': A Paradox Regained." In Schwartz and Estess 1983, pp. 61–74.

Lentricchia, Frank. 1983. *Criticism and Social Change.* Chicago: Univ. of Chicago Press.

Lowell, Robert. 1947. "Thomas, Bishop, and Williams." *Sewanee Review* 55 (July–September): 497–99.

———. 1983. "For Elizabeth Bishop 4." In Schwartz and Estess 1983, p. 207. (First published in Lowell's *History,* p. 198 [New York: Farrar, Straus, and Giroux, 1973].)

———. 1987. *Collected Prose,* ed. Robert Giroux. New York: Farrar, Straus, and Giroux.

McClatchy, J. D. 1984. "Some Notes on 'One Art.' " *Field: Contemporary Poetry and Poetics* 31 (Fall): 34–39.

MacMahon, Candace W. 1980. *Elizabeth Bishop: A Bibliography, 1927–1979.* Charlottesville: Univ. Press of Virginia.

Mazzaro, Jerome. 1985. "The Poetics of Impediment: Elizabeth Bishop." In Bloom 1985, pp. 23–50. (First published as Chap. 7 of Mazzaro's *Postmodern American Poetry* [Urbana: Univ. of Illinois Press, 1980].)

Merrill, James. 1979. "Elizabeth Bishop, 1911–1979." In Schwartz and Estess 1983, pp. 259–62. (First published in *New York Review of Books,* 6 December 1979, p. 6.)

Merrin, Jeredith. 1990. *An Enabling Humility: Marianne Moore, Elizabeth Bishop, and the Uses of Tradition.* New Brunswick, N.J.: Rutgers Univ. Press.

Millier, Brett Candlish. 1989. "Modesty and Morality: George Herbert, Gerard Manley Hopkins, and Elizabeth Bishop." *Kenyon Review* 11 (Spring): 47–56.

Moore, Marianne. 1983a. "Archaically New." In Schwartz and Estess 1983, pp. 175–76. (First published in *Trial Balances,* ed. Ann Winslow, pp. 82–83. [New York: MacMillan, 1935].)

———. 1983b. "A Modest Expert: *North & South.*" In Schwartz and Estess 1983, pp. 177–79. (First published in the *Nation,* 28 September 1946, p. 354.)

Moss, Howard. 1977. "The Canada-Brazil Connection." *World Literature Today* 51 (Winter): 29–33.

———. 1985. "A Long Voyage Home." Review of *Elizabeth Bishop: The Collected Prose,* ed. Robert Giroux. *New Yorker,* 1 April 1985, p. 104.

Mullen, Richard. 1982. "Elizabeth Bishop's Surrealist Inheritance." *American Literature* 54 (March): 63–80.

Newman, Anne R. 1983. "Elizabeth Bishop's 'Roosters.'" In Bloom 1985, pp. 111–20.

Nyquist, Mary. 1985. "Musing on Susanna's Music." In Hošek and Parker 1985, pp. 310–27.

Ostriker, Alicia Suskin. 1982. "Thieves of Language: Women Poets and Revisionist Myth-Making." *Signs* 8 (Autumn): 68–90.

———. 1986. *Stealing the Language: The Emergence of Woman's Poetry in America.* Boston: Beacon Press.

Page, Barbara. 1981–82. "Shifting Islands: Elizabeth Bishop's Manuscripts." *Shenandoah* 33, no. 1: 51–62.

Parker, Robert Dale. 1988. *The Unbeliever: The Poetry of Elizabeth Bishop.* Urbana: Univ. of Illinois Press.

Paz, Octavio. 1983. "Elizabeth Bishop, or the Power of Reticence." In Schwartz and Estess 1983, pp. 211–13.

Perloff, Marjorie. 1977. "Elizabeth Bishop: The Course of a Particular." *Modern Poetry Studies* 8 (Winter): 177–92.

Pinsky, Robert. 1979. "Elizabeth Bishop, 1911–1979." In Schwartz and Estess 1983, pp. 255–58. (First published in *New Republic* 181 (10 November): 32–33.

Poe, Edgar Allan. 1984. "The Poetic Principle." In *Edgar Allan Poe: Essays and Reviews,* ed. G. R. Thompson. New York: Library of America.

Pound, Ezra. 1954. *Literary Essays,* ed. T. S. Eliot. London: Faber and Faber.

Procopiow, Norma. 1981. "Survival Kit: The Poetry of Elizabeth Bishop." *Centennial Review* 25 (Winter): 1–19.

Rich, Adrienne. 1979. "When We Dead Awaken: Writing as Re-Vision." In Rich's *On Lies, Secrets, and Silence: Selected Prose, 1966–1978,* pp. 33–49. New York: Norton.

———. 1983. "The Eye of the Outsider: The Poetry of Elizabeth Bishop." *Boston Review* 8 (April 1983): 15–17.

———. 1986. *Blood, Bread, and Poetry: Selected Poems, 1979–1985.* New York: Norton.

Sanders, Charles. 1982. "Bishop's 'Sonnet.'" *Explicator* 40 (Spring): 63–64.

Santos, Sherod. 1984. "The End of March." *Field* 31 (Fall): 29–32.

Schwartz, Lloyd. 1991. "Elizabeth Bishop and Brazil." *New Yorker* 30 (September): 85–97.

Schwartz, Lloyd, and Sybil Estess, eds. 1983. *Elizabeth Bishop and Her Art.* Ann Arbor: Univ. of Michigan Press.

Scott, Nathan A., Jr. 1984. "Elizabeth Bishop: Poet without Myth." *Virginia Quarterly Review* 60 (Spring): 255–75.

Shelley, Mary Wollstonecraft. [1831] 1965. *Frankenstein, or the Modern Prometheus.* Reprint. New York: Signet. (First published 1818.)

Sidney, Sir Philip. 1962. *The Poems of Sir Philip Sidney,* ed. William A. Ringler. Oxford: Oxford Univ. Press.

Spiegelman, Willard. 1985. "Elizabeth Bishop's 'Natural Heroism.'" In Bloom

1985, pp. 97–110. (First published in *Centennial Review* 22 [Winter 1978]: 28–44.)

———. 1992. "Elizabeth Bishop: 'The Things I'd Like to Write.'" *Gettysburg Review* 5 (Winter): pp. 62–70.

Stepanchev, Stephen. 1965. *American Poetry since 1945*. New York: Harper and Row.

Stevens, Wallace. 1954. *The Collected Poems*. New York: Alfred A. Knopf.

Stevenson, Anne. 1966. *Elizabeth Bishop*. New York: Twayne.

———. 1980. "Letters from Elizabeth Bishop." *Times Literary Supplement,* 7 March 1980, p. 261.

Talbot, Kathrine [Ilse Barker]. 1959. *Return*. London: Faber.

———. 1971. "The Lion of Heyst." *Paris Review* 13 (Winter): 117–23.

Travisano, Thomas. 1988. "Fables of Enclosure: *North & South I*." Chap. 2 in his *Elizabeth Bishop: Her Artistic Development,* pp. 17–51. Charlottesville: Univ. Press of Virginia.

———. 1991. "Heavenly Dragons: A Newly Discovered Poem by Elizabeth Bishop." *Western Humanities Review* 45 (Winter): 28–33.

———. 1992. "Emerging Genius: Elizabeth Bishop and *The Blue Pencil*, 1927–1930." *Gettysburg Review* 5 (Winter): 32–47.

Twain, Mark. 1935. *Mark Twain's Notebook,* ed. A. B. Paine. New York and London: Harper's.

Valentine, Jean. 1984. "Sonnet." *Field: Contemporary Poetry and Poetics* (Fall): 45.

Vendler, Helen. 1977. "Recent Poetry: Eight Poets." *Yale Review* 66 (Spring): 407–24.

———. 1983. "Domestication, Domesticity, and the Otherworldly." In Schwartz and Estess 1983, pp. 32–60.

Wehr, Wesley. 1981. "Elizabeth Bishop: Conversations and Class Notes." *Antioch Review* 39 (Summer): 319–28.

Wenzel, Helen Vivienne. 1981. "The Text as Body/Politics: An Appreciation of Monique Wittig's Writings in Context." *Feminist Studies* 7 (Summer): 264–87.

Williams, Oscar. 1983. "North but South." In Schwartz and Estess 1983, pp. 184–85. (First published in the *New Republic* (21 October 1946), p. 525.)

Williamson, Alan. 1983. "*A Cold Spring*: The Poet of Feeling." In Schwartz and Estess 1983, pp. 96–108.

Wittig, Monique. 1981. "One is Not Born a Woman." *Feminist Issues* 1 (Winter): 47–53.

Wood, Michael. 1977. "RSVP." *New York Review of Books,* 9 June 1977, p. 29.

Contributors

JACQUELINE VAUGHT BROGAN is professor of English at the University of Notre Dame. She is the author of *Stevens and Simile: A Theory of Language* (1986) and *Part of the Climate: American Cubist Poetry* (1991). She has published several articles on the topic of femininity in poetic voice.

BONNIE COSTELLO is associate professor of English at Boston University. She is the author of *Elizabeth Bishop: Questions of Mastery* (1991). In 1982 she won the Explicator Award for her book *Marianne Moore: Imaginary Possessions*.

JOANNE FEIT DIEHL is Henry Hill Pierce Professor of English at Bowdoin College. She is the author of *Elizabeth Bishop and Marianne Moore: The Psychodynamics of Creativity* (1993), *Women Poets and the American Sublime* (1990), and *Dickinson and the Romantic Imagination* (1981).

LEE EDELMAN is associate professor of English at Tufts University. He is the author of *Transmemberment of Song: Hart Crane's Anatomies of Rhetoric and Desire* (1987) and *Homographesis: Essays in Gay Literary and Cultural Theory* (1993). He has published many essays on modern poetry, lesbian and gay studies, and literary theory, including essays on Elizabeth Bishop, John Ashbery, and Wallace Stevens.

LORRIE GOLDENSOHN is visiting associate professor of English at Vassar College. She is the author of *Elizabeth Bishop: The Biography of a Poetry* (1991). She has published several essays on Bishop, including "Elizabeth Bishop: For a World 'minute and vast and clear,'" in *Pequod* and "Elizabeth Bishop: An Untitled, Unpublished Poem" and "Elizabeth Bishop's Originality," both in the *American Poetry Review*. "It is marvelous," the Bishop poem that Goldensohn found in Brazil in 1986, was chosen for inclusion in *The Best American Poetry, 1989*, edited by Donald Hall and Daven Lehman. Goldensohn has also published two books of poetry.

VICTORIA HARRISON is assistant professor of English at the University of California at Santa Barbara. She is the author of *Elizabeth Bishop's Poetics of Intimacy,* (1992). She has published several essays on Bishop in *Twentieth Century Literature* and *Contemporary Literature*. The author of essays on Gertrude Stein, Marianne Moore, and Mina Loy, she is currently working on a book about the relational subjectivity of modern women's poetry.

MARILYN MAY LOMBARDI is associate professor of English at the University of North Carolina at Greensboro. She is the author of *The Body and the*

Contributors

Song: Elizabeth Bishop's Poetics (1994) and of recent articles on Mary Shelley, William Godwin, and Edna St. Vincent Millay. Her essay for this volume first appeared in *Twentieth Century Literature*.

JEREDITH MERRIN is associate professor of English at Ohio State University. She is the author of *An Enabling Humility: Marianne Moore, Elizabeth Bishop, and the Uses of Tradition* (1990) and contributed a chapter on Moore and Bishop to *The Columbia History of American Poetry*. Her poems have appeared in *Ploughshares, Kenyon Review,* and elsewhere.

BRETT CANDLISH MILLIER is associate professor of American Literature and Civilization at Middlebury College. She is the author of the biography *Elizabeth Bishop: Life and the Memory of It* (1993) and she has published essays on Bishop in *The Kenyon Review, The New England Quarterly,* and *Verse.*

BARBARA PAGE is professor of English and chair of the department at Vassar College. She is former director of the women's studies program. The author of several essays on Elizabeth Bishop, Page was instrumental in Vassar's decision to acquire the Bishop papers for its library. Her essay "Shifting Islands: Elizabeth Bishop's Manuscripts" (*Shenandoah,* 1981–82) was among the first based on the manuscript collection.

THOMAS TRAVISANO is associate professor of English at Hartwick College. He is the author of *Elizabeth Bishop: Her Artistic Development* (1988) and of recent essays on Bishop's juvenile prose and poetry for the *Gettysburg Review* and the *Western Humanities Review.*

Index

Index